GENDER, SYMBOLISM AND ORGANIZATIONAL CULTURES

Silvia Gherardi

SAGE Publications
London • Thousand Oaks • New Delhi

First published in 1995

SAGE Publications Ltd
6 Bonhill Street
London EC2A 4PU

SAGE Publications Inc
2455 Teller Road
Newbury Park, California 91320

SAGE Publications India Pvt Ltd
32, M-Block Market
Greater Kailash – I
New Delhi 110 048

British Library Cataloguing in Publication data

A catalogue record for this book is available from the British Library.

   ISBN 0–8039–8910–5
   ISBN 0–8039–8911–3 pbk

Library of Congress catalog record available

Typeset by Mayhew Typesetting, Rhayader, Powys
Printed in Great Britain by The Cromwell Press Ltd,
Broughton Gifford, Melksham, Wiltshire.

Contents

Introduction

The knowledge yielded *by* the category 'gender' *about* gender is one of the clearest examples of reflexive knowledge – by which I mean the social process of knowledge production which changes the knowing subjects and the conditions under which the phenomenon is produced. And this calls to mind a minor episode in my private life which relates to the writing of this book.

When I began to consider the idea, I inspected the shelves of my bookcase, where, year after year, I had collected feminist writings and accumulated material ranging from political pamphlets to notebooks of jottings taken during in-the-field research into organizations; notebooks intended one day to provide the raw material for a book on gender and organizations. The experience was like leafing through a family photograph album, looking at the pictures of the past and marvelling over the way we used to be, the things we thought, the language we used. The books from the 1970s touched me deeply. By now they were historical texts, and the passionate debate of those years had subsided. Other books, instead, were still riven with violent emotions and echoed with the harsh voices of discord, controversy, separation and difference. I was intensely moved by the transformation of everyday life and social analysis brought about, in just twenty or thirty years, by the change in the discourse practices with which we socially construct the meaning of gender. I have been able to retrace the stages of this transformation in my personal and professional biography. At the end of the 1970s, I confidently proclaimed myself a feminist. I studied female work in terms of female occupation and labour market participation. In the 1980s, differences among women and among feminisms induced me to draw on women's studies and to separate my politics from my study of women's work within the broader context of organizational research. It was in those years that the word 'gender' first made its appearance in Italy; a word which translated awkwardly into Italian but which nevertheless opened up new horizons. We 'discovered' that men too have a gender and that sex too is a cultural category. In the meantime, the cultural and symbolic approach moved to the forefront of organizational studies, while my reading of the French philosophers convinced me that a postmodern world was now upon us.

Professionally, I belong to the occupational community of academic sociologists, and I identify myself with an approach which pivots on the interpretative act and on social interpretations. Assuming, therefore, that interpretative procedures constitute a rigorous method for knowledge-production, the task of sociology is to develop new metaphors and languages with which to handle intersubjectively meaningful experiences. From this point of view, writing and reflecting on gender helps to change gender relations. My hope is that these processes will evolve in such a manner and with such a speed that the original grammatical meaning – or a wholly new one – will be restored to the term gender, thereby rendering this book obsolete.

I have tried to use a different language, one within the bounds of my expressive capacities and within the limits of social convention, in order to respect the reader's legitimate expectation of a text dressed in the mental clothing of science. I have exploited the interstices in the script to elicit the experiences of the reader, which may be both similar to and radically different from mine, and to propose various perspectives on the same facts. Another reason for not using a systematic and linear style relates to the subject-matter of the book, which is, it will be seen, the shifting boundaries between the symbolic universes of male and female as areas of experiential and cognitive ambiguity. Is it possible to speak unambiguously about ambiguity? I believe not. Consequently I have tried to develop an indirect discourse which suggests lines of thought, draws comparisons and elicits insights, rather than pursuing linear arguments which are expounded analytically.

More than the subject-matter of science, gender is common experience and common sense – but also banality, in that it is a construct taken for granted. My intention, therefore, is that this book should hold a mirror up to a reality which is, so to speak, a flux of experience in consciousness. I have tried to avoid writing a book which talks about other books and caters to an increasingly self-referential community. For this reason I have restricted the bibliographical references, providing instead a wide range of examples taken from my research and anecdotes from my private life, since these represent simple everyday experience. Again for this reason, my syntax adheres to the first person 'I'. My use of 'we' is not a discourse marker for the disembodied Author; it serves to denote a community, or to create an ideal communality with the Reader and others. The impersonal Author is, by definition, always objective, dispassionate, cold; an entity methodically concluding one argument before beginning another. By contrast, I have tried to preserve some human warmth in the episodes that constitute my research 'data' or my logical arguments. Moreover, I have endeavoured to introduce a touch of irony, and sometimes sarcasm, which metacommunicates to the Reader the fact that every text, including this one, is open to many interpretations. Arguments never reach a closure; they are ongoing conversations which any reader is able to conclude in the way that s/he finds most congenial, and my own conclusion is no better than any other. It is precisely because of this interpretative 'openness' of every text that I have sought to broach many more arguments and many more lines of thought than I have sought to close.

Much has been said and written about scientific language as a specific literary genre, about its function of providing *a posteriori* legitimation and rationalization for the scientific method, about the legacy of positivism and its imposition of a uniform script on experimental science, about the annihilation of the author and the passivity of the reader. However, we have few examples of how to write 'differently', mainly because the scientific community – colleagues and reviewers – is strongly biased towards the 'normalization' of language. We do have, though, a metaphor which proposes a new alliance between Authors and Readers, where the former are not forced to dehumanize and cancel themselves from the text to maintain their author-ity, and the latter are not forced to think themselves into insignificance, as the passive receptors of somebody else's thoughts.

The metaphor of text and of textual cooperation (Eco, 1979; Brown, 1977) declares that society is a text written by concrete human authors, and that accordingly it must be read and not merely observed. The point, therefore, is not to search for the truth but 'to create with the reader a new textual space and a new rhetorical practice that, once established, would enable both Rhetor and Reader to transcend the ontological assumptions and cognitive and behavioural norms that have served in part as their prison' (Brown, 1989: 54).

This book examines gender relations both as regards practices (and therefore the way in which these relations are or may be constructed differently) and as regards their existence and action independently of subjects; that is, as forms of thought and language, and as cultural symbols. Discourse on gender – any discourse whatever on gender – is political discourse. Just as there are discourse practices which sustain an order based on inequality, so there are others which sustain an order based on difference. Within the discourse structure of difference (the reference here is to Derrida's celebrated neologism '*différance*'), gender is not solely static difference: it is also processual difference as the contingent historical construct of a community. This entails that moral decisions must be taken on which gender relations are social practices and which discourses legitimize them. I shall accordingly argue that any discourse on gender produced at any particular moment by any specific culture is part of civic discourse. This holds, in my view, both for a society and its institutions, defined as crystallizations of forms of thought, and for smaller human groupings like organizations, which express a number of work cultures and comprise social constructs on workplace gender relations. Labour law, for example, provides a clear illustration of the relationship among social institutions which assimilate and normatize demands for equality voiced by civil society while simultaneously promoting an egalitarian culture by constraining work behaviour.

It is my intention to argue that organizational cultures differ according to their gender regimes and, consequently, according to the social patternings that they give to gender citizenship. As forms of communicative behaviour, organizations are constrained and shaped by the grammar of the social structure. But they are also constituted by – and constitute – the discourse practices that occur within them. How gender is 'done' in an organization is a crucial cultural phenomenon; and how it can be 'done' differently is a challenge to all those who work for organizations, and indeed to the civilizing process itself. If we are to escape the gender trap, if we are to free ourselves of the idea that there exist two and only two types of individual, if we are to ensure that social differentiation is no longer based on sexual differentiation, we must destabilize all thought which dichotomizes (either male or female) and hierarchizes (male as One, as the norm, and female as the Other, the second sex). Holistic thought reformulates the relation as interdependence, inseparability, ambiguity; and it recasts gender practices as dual presence, intersections, reciprocity. From biological destiny, gender may develop into discourse position.

The first chapter of the book introduces the reader to the idea that organizations, despite their claim to be neuter and neutral, are structured according to the symbolism of gender. Their culture is gendered. I set out my theoretical approach to the organization as a cultural system and I anticipate what is meant by symbolic analysis.

The second and third chapters propose two metaphors with which to explore the pervasiveness, elusiveness and ambiguity of gender in organizational cultures: the sexual contract and the alchemic wedding as symbols of the immanence and transcendence of gender relations.

The sexual contract is a metaphor for immanence, for the conflict of interests, for the female contraposed to the male, for static difference. As such, it represents the ambiguous link between gender and sex, as well as the covert action of the ties between sexed bodies typical of the private sphere in the public one. It is a metaphor which enables us to explore organizational sexuality as a specific form of public sexuality which obeys a specific expressive code.

The alchemic wedding is a metaphor for transformation, transcendence, the separation and inseparability of the male and the female; it stands for plurality and the relaxing of the principle of non-contradiction, for dynamic difference. It is an image which takes us beyond gender construed as two symbolic, mutually exclusive universes of meaning, and it displays a plurality of cultural models of femaleness (which I depict in terms of the Greek female gods) and a plurality of interpretations of the woman/work relationship. Independence, rationality, autonomy are male attributes in a system of dichotomous representation: Artemis (independence), Athena (rationality) and Hestia (autonomy) are its female embodiments, and every cultural model of femaleness activates a corresponding model of maleness. Many work couples, as the chapter shows, display cultural work patterns based on the interdependence of the conceptions of gender.

The organization is founded on asymmetric power relations, and it solicits, activates and exploits the eroticism of dependence: the boundary between public/private, spontaneity/imposition is an extremely fine one. In the social construction of gender, the great binary opposites of nature/culture, physicality/spirituality, separation/inseparability act as conflicting forces which at times impose a static difference – based on the principle of non-contradiction – and at times a dynamic one based on the re-emergence of the excluded term in creative game-playing which differentiates meanings over time. On these two pairs of forces rests the symbolic order of gender described in the fourth chapter.

People weave together the symbolic order of gender in an organizational culture as they construct their understanding of a shared world or of difference. I illustrate this notion by describing six ideal-types of organizational culture which depict the initial impact of female intruders on various cultural patterns of male hegemony preservation. The paradox of being an organizational citizen by right and an outsider by fact may suggest ways to make an organizational culture more woman-friendly or, alternatively, why this may not be possible.

The fifth chapter examines the construction of gender through interaction and discusses possible cooperation between men and women in acknowledging difference and combating second-sexing and inequalities. The argument is that the production of gender in the workplace – in a setting, that is, where the female presence overturns the symbolic order based on mutual exclusion – passes through a two-stage ritual comprising celebration work (which asserts static difference) and remedial work (which affirms dynamic difference). Suggested as resources for analysis of further cleavages in gender relations are hypocrisy, irony, trust and embarrassment, since these, in different ways, protect the multiplicity of the self as identities, and identifications are explored which, although they do not deny gender identity, seek different kinds of social differentiation. Gender, therefore, may be one of the forms that difference assumes; but it is not the only one and it is not always the most important.

Gender used to be the paramount form of social differentiation in simple societies because it gave rise to a sexual division of labour. In the more complex societies of today, however, and with the spread of the dual presence into almost all societal areas, social differentiation is more articulated and more tightly enmeshed with other dimensions (most notably, class and race). The civilizing process, whereby customs once considered 'natural' are no longer acceptable, is also changing the classic social distinction of gender. Gender inequalities are becoming an embarrassment, and it is increasingly difficult in democratic societies to come up with moral justification for gender as a social destiny. Yet the civilizing process is ambiguous in its effects, and history teaches us that it is a process based on the suppression of instincts. Emancipation, liberation and repression, therefore, are much more closely interwoven than mutually exclusive.

Lastly, the Conclusions to the book propose a metaphor which encompasses the previous analysis in its entirety: gender citizenship. Citizenship and gender are potent symbolic constructs linked by a web of historical and political meanings. If organizational life is a common good in which all, although with different responsibilities, share, then the social construction of the meaning of gender citizenship is the moral responsibility of the historical community and a constitutive theme of its civic discourse.

Each chapter of the book is intended to merge with the next; in this they resemble the acts of a play, each of which involves a change of scenery but each of which has a meaning which can only be understood within the overall context of the work. The reader will find that the chapters do not end with those paragraphs of summary so useful for the rapid and superficial skimmer. This may frustrate the reader, but something functionally similar to a summary is provided by the brief stories which preface each chapter and which, in a certain sense, are its 'parable'.

Finally, I must thank the many people to whom I owe a debt of gratitude for their help in my writing of this book. My thanks go first to all those whom I met in the course of my research and with whom I began my conversation on gender and organizations. I still carry the mental image and the warmth of a relation which continues over time and through words. Words, however, which belong to an acquired language in which I could not have expressed myself without the fine linguistic intuition of Adrian Belton, without whom I could not have overcome the barrier of linguistic difference.

I also extend my thanks to any colleagues in the Dipartimento di Politica Sociale who discussed many of the ideas presented here. I am particularly indebted to Chiara Saraceno, who created the Centro per lo Studio delle Strutture di Genere, some years ago in the Dipartimento, and whose work has been so influential in changing gender relationships in my workplace and in our professional community.

However, this book would probably never have been written without the patient insistence of Sue Jones who, at Lancaster in 1992, saw that I had a book to write before I realized that it was in gestation.

Finally I express my gratitude to all those who read, as a whole or in part, the first draft of the manuscript and made such constructive suggestions: Giuliana Chiaretti, Barbara Czarniawska-Joerges, Celia Davies, Sue Jones, Alberto Melucci, Vittorio Mortara, Chiara Saraceno, Linda Smircich, Antonio Strati and an anonymous reviewer. Of course, I alone am responsible for what is written in the following pages.

1
Organizational Symbolism, Culture and Gender

I was a skipper and a woman. On the suggestion of my coach, for my first national regatta I raced with a female crew. I came first in the women's event, and how my heart raced at the prizewinners' ceremony when, after the largest cup had been handed to the winner, the medium-sized cup to the runner-up, and the smallest cup to the crew placed third, the name of my boat followed by my own name were announced over the loudspeaker. I walked proudly out of the crowd and mounted the rostrum. But when I finally received my prize I found it was a bottle of eau-de-Cologne, Roger e Gallet 4711; the very same cologne that my father used. My head swam and tears sprang to my eyes, but I refused to let 'them' see my disappointment. I had my pride to protect. But what pride? As a skipper? As a woman? I thought that a mistake must have been made, that at the next regatta there would certainly be a trophy or at least a medal for the best female crew. I continued to race, always with female crews, and I accumulated a fine collection of men's toiletries which I duly passed on to my father. No mistake had been made! I stopped sailing with other women and concentrated on winning a real cup. A male cup.

Feminism did not exist in those days. I attended a *liceo scientifico* (the Italian scientific high school), and I vaguely felt that, with seven girls and twenty-three boys in the class, science was not a subject for women. I had no doubt, though, that I was just as good as the boys. Perhaps better, because I outclassed them at school and at sport. Yet there was something that I found impossible to understand and which still deeply offended me: why announce the best female crew and not award it a cup, even a small one? Why not give a male perfume to the male crew and a female one to the female one? No one came up with a sensible explanation; indeed I was dismissed as over-sensitive and as a troublemaker.

Only years later, with the advent of feminism, did I realize that the trophy that I had failed to win was part of a patriarchy system. I felt better: I was not wrong and my sense of injustice had a name, hence it existed!

It took many more years before I realized that my trophy was an organizational fact. A regatta is the joint product of a number of sports clubs belonging to a state-funded federation financed by membership fees. This is an organization which draws up a calendar of regattas, which hierarchizes them into local, provincial, regional, national levels; an organization which helps, through sport, to shape the moral character of future generations, and which employs ex-champions in voluntary work as they hand on their example and their experience.

As a sport, sailing treats women very liberally. Regattas are not segregated by sex, a woman can skipper a male crew, and there are even special prizes for female crews. Are not these the features of a democratic organization offering equal opportunities and, indeed, committed to a programme of affirmative action? As an ironic organizational consultant I would only suggest replacing the eau-de-Cologne with Chanel Number 5.

This episode from my past came unexpectedly to mind during a recent meeting with five top bank executives in Milan, who were seeking my advice on how to encourage women to embark on careers in management. They asked me in bewilderment: 'Why aren't women interested in careers?' They had just described the bank's twenty-year policy of openness to women in the following terms: at first, only a few women were employed in the bank, and they worked in the innermost offices out of the public's sight. They were hidden away because the clientele might feel uncomfortable discussing money matters with a woman. The bank later placed women at the cash desks, because, it felt, customers appreciated a demure presence behind the counter. Now that many of the bank's executives were about to retire, there was a shortage of suitably qualified personnel to take their place. Women workers were now in the majority in the bank, there were now many more women graduates in Italy than in the past; but, the executives claimed, they were not interested in competing for managerial positions. They refused to move to the provinces, where they could gain experience and begin climbing the career ladder.

Practically this same generation of women, therefore, had first been sequestered in purdah like Arab women, then they had been displayed as ornamentation, and now they were being asked to work alongside unattractive old dodderers nearing retirement. During my first round of interviews I realized very forcefully that I was witnessing precisely what Watzlawick *et al.* (1967) describe as a situation of paradoxical communication. Apparently, the bankers were simultaneously inviting women to become their peers, expressing their distrust of equality, and implicitly threatening those who dared imagine that they could change the rules of the game. The bankers wanted to change matters by offering incentives to women through a classic form of affirmative action: removing the obstacles against hiring, offering maternity leave, and bringing work and home closer together. Except that the women who might have been interested in a managerial career were already long past the age when they had to cope with child-rearing, and if they showed any interest in the proposal it was only to express solidarity with other women. Hence their explicit distaste for the perfume of power, which only masked the unpleasant odour of contempt for women.

As a consultant, before accepting the commission, I tried to redefine th
problem in terms of the invisible cultural barriers – the glass ceiling –
which trap women below the executive-level threshold. I proposed a
methodology which would reveal the meanings of the reward system for
these male managers and for potential female managers, so that the values
they attributed to male and female could be specified. Needless to say, I
and the bankers failed to reach any sort of agreement. I even failed to
convince them that men *also* should be interviewed, and I was unable to
reassure them that being interviewed by a male would protect them against
misinterpretation and possible accusations.

For my part, this egregious experience was illuminating because it finally
convinced me that if an organizational culture expresses a gender regime
which systematically devalues everything connected with the female, the
organization can never become democratic, whatever affirmative action it
may introduce, and whatever equal opportunity legislation may be
promulgated. I thus began to think in terms of gender citizenship: the right
to have gender values respected within a culture that acknowledges all
differences. In the final chapter of this book I shall show how diverse
organizational cultures give voice to diverse forms of citizenship. For the
moment, however, the problem is how they symbolically construct the
male and the female.

As a scholar of organizations who had chosen a cultural approach to
their study, and as a woman no longer in her youth, I conducted various
surveys of female work (Gherardi, 1978, 1982, 1991, 1994; Gherardi and
Masiero, 1988). In the course of my organizational research, I interviewed
groups of female or mixed workers and annotated my field notes with a
wide selection of thoughts, anecdotes, jokes and sayings which related in
some way or other to gender differences. I never made systematic analysis
of these jottings because I reacted with horror to the view that women do
things differently because they are women, and because I was obsessed
with the thought that I might be interrogated by the classic quantitative
researcher: how many women, where, of what age, compared with how
many men? And if I didn't have a control group, what would become of
me?

As I grew older, I discovered grounded theory and the scientific validity
of qualitative methods, eventually co-authoring with Barry Turner
(Gherardi and Turner, 1988) a booklet entitled *Real Men Don't Collect
Soft Data*. My experience gained from teaching courses for women only
and my ongoing researches on gender expanded my research material until
I became sufficiently confident in my ideas for Sage to honour me with the
invitation to write this book. In doing so, I shall seek to be as rigorous in
my argument as I am simple in my style, since my overall purpose is to
'show' gender in organizational life, how it is 'done' in everyday routine,
and how it could be 'done' differently.

Since it is extremely difficult to do simple things well, I shall first have to
establish my premises. For example, that gender has something to do with

organizations and with organizational cultures. And that both gender and culture relate to ambiguity, and this to science, and that it is not possible to talk unambiguously about ambiguity.

Although there is no answer to the disquieting question of whether we are the same species with two sexes or two different species, we may nevertheless agree that, in general although not always, sexual difference is a datum that can be taken for granted.

Yet this banality of sexual attribution is less self-evident than might appear (Butler, 1990; Lorber and Farrell,1991). Even the earliest traces of civilization reveal a cultural elaboration of sex difference which associates each sex with specific attributes, qualities and symbols. It is a linguistic artefact which enables us to talk about symbolic universes of meaning which do not necessarily correspond to sexed bodies or, therefore, to a female and male nature. Culture is a historical product whose elements have differing properties of permanence and change: all known cultures possess systems with which to signify sexual difference. Hence, although male and female are universal symbols, the contents of male and female are simultaneously specific to particular historical cultures, to subcultures, and to individual people. The irony of the human condition, or of human knowledge, is that we forget the 'human' operations that generate knowledge of the world, and that we believe that a world of essences lies 'out there' beyond our possibilities of knowledge (or that it is not mediated by language). A nature separate from culture. Essentialism, in fact, reiterates language's structure of contraposition by founding it either on biological determinism or on cultural determinism (Flax, 1987).

So far as the relationship between people of different sexes is concerned, for example, it is still very difficult to define the link between sex and gender and to establish whether one, the other, or both are 'natural' or 'cultural' facts. For a certain period it was customary in the feminist literature to distinguish sex from gender by assigning the former the status of a natural fact, as a mere biological distinction constituted by different genital organs; gender, on the other hand, was a cultural fact, the differentiation of masculinity and femininity as the social construction of different destinies.

But once doubt had been cast on the concept itself of nature, on the social construction of knowledge (biological knowledge in particular), and on the social and organizational processes that derive from the definition of sexual membership, gender came to be viewed as a specific social relation. In genetics the attribution of sex is a more difficult undertaking than that normally confronted by clinical obstetrics at the birth of a baby – the moment when a social and organizational process assigns a birth certificate to the infant which fixes it as a member of one or other of the sexes. In fact, the social categorization of a human being on the basis of sex comes into operation prior to birth, because ecograph technology can be used to control individual life even before the human being exists. Thus many unborn girls, potential members of cultures or religions which devalue the female, have their social destinies marked out even before become human beings.

The concealed cognitive process at work here is the social belief ...... anatomical difference gives rise to two, and only two, distinct types of human being: men and women. Thus if gender is thought in terms of either/ or, we perpetuate a social belief that only two human types exist and only two can exist. Gender as a structure of binary opposites has been the most potent of all symbols of differentiation: since the earliest beginnings of civilization, since the most ancient and simplest cultural elaboration, difference has been symbolized in compliance with the tenets of gender difference. The cultural production of male and female symbolic universes has entrenched belief in the universal essences of masculinity and femininity. Historical interpretation of social practices has traditionally acted as a corrective to the hypostatization of gender by demonstrating that the actual contents of masculinity and femininity, as well as the social relations (the sexual division of labour and child-rearing) based upon them, have changed historically and culturally. But although the historical perspective may blunt essentialist determinism, the power of the symbolization of difference as gender difference and binary opposition still remains intact.

Gender and organizational culture

It is a common experience on entering an organization for the first time – as a user, consultant or researcher – to be struck by the pervasively masculine or pervasively feminine atmosphere of the surroundings. Sometimes the physical environment, the exterior of the building or the interior décor give an impression of strength and virility or, alternatively, one of care and intimacy. When the architecture and the design of the rooms emphasize straight lines and height, or conversely curves and breadth, the observer is reminded of the archetypes of masculinity and femininity. Not just the physical reality of environments but language, too, possesses this evocative power. Thus business reverberates with the great male saga of conquest (of new markets) and of campaigns (to launch new products), while services echo to the language of care, of concern for needs and of relationality.

On entering an office, all our senses convey to us its greater or lesser acceptance of the values of either gender; yet it is extremely difficult to express in words how we decode that complex phenomenon which, for the sake of brevity, we may call 'organizational culture'. It is equally difficult to legitimize 'scientifically' the set of sensations that evoke within us this feeling of an organization's male or female personality. Fortunately, however, we know much more about it than we think we do. We possess what Polanyi (1958) has called 'tacit knowledge' to denote both what we have learnt and forgotten, and what we know at a pre-conscious or unconscious level.

Being part of a culture has often been compared metaphorically to a fish living in water: fish not only find it 'natural' to move through their element (which to us is 'alien'), but they are also the last to notice the water through which they are swimming. This metaphor concerns what is 'taken for granted' (Schutz, 1971) in cultural construction and what has become 'natural', but it also emphasizes the macroscopic dimensions of a phenomenon which we do not see, and the poverty of the tools with which we analyse and communicate it. Gender is one such cultural construct.

For example, during the Italian *Carnevale* (the word 'carnival' means, in fact, the temporary suspension of everyday norms), men and women frequently dress as members of the opposite sex. Usually, however, the observer rapidly sees through the disguise because this caricature of gender strikes him or her as 'non-natural'. For those wearing the costumes, cross-dressing is often an experience which gives them insight into the long process of the cultural learning of gender. The humour generated by gender swapping (one thinks here of films like *Some Like It Hot* or *Tootsie*) is effective precisely because it subverts a logical and natural relation, namely that between sex and gender.

Changing gender, as in the transvestism of *Carnevale*, yields an experience of the Other (Cassano, 1989). So too do other experiences, such as falling ill, or spending time in prison, or pretending to be a different age, or living a different lifestyle. *Carnevale* is closely bound up with enjoyment, of course, but the experience of the Other may play a major role in revealing the tacit rules of an organizational culture in more serious contexts as well. For example, it can be recommended as an illuminating experience in the training of young doctors specializing in geriatrics. By being obliged to wear special devices which restrict their movement, reduce their hearing, and blur their vision, the young doctors are placed in the patient's situation of dependence upon others. If this was an episode in a film, it would be grotesque and amusing; yet as the 'learning' of a situation in which the dependence relationship is 'reversed' with respect to the habitual conception of the patient/doctor role relationship, the experience may be painful.

What I wish to argue here is that both gender and organizational culture are phenomena which the analytical and atomizing mentality of organizational studies finds difficult to grasp. Yet our direct experience tells us that organizational cultures – as holistic phenomena – are strongly 'gendered'. Organizations themselves, therefore, are gendered, and organizational processes are ways of organizing gender relations.

Gender not only provides a key for interpretation of organizational cultures, it is one of their distinguishing features. Not all researchers into organizational culture have adopted an interpretative approach which examines the production and consumption of meanings; many have stuck to a functionalist approach, questioning the utility of that 'thing' called culture. For those who adopt a cultural intepretative approach, culture consists of the taken-for-granted and problematic webs of meaning that people produce and deploy when they interact. These systems of meanings are shaped by more general culture and by the institutions and organizations of society at large.

Without wishing to enter into polemic with other points of view, I merely point out that I prefer an interpretative definition of organizational culture such as the following:

> An organizational culture consists of the symbols, beliefs and patterns of behaviour learned, produced and created by the people who devote their energies and labour to the life of an organization. It is expressed in the design of the organization and of work, in the artifacts and services that the organization produces, in the architecture of its premises, in the technologies that it employs, in its ceremonials of encounter and meeting, in the temporal structuring of organizational courses of action, in the quality and conditions of its working life, in the ideologies of work, in the corporate philosophy, in the jargon, lifestyle and physical appearance of the organization's members. (Strati, 1992a: 578)

I prefer this definition to others because it refers not only to non-material things like values (what people think), to such concrete things as what people say when they meet, but also to something so apparently banal as appearance (sex, I would add) and the symbolic message it transmits (the social construction of gender).

For example, has the reader ever met a woman manager with long hair worn loose to the waist? Would he or she prefer to think that medium-length hair is dictated by personal and practical considerations; that it is the result of a tacit organizational norm enforced by the gate-keepers of the organization; or that it has something to do with the symbolic significance of hair (Synnot, 1987)? All three explanations are plausible (they may even be correct), but I would argue that cropped hair conveys an impression of excessive masculinization, whereas over-long hair has a 'sexiness' that clashes with the role of woman manager and the authority that this confers. I have frequently asked women about the length of their hair. Putting such a question during a conversation/interview among women is not as bizarre as it might seem (I would also add that my sex and appearance – I wear my hair medium-length – make it easier for me to ask it). Replies have referred to 'personal' choice and to taste, but also to a sensation for which I use the shorthand expression 'being out of tune'. The woman is unaware that she is obeying a rule. Although she cannot explain herself properly, she feels that otherwise her hair would be wrong, it would be odd, it would clash.

The French use a term, *bon ton*, which efficiently sums up the notions of what is 'in tune', tasteful and in compliance with the dictates of etiquette. Organizational culture, too, expresses itself through the code of *bon ton*. Although participants may believe they are expressing purely personal tastes and inclinations, knowledge of what matches and what clashes with the organization's style – as well as with a particular occupational community within it – is an organizational fact (an acquired skill). Ever since Monsignor Della Casa wrote his *Galateo* in 1558, etiquette has laid down a rigid and clearly defined division of roles between the sexes – however much manners and ceremonies may differ from one local culture to another.

Although organizational culture approves of medium-length hair (or any other female attribute), for women in positions of authority, this is not to say that all women comply. One notes with interest that those who refuse to do so are more fully aware of resisting a social pressure that tells them that, if they display the attractions of their sex at work, they will not be taken seriously. My replies from long-haired women told me that there exist other forms of resistance, cheerful defiances of custom, declarations of irreducible femaleness. These are minor matters, signals of rebellion and statements of personality which counteract the depersonal-izing (and desexualizing) pressure applied by the organization: make-up, red nail-varnish, a gaudy dress, a short skirt. The young men behave similarly; they sport beards or ponytails, or they pin colourful badges to their sober suits. These are all forms of resistance to organizational pressure.

Nevertheless, there is a gender-based difference. When femininity is attractiveness, and when it is not to the direct advantage of the organiz-ation (as, for example, in customer relations or when embodied in a service or product), then an organizational rule may come into effect which, paraphrasing Thompson (1967) and the gist of numerous texts in the organizational literature, runs as follows: The 'rational' woman may be pleasing and moderately feminine, but she should not be attractive; if she is, she will not be taken seriously, she will find it more difficult to compete with her male colleagues, she will arouse suspicions of collusion in harassment, and so forth.

It may seem trivial to adduce arguments like these to demonstrate something as evident as the fact that organizational culture is gendered; but if one consults the literature on women in management – see Calás (1988) for a critique – it can all be translated *à la* Thompson into a manual on how women can 'fit in' with management so that formal equality and cultural assimilation deny the diversity of gender. As at *Carnevale*, organizational women are cross-dressed and pretend to be genderless.

Order presupposes a system of coherences, of stable expectations. The symbolic order of gender presupposes that women are female and that men are male; that the former are private, the latter public; that the former are employed in reproduction, the latter in production; and so on. Since organizations are public sites of production, they are necessarily male: women 'do not work'. Indeed, 'housewife' means (used to mean) 'non-worker'; not 'unemployed', however, since being unemployed presupposes being a worker.

If, therefore, women happen to work in organizations, that they do so is purely a concidence, an exception, a historical accident, a matter of little importance, temporary, secondary. If an organization consists of only

women it is a female organization, addressing women, providin'
in support of reproduction, housework, child-rearing. 'True' org
are only male.

Occupational segregation expresses this coherence: women do women's
tasks, in organizations they occupy female posts, they perpetuate the
symbolic system of subordination, of subservience. The upper part of
the organization is male, the lower part is female. Any career development within this coherence takes place within the system of segregation.
Occupational segregation protects women against male competition, it
legitimizes their presence in the organization. When women occupy female
positions they endeavour to be discreet, almost invisible. The symbolic
order of gender can cope with this minor contradiction. But there may be
more female positions in an organization than there are women.

The attributes of femininity are ingrained in the subordination relationship: caring, compassion, willingness to please others, generosity, sensitivity,
solidarity, nurturing, emotionality, and so on. These are attributes that also
belong to other marginalized or dependent categories of people. Since they
are the attributes of the powerless, it is possible to occupy a feminine
position, not because of biological destiny but because of a political and
organizational social dynamic. The 'lean organization', amongst other
things, expands female work positions. The logic of quality rediscovers the
characteristics of care, and as Kanter wrote (1977), the structural arrangement of the work position predetermines similar behavioural patterns.
While resisting an over-simple determinism between gendered positions and
gendered behaviours, we may nevertheless assert that patterns of work
identity, either male or female, depend as much on the job as on the person.
Jobs with little autonomy, responsibility or interest, with few or no career
prospects, are likely to display patterns of so-called 'female work behaviour': instrumentality, low commitment, investment in life outside work,
and so forth. So, should the femaleness of an organization be specified
according to the number of women who work for it, the number of female
jobs it contains, or the structural demands for female behaviour that it
makes?

Ferguson writes (1984: 95): 'Women are not powerless because they are
feminine; rather, they are feminine because they are powerless, because it is
a way of dealing with the requirements of subordination.' The same
reasoning can be applied to the male, and indeed it is to be found in a
great deal of the literature on how women can be helped to fit in with
organizations or management. The upshot is that they too are able to
behave 'properly'. Although these considerations tell us a great deal about
the gender of the normative model, they are too hackneyed and imprecise.
We are obliged, in fact, to conclude that if a symbolic order of gender is to
be found in an organization, distribution by sex is not its only indicator
(or not its best one), and that we should instead map work positions
according to gender. Not only would it thus transpire that organizations
are much more female than they claim to be, but also that the power

imbalance is much more marked than the alleged democratism by which it is legitimized.

It may be superfluous to insist yet again that organizations are not distinct from society, and that they internally reflect the patriarchal system of their environment; a patriarchal system which, combined with technocracy (Burris, 1989), assigns women to a subordinate system and forces them to adapt to the inequality of the genders. As Alvesson and Billig (1992: 80) point out,

> if a particular group, in this case women, is consistently forced to adapt/ resocialize to a much higher degree than another group (men) in order to attain better life chances accompanying career and promotion in bureaucracies, then issues of political interests, fairness, domination and equality enter the picture.

Alvesson and Billig also stress that not all organizations are the same; nor are all female conditions the same. In other words, there are organizational cultures which are more or less women-friendly, just as the structuring of gender varies among organizations, within individual organizations, among organizational roles and within the same occupation.

There are, for example, gender differences among organizations: the world of business is more male than the civil service or, as Mennerick (1975) has pointed out in a study of travel agencies, women tend to enter less prestigious organizations even within non-stereotyped sectors of work, and they are more likely to occupy management positions in less prestigious organizations compared with more prestigious ones. Moreover, within an individual organization, high-level positions are male, whereas lower-level ones are female and pertain to different social classes. Hence female jobs occupy a subordinate position reinforced by class and race. Again, different departments have different gender connotations: production departments are usually more male than personnel and administration ones. Although these features may vary from one organization to another, every organization has some departments which are more male, and others which are more female, according to their strategic and reputational importance.

Perhaps there is a simple rule of thumb – approximate, unscientific but nevertheless practical – which can be applied to reveal the gender features of organizations and occupational roles. The rule runs as follows: Look at the power structure and at the reputation system. When these are clear, then gender appropriateness is also clear.

However, the relationship between the gender of the occupational position, the sex of the organization's workers and the gender relation that ties them together, is much more complex than this. For example, if job tasks and their performance are analysed, the same job performed by men and by women gives rise to different forms of work. Or again, men doing female jobs, like male nurses or nursery school teachers, soon manage to carve out different career paths and to masculinize the occupation. The boundaries between male and female jobs are changeable, blurred and fragile.

Even within the same occupation, gender connotations alter as one climbs the prestige ladder. As Podmore and Spender's (1986) study of the legal profession has shown, men are more frequently employed in more prestigious jobs in commercial law, or criminal case law, and they work with male clients. Women more often do desk work, handle matrimonial lawsuits, deal with women and devote themselves to tasks which require 'caring qualities'. The same division between male and female jobs occurs in the other free professions, regardless of whether they are inherently male or female.

Culture, gender and power are therefore intimately bound up with each other in organizations as well as in society. Difficulties of conceptualization arise over gender and organizational culture because of: (a) the *pervasiveness* with which gender and culture permeate language, thought, social structures and organizational facts; (b) the *elusiveness* of their definition in relation/contrast to a difficult concept of 'nature'; (c) the *ambiguity* of a symbolic universe which resists being ordered according to a single criterion.

Interestingly, organizational theories – which we can take to be a specific kind of literature, a cultural product – claim to be gender neutral, to refer to genderless organizations employing disembodied workers. However, there is an implicit subtext to this literature which assumes that workers are male, that managers are men with virile characteristics, and that organizations are the symbolic locus of production just as the home is the locus of reproduction. The feminist critique of traditional organizational theory targeted precisely this purported neutrality, charging that organizational theories are gendered (Hearn and Parkin, 1983; Hearn *et al.*, 1989; Mills and Murgatroyd, 1991; Mills and Tancred, 1992; Savage and Witz, 1992) and in a manner such as to perpetuate male domination and gender-based social inequality.

Gendering organizational analysis is also a project of study which incorporates a gender perspective. Like other disciplines prior to organizational studies, it began by including female experience in its description of organizations. A gap was filled, and this was important; nevertheless, it is not only women who possess a gender, nor are there only two types of human being, nor is there continuity and coherence between sex and gender membership. There is still a long way to go. Thus, when one discovers that the purported 'gender neutrality' of organizations is a falsehood (Ferguson, 1984; Calás and Smircich, 1992b), one must learn to recognize the prestructuring of management, workplaces and organization in gender assumptions, rules and values, without forgetting that gender is a pervasive symbol of the power relation. I maintain that it is necessary to understand how an organization attributes meaning to male and female if analysis of the experiences of men and women in gendered organizational processes is to be possible.

ςendered processes are concrete organizational activities, both material
ἱ ideological, whereby 'advantage and disadvantage, exploitation and
ὑɔntrol, action and emotion, meaning and identity, are patterned through
and in terms of a distinction between male and female' (Acker, 1990: 146).
    The organizational production of gender – according to Acker (1992:
253) – can be described in terms of four sets of processes:

1. the production of gender divisions, i.e. the gender patterning of jobs,
    wages, hierarchies, power and subordination;
2. the creation of symbols, images and forms of consciousness which
    explicate, justify or oppose gender divisions;
3. the interactions among individuals in the multiplicity of forms that
    enact dominance and subordination, create alliances and exclusions;
4. the interior mental work of individuals as they consciously construct
    their understandings of the organization's structure of work and
    opportunity.

Gender, therefore, is socially produced by processes in which organizations actively participate and by which these organizations are shaped:
practices 'make' gender in that they produce and reproduce social relations
and material culture and the artefacts that sustain them. The meaning, the
social representations and the rhetoric with which these practices are made
accountable to those engaged in them and to all others constitute the
organizational culture as textuality which moulds the subjectivity of these
individuals and their audiences.
    The divide between a social reality organized on gender relations and
gender-neutral thought, both within organizations as they think and speak
of themselves, and within the body of organizational theory, is an odd
paradox which must be addressed because it says a great deal about the
social relation that it represents. Or rather, it conceals a great deal about
this relation, because the claim of neutrality is a social activity specifically
designed to suppress knowledge and to exercise control, most notably
through the impersonal and objectivizing practices of large organizations.
De-gendering is a social practice which exposes the power structure erected
on the claim to universality and on suppression, not of gender but of only
one of the (only) two genders. Silencing gender knowledge is a practice of
power, as the title of Smith's (1990) book – *The Conceptual Practice of
Power* – reminds us.
    Organizations are among the chief agents of these practices; practices
which are ever more textually mediated (Smith, 1993) through written
bureaucratic rules, computer programs which control the production and
reproduction of management routines, managerial expertise which maintains organizational hierarchies by rules either written or inscribed in
organizational discourse.
    Considerable efforts have been made in recent years to produce an
organizational literature which genders organizational analysis, thereby
revealing the suppressed gender subtext and the meanings concealed by

claimed neutrality. This literature is engaged in a dialogue with research that assumes gender neutrality. Both of these lines of inquiry are forms of the legitimation of gender relationships – even if different – both of them are based on power structures, even if they are antithetical. The intention of this book is less to argue the importance of deconstructing the claim to neutrality than to expose the alleged uniformity of gender predicated by the literature on gendering organizational analysis.

Organizational cultures are gendered, and they claim to be de-gendered because they are committed to principles of universality. A cultural approach to organizational cultures investigates how the symbolic construction of gender comes about, how it varies from one culture to another, and how the preferences system sustains social thought on gender. The next section describes this cultural approach in more detail.

A cultural approach: the dragon ripping down the organizational chart

The number of articles catalogued under the heading 'culture' amounted to some 2,550 in 1990 (Alvesson and Berg, 1992). The last ten years have seen the birth of the cultural approach to organizations, its enormous expansion, and – in the opinion of some – its demise (Smircich and Calás, 1987). Many of these articles were surveys, and to these I refer readers who wish to broaden their knowledge of the subject: I do not intend here to embark on yet another purely illustrative review (Allaire and Firsirotu, 1984; Ouchi and Wilkins, 1985; Knights and Willmott, 1987; Jeffcut, 1994; Martin and Frost, 1995).

In this section I shall set out a conception of the cultural approach to organizations in the tradition of symbolist thought, with principal reference to the European cultural and philosophical legacy of Cassirer (1923) and to the heritage of symbolic interactionism (Mead, 1934; Goffman, 1967; Denzin, 1992).

It is extremely difficult to define the cultural approach, for it has become a field in which it is easier to draw distinctions than to unify. Corporate culture, organizational cultures or subcultures, cultural organization, the postmodern approach to organizational culture: these are some of the labels adroitly deployed by Linstead and Grafton-Small (1990). For the moment, I am interested in the features shared by the many approaches to cultural production – and organizations are a cultural product – and which differentiate them from others which reify culture and search for its properties.

Appropriate here is a definition as broad in its scope as the title of an article by Czarniawska-Joerges (1991): culture is the medium of life. Drawing on Latour's (1986) distinction between an ostensive and a performative definition of society, Czarniawska-Joerges draws a parallel distinction between an ostensive definition of culture that assumes that, in principle, it is possible to discover properties that are typical of a given culture and that can explain its evolution, although in practice they might be difficult to detect, and a performative definition which assumes that, in principle, it is impossible to describe properties characterizing any given culture, but in practice it is possible to do so. Under an ostensive conception of culture, actors are useful informants and social researchers, using appropriate methodology (what Denzin, 1992, calls 'ethnomethodological voyeurism'), uncover opinions, beliefs, myths and rites and arrange them into a picture. Under a performative conception, there are no actors who know any more or any less, and researchers ask the same questions as any other actor, although they might use a different rhetoric in formulating their answers. Thus 'ostensive definitions are attempts to *explain principles*, whereas performative definitions *explore practices*' (Czarniawska-Joerges, 1991: 287).

I therefore use the term 'cultural approach' to refer to a performative definition of organizational culture as the system of meanings produced and reproduced when people interact. An organizational culture is the end-product of a process which involves producers, consumers and researchers. Thus the construction of meaning is purposive, reflexive and indexical.

I shall refer to the cultural studies conducted by SCOS, the acronym for the Standing Conference on Organizational Symbolism; analyses presented at SCOS conferences, but which have only in part appeared in the official journals. My intention is to show that the cultural approach is neither functionalist nor structuralist but springs from the paradigmatic breakdown (Turner, 1990b; Gherardi and Turner, 1988) which, in the 1980s, prompted organization scholars to look for analytical tools other than those of the dominant structural-functionalist paradigm (Burrell and Morgan, 1979; Linstead and Grafton-Small, 1990).

In 1981, in fact, within the European Group for Organizational Studies, an organization was set up which embraced the cultural approach, in the broadest sense of the term and without claiming to establish an orthodoxy or seeking to lay down the canons of a new creed. What is distinctive about SCOS is the fragmentation and plurality of its voices – which is, perhaps, the only factor that unifies its members. One thus understands the difficulty of presenting as a unitary phenomenon what is an ongoing debate among many and conflicting points of view. I shall attempt to do so by examining the logo of this cultural organization. More comprehensive illustration of SCOS's work can be found in Alvesson and Berg (1992) and in a number of anthologies containing its most representative output (Pondy *et al.*, 1983; Turner, 1990a; Gagliardi, 1986a, 1990; Frost *et al.*, 1985, 1991).

Within the broader cultural approach, organizational symbolism is an area of research more sketched than thoroughly explored. It is a set of intuitions more than a methodology, and as such is graphically depicted by a dragon tearing up an organization chart, the symbol of organizational rationality. Since 1984, the dragon has appeared on posters for SCOS annual conferences, on its various brochures and gadgets, and it may be taken as the organization's official logo. *Dragon* was also the name of a journal published between 1985 and 1987 which collected numerous articles on organizational symbolism.

I shall argue that the dragon is a root metaphor for the cultural approach to organizations. The dragon is a potent symbol, one common in both Western and Eastern cultures and which represents the beast *par excellence*, the adversary, the devil. Combat with the dragon is the supreme test. Yet, on the other hand, the tamed dragon with five legs is the Chinese emblem of imperial power, of wisdom and of rhythmic life.

Dragons were conventionally portrayed with the bust and legs of an eagle, the body of an enormous serpent, the wings of a bat, and a coiled tail with an arrow-shaped tip. These images represented the fusion and confusion of all the elements and all the faculties: the eagle stood for celestial power, the serpent for occult and subterranean power, the wings for the flight of the intellect, and the tail for submission to reason.

Ambiguity and duality are the distinctive features of every symbol, since the symbolic function resides simultaneously in the force of coagulation (i.e. in the synthesis, by images and correspondences among symbols, of a multiplicity of meanings into one) and in the force of dissolution (i.e. in a return to chaos, to the mixing of meanings, to dissolution).

Thus the SCOS dragon 'was meant to symbolize the ambiguity of corporate or organizational cultures. On the one hand there was the terrifying, collective "beast" lurking beneath the smooth corporate surface; on the other hand, the dragon was to symbolize the ancient and inherited wisdom built into social structure and artifacts' (Alvesson and Berg, 1992: 3). SCOS folklore has developed a real and proper 'draconological discourse' (Sievers, 1990). And from this organizational symbolism we may deduce that the dragon is present to the consciousness of those who study organizations using a cultural approach as the intellectual unease provoked by the fact that, although rational explanation and refined theory have their logical and empirical foundations, there still remains the unexplored continent of shadowland, where the most interesting phenomena of organizational life occur, and to which the concepts and languages of normal science do not apply. Science and scientific discourse are based on distinction, on separation, on analyticity and on logico-temporal sequence; their subject-matter, by contrast, is untamed, its causations are multiple and reciprocal, its boundaries are uncertain and constantly shifting, and the very action of studying such matters transforms them before our eyes.

This discussion of the dragon brings to mind another metaphor for organization, one which has enjoyed great popularity among organization scholars and which, originally, was a Zen story. People who had been blind from birth were taken to an elephant (an organization) and asked to describe it by touch: those who felt the trunk described it as a serpent, those who touched an ear described it as a great bird with wings, and so on. The dragon, the elephant and other similar stories simultaneously express both the idea that the organization is a totality and the difficulty of describing it as such: order and chaos can appear together, but what concepts can we employ to assert that something can both be and not be at the same time? Being and non-being dissolve and coagulate like alchemic principles, like the words tattooed on the arm of the devil in the fifteenth arcanum of the *tarot*; the dragon biting its own tail in the Uroboros of the Gnostics as the symbol of every cyclical process; and, again for the Gnostics, the igneous dragon symbol of Kaos and therefore of the 'path through all things', the principle of dissolution, hard and soft, hot and cold. These too may be routes to knowledge of organizations.

Understandably, generations brought up to believe the myth of science, to trust in the rational thought which vanquishes the obscurantism of faiths, and to be confident in technology's ability to resolve all problems, recoil in horror from the dragon, and reject symbolism as a legitimate source of knowledge. Before we dismiss this latter possibility, however, we must be pragmatic: we must assess whether or not organizational symbolism can throw fresh light on organizations, or help us to see something already known from a different vantage point. Indeed, a precedent already exists. Until only a few years ago, no one had explored the potential of metaphorical thought in science (Black, 1962; Brown, 1977; Ortony, 1979). And since the work of Morgan (1986), organizational studies have learnt to explore increasingly complex metaphors: from the organization-as-machine to the organization-as-hologram, to the organization-as-brain. Therefore, the organization-as-dragon may provide a metaphor for what is hidden, suppressed, slumbering beneath the surface, the irrational, the feminine, the devouring mother.

The symbology of the organizational dragon as the beast of dread condenses everything that is unconscious, everything that lies in the deeps, within the bowels of the structure, everything that may rise up to assault the conscious ego, the seat of rationality. Organizational scholars have always been aware of the dark side of organizational life, as expressed in the dichotomies of formal/informal, on the stage/behind the scenes, upper world/underworld; or in the spatial symbolism where above = managerial world = rational planning, below = workers' world = resistance = irrationality; or in the cognitive patterns where top-down = rationality moving downwards towards its implementation, bottom-up = institutionalization of social practices. In its battle to repel chaos and the irrational, management reincarnates St Michael or St George, although it is less aware of the gender symbolism implicit in the dragon.

In its positive symbology, the dragon blends the ego with the richness and the creativity of the unconscious to produce a richer 'subjectivity'. The dragon ('culture' for Smircich, 1983: 347–8):

> promotes a view of organizations as expressive forms, manifestations of human consciousness. Organizations are understood and analyzed not mainly in economic or material terms, but in terms of their expressive, ideational, and

symbolic aspects. Characterized very broadly the research agenda stemming from this perspective is to explore the phenomenon of organization as subjective experience.

This is the romantic dragon (Ebers, 1985) that we have inherited from the cultural tradition of the nineteenth century; the healer of profound conflicts because it shows 'the organization's expressive and affective dimensions in a system of shared and meaningful symbols' (Allaire and Firsirotu, 1984: 213) and because it has transcendental functions for a humankind 'emotional, symbol-loving and needing to belong to a superior entity or collectivity' (Ray, 1986: 295).

Culture conveys into organizational analysis subjectivity, emotionality, ambiguity and sexuality, all themes associated with the symbolism of the female in its fundamental psychological ambivalence: the good mother and the devouring mother.

In other words, the field of studies which falls under the umbrella term of 'culture' can be depicted as a monster with five heads, each of which is quite distinct from the others, but all of which are connected to a body in which they find unity and a common life source. We may take that these five heads to represent, respectively, five approaches to organizational culture (Alvesson and Berg, 1992: 93):

– *The head as culture*, which possesses four eyes, each of which looks at: (i) the corporate culture, i.e. culture as one of many organization variables; (ii) culture as a system of values and beliefs which links with a deeper level of basic assumptions shared by the members of an organization; (iii) cultural cognitivism which regards the system of cognitions and shared forms of knowledge; (iv) cultural artifacts which relate to unitary symbol systems unique to an organization and which function as 'culture bearing milieux'.

– *The head as meaning construction*, which possesses two eyes swivelling between organizations as shared meanings or as constructions and deconstructions of meaning.

– *The head as ideology*, which considers what positions or actions are correct, what behaviour or attitude is legitimate. This head has two ways of thinking ideology: a) neutrally, as a specific philosophical system, i.e. the corporate ideology of an organization; b) pejoratively, as political ideology which legitimates the interests of dominant groups.

– *The head as pyschodynamics*, which considers the way in which the culture phenomenon is related to unconscious and primitive aspects of human behaviour. This head has two eyes which look at shared fantasies and the organizational members' projections of their inner impulses and contradictions, and at the archetypes made manifest in the myths, rituals or other 'cultural blinders' inherent in the unconscious of organizations.

– *The head as symbolism*, which generates a symbolic picture of the organization. This head also has two eyes: one to see the particularism of symbols, the other to see their universalism.

As well as its five heads, the dragon also possesses a body, which sweats and emits steam. Following Chetwynd (1982: 138), this suggests the transformation of solid matter into energy: work activity and heat are symbolically linked through fire and the rhythm of breathing. Fire symbolizes the working order of the world, the energy of the body, the life forces of the cosmos; an image of love and therefore of union. The rhythmic flow of breath unites the inner and the outer realm; but it is also an image of the invisible flow of mental energy, which lasts as long as we breathe.

We now know a great deal about the organization/dragon, but one intriguing question is still unanswered: what sex is the animal?

Very little is known about the sex of the dragon; draconology is somewhat reticent on the matter. There are, though, two kinds of dragon. The cosmic dragon is the incarnation of chaos, it cannot be regarded as an animal and hence does not have a sex. Mythological dragons, instead, are animals which live in caves and wander the mountains and lakes 'leaving behind them stink and slime' (Sievers, 1990: 212). Yet we do not know whether there are male and female dragons, or whether they are single-sexed. The same problem arises over psychic mythodragons, which, although inhabitants of the human inner world, cannot be acknowledged as such and must therefore be projected on to objects in the outside world.

With so little known directly about the sexual and reproductive life of dragons, we may indirectly deduce their gender by considering the relationships that humans have established with these strange beasts.

Sievers (1990: 213) lists five practical ways to cope with a dragon:

1.   the heroic way: 'You have to kill him!'
2.   the magic solution: 'Kiss him!'
3.   the Chinese version: 'It is the emperor of wisdom and rain!'
4.   the science fiction approach: 'Ride him!'
5.   the lonely child solution: 'Let's be friends.'

The second and the fourth solutions are similar: 'Tame him!' So too are the third and the fifth: 'Ingratiate yourself with him!'

But by far the best known relationship with the dragon is heroic combat and the dragon's slaughter (Dégot, 1985), with the victor then absorbing its strength or, through a drop of its blood, achieving supreme knowledge. A broad array of Christian male saints, apart from St George and St Michael, have fought with dragons; but only two female ones: St Martha, who vanquished the dragon with holy water, and St Margaret, whose burning cross slew the monster. Male saints instead confront the dragon with a variety of weapons and in open combat. Combat is generally a type of social relation which arises among men, and it is valued more highly, the more it takes place between equal adversaries and according to the chivalric code. A man and a beast cannot share the same code of honour (cultural product) in combat, and there is nothing to prevent the beast from being female but ferocious and wicked. Yet combat is an activity which is assumed to be male and generally conceptualized within a male symbolic universe. Even the magic solution presupposes that it is a male dragon which is tamed – either by the Russian sorceress Marina or by the French ghost Lady Succube (Sievers, 1990: 218). The dragons of science fiction, too, are tamed, albeit by other means.

Finally, a third form of relationship can be established with the dragon: ingratiation, in both its Chinese version of the invocation of rain, and the childish one of soliciting friendship. These three relational modalities – combat, domestication, ingratiation – conjure up the idea of a male being. But whereas the first two modalities are behavioural strategies which belong to a male symbolic universe, even when the dragon is tamed by a woman, the third strategy is inscribed in a female universe and attributed to women, to people socially marginalized and generally powerless. I shall develop this topic later.

There are also good grounds for arguing that the dragon symbolizes the female gender: 'since the Middle Ages the dragon became a container for the often conscious anxieties related to sexuality . . ., a symbol of the pleasure of the flesh and lasciviousness which then had to be projected by men into women' (Sievers, 1990: 217). In the Jungian psychoanalytic tradition, the dragon is the archetype of the 'great mother', of the most inaccessible level of the collective unconscious.

The image of the Madonna with the dragon subdued beneath her feet is a symbol of the wholeness of the female self, and so too in the Christian tradition is the image of Mary crushing the head of the serpent (synonymous with the dragon).

The dragon ripping up the organization chart in the SCOS logo more closely resembles an inhabitant of the human inner world than a frozen symbol of corporate identity, like the flag of the Dragoon Guards. It therefore belongs to the subterranean world of shadows, of the intuitive, of the female and of what has been erased.

Corporate identity belongs to the domain of the conscious, of the public and of the rational, whereas the dragon is the Jungian shadow, the unaccepted split-off part of it, irrational and emotional reality. Bearing in mind the three ways to handle the dragon – slay it, tame it or ingratiate oneself with it – let us look very briefly at their treatment in the literature on gender and the organization.

First of all, it is extremely difficult to take seriously the contention that 'gender and organization' is truly a neglected topic, given that so many articles have been written to make precisely this point. It may be that this view is only the romantic expression of nostalgia or, even worse, the grumbling of those who have been excluded. Broadly speaking, the literature adopts one of two equally good strategies to cope with the problem of gender: the functionalist strategy of treating gender as just one variable amongst others, and therefore to be considered only when the need arises (Hearn and Parkin, 1987), and the emancipationist strategy which emphasizes the fundamental 'sameness' of men and women and which underrates sex differences in work and positions within organizations (Kanter, 1977).

Equal opportunities and equal rights are consequently the preconditions for women to become as good as men. The literature contains a broad strand of prescriptive recipes on how to tame the dragon. I refer to the 'fit-in' school of thought, which instructs women on how to enter organizations and management. Evidently it is taken for granted that women and organizations do not 'fit' together naturally, especially at managerial levels, and that women must therefore be socialized to roles, jobs and organizations that are by definition neuter.

Another way of taming the dragon is to exploit, to the organization's advantage, the sexual division of labour in a society which differentially socializes men and women to diverse roles in family life, in order to obtain cheap labour from women (Clegg and Dunkerley, 1980; Saraceno, 1987) and a stable male labour force to be assigned the best jobs.

There is, finally, the strategy of ingratiating oneself with the dragon by recognizing the increasing feminization of all work, especially white-collar occupations. This strategy acknowledges the strategic importance of service, understood both as the tertiary sector and as the factor 'service' within the industrial sector, and therefore positively evaluates the different skills deployed by women because they have been socialized differently and because their skills are valuable to organizations. Following Chodorow (1978) and Gilligan (1982), the difference between the sexes which appoints women as carers and assigns to men a greater 'denial of relation' is an incentive to organizations to appropriate what is good (for them) in women and to preserve it.

I have employed the symbology of the dragon to convey multiple messages, but mainly to provide the reader with a first insight, more empathic than analytical, into organizational culture viewed from a cultural standpoint. I have sought to give an idea of the plurality and fragmentation of the subject, to show that various textual strategies can be used to address gender, depending on how the relationship between gender and organization is conceived. I have moved on various levels because symbolic understanding allows exploration of the area that lies between being and non-being. Whereas in the next section I shall give analytical treatment of what is meant by symbolic understanding, here I have used a symbol as if its meanings were boulders in a river. By stepping from one to the other I have moved from functionalist analysis to symbolic analysis. These stepping stones have been a scientific community, SCOS, as a cultural community or a community of practice, depending on how one wishes to define it, which has symbolically broken with the rationalist paradigm: the dragon unmasks what the organization chart conceals. The dragon has five heads, five different approaches to organizational culture, with a single shared body and a sex. Then, in order to jump to the next stepping stone, I have asked what this symbol represents for the community which has chosen it for its logo. A possible interpretation is that the female hides behind the organization chart, but the female is both seductive and terrifying. An alternative interpretation is that the cosmic dragon represents chaos; it has no sex, it is Uroboros, the eternal flux, indeterminacy, and symbolizes process, becoming, the passage from organization to organizing.

Ambiguity in symbolist understanding

The ambiguity of language gave patriarchy its principal justification, expunged the female from history, and introduced systematic gender biases into the construction of scientific theories. Not coincidentally, feminist scholars in all the scientific disciplines (Dubois *et al.*, 1987) have denounced the sexism of language: first in history and anthropology, then in the fields of education, philosophy and literature, in the natural sciences too (Harding, 1986b) and finally in organization theory (Mills and Tancred, 1992; Calás and Smircich, 1992a). But is ambiguity inimical to science, or does it instead provide a rich source of knowledge about the complexity of the real?

There are a variety of facets to the ambiguity of life: empirical ambiguity as ambivalence, i.e. the simultaneous presence of opposites or profound contradiction; ambiguity as the indeterminacy or the contradictoriness of information, its inexactness, scarcity and high uncertainty; ambiguity as the psychological resource which increases cognitive flexibility and enhances innovative insight (Levine, 1985). The study of organizations has undervalued the ambiguity of organizational life. In using the term 'ambiguity of life' (as opposed to the ambiguity of language) I refer to the fact that a situation may have two or more meanings, or it may simply be unclear or confused: people hold contradictory expectations, consequences are vague, opinions are muddled and coloured by contrasting feelings. If, for simplicity's sake, we consider two organizational actors – management and workers – it is highly likely that every organizational event that affects their respective lives in significantly different ways will constitute, in reality, two distinct events. It will give rise to at least two different interpretations, and as a situational stimulus trigger different courses of action. The irreducible plurality of organizational facts has been simplified out by organizational studies and by the view that those who wield more power in defining reality can control more resources, and thus exert more influence.

In organization studies, Merton (1957) regarded the ambivalence of actions as a methodological problem to be addressed in the development of more comprehensive research methods which included, for example, both the manifest and the latent functions of bureaucratic action. Crozier and Friedberg (1977) subsequently used ambivalence to distinguish between the strategies of actor and the system. In sociology, Simmel (1908) was the writer most sensitive to the ambivalences of human behaviour and to the duality inherent in interaction: conformity and individualism, antagonism and solidarity, complicity and rebellion, freedom and constriction, closeness and distance, public and private. Ambiguity as indeterminacy and as a pyschological resource has been analysed by students of organized anarchies, of the garbage-can decision model, of leadership in situations of ambiguity (Cohen *et al.*, 1972; Cohen and March, 1974), of organizational learning (Levitt and March, 1988) and of organizational thought (Sims and Di Gioia, 1986).

One of the foundations of the modern age is the myth of univocality: the exact sciences, sociology and politics invariably insist on rigorous language, on unambiguous terminology, on standard and universally comprehensible discourse. The heroes of the struggle against ambiguity were Galileo, Descartes and Newton, who founded modern science on univocal discourse, on the scientific definition of categories and on the formalization of theories. Indirect, metaphorical and allegorical expressions were regarded as provisional, as subordinate, as embellishments; or else they were dismissed as expressive forms which belong to the realms of poetry, literature, philosophy, to the humanities in general, and which only enfeebled scientific enquiry.

Intrinsic to the history of ideas in the modern West is what Morin (1974) has called the 'morbid rationalism' made manifest in the endeavour to have the real coincide with the rational, to discard the event because it represents the unknown, and to reject rich, polysemous and polyphonic language because it is uncertain: 'the stuff of literati', not of 'the hard-headed men of science'. Yet this has not always been so in the history of human thought. Indeed the 'flight from ambiguity', as Levine (1985) has termed it, is a modern process which received its major impetus from the rise of Western bureaucracy. Prior to the seventeenth century, most of human knowledge derived from exploration, from accounts of voyages, from conversation and from interior reflection on life and the social. Language was vivid, evocative, analogical and ironic: it enabled the reader to enter and share the experience of the writer.

In the eighteenth century, technological and productive development increased the use of money, so that human interactions were conducted according to calculations of economic convenience. Nascent administrations drew up precise codes of conduct using bureaucratic-legal language. Finally, with the rise of the capitalist mind-set came the triumph of the patterns of thought required by planning and efficiency. Philosophical certainty resided in the deductive-mathematical method: Locke maintained that words must be purged of their obscurity; Hume urged the expulsion of vague generalizations and misleading metaphors; Newton proposed a standard terminology, concise and exact, as the sole expression of verifiable knowledge. Early social science aspired to the rigour of positivism: Durkheim sought univocal concepts with which to capture the true nature of things; Pareto endeavoured to eliminate imprecision from the use of words; and Weber was worried that terminological ambiguity might impede construction of his ideal types.

According to Levine (1985), this aversion to the ambiguity of reality and language has led to systematic undervaluation of the conceptual ambiguity of the terms used by modern science in constructing its models and, more importantly, to its consistent failure to observe and represent ambiguity as an empirical phenomenon.

Different cultures assign different values to the capacity of language to convey personal associations, to generate paradoxes, allegories, puns, and to contain hidden, symbolic and metaphorical messages. Traditional and premodern cultures (in Asia, Africa and China), but also modern cultures like Japan's, consider language as constituting expository riches, and they cultivate it as an art in complex forms of courtesy and reciprocity. Their tolerance of ambiguity has enabled these cultures to give an original and flexible elaboration to contact with different worlds, generating new symbolic equilibria (Levine, 1985). De Saussure attributed to *parole* this capacity constantly to change with the community of speakers, thereby assimilating social change and transformations in economic power among classes and between genders.

We can therefore describe – following Levine (1985: 37) – the differing tasks performed by ambiguous discourse and univocal discourse as follows. Both fulfil a cultural function as well as a social function in the context of everyday life. Both relate to a reality either external or internal to the communicating subject (see Figures 1.1 and 1.2). When ambiguity is used to represent intimate realities, it performs, through allusion, an expressive function; when, through opacity, it is used to disguise inter-actions and opinions it performs a protective one. When ambiguity represents external reality, through evocation, it yields enlightenment; when it serves to conceal these realities, through vagueness, it has a socially binding function.

Enlightenment is the feeling that one is approaching a deeper-lying truth; it is the experience of opening one's mind; it is the expression of a mystical relationship with the world. Science is enlightenment's exact opposite, since in both its ratiocinative and empirical dimensions it predicates an opposition between the knower and the known in order to dominate reality. Scientific truth is whatever can be formulated in clear definitions and precise propositions. The mystical relation with the world, by contrast, requires some sort of surrender to the universe, an intimate participation in the oneness of reality, a state of harmonious fusion with it. Science exalts cognitive mastery over the world – the action, the active being, the agent. Mysticism exalts participation and fusion; it is passive-ness in the sense of rendering oneself passive, open, receptive. Both, I believe, are forms of action which are evaluated differently, and to both correspond different attributes of gender.

I turn to the social functions of univocal and ambiguous discourse in the representation of external reality: 'Univocal communication has the properties not only of being literal, affectively neutral, and public, it is also precise. Ambiguous expressions, by contrast, can be vague' (Levine, 1985: 35). Vagueness performs some sort of socially binding function. It is used to build consensus and to create collective identity: there would be no

	EXTERNAL REALITIES	INTERNAL REALITIES
CULTURAL FUNCTIONS	Enlightenment through intuited indeterminacy (mysticism)	Expressivity through evocative allusions (metaphor)
SOCIAL FUNCTIONS	Bonding through diffuseness (solidaristic symbolization)	Self-protection through opaqueness (secrecy, deception)

Figure 1.1   *The functions of ambiguous discourse*

Source: Levine, 1985: 35

	EXTERNAL REALITIES	INTERNAL REALITIES
CULTURAL FUNCTIONS	Cognitive mastery through determinates (secular science)	Disciplined expression through literalness (prosaic language)
SOCIAL FUNCTIONS	Discrimination through specificity (specification of claims)	Self-disclosure through transparency (publicity, honesty)

Figure 1.2   *The functions of univocal discourse*

Source: Levine, 1985: 37

politics nor culture nor ideology without ambiguous language (March, 1981).

In organizations, functional specialization, occupational segregation, and the rationalization of activities used to be based on univocality in order to improve the performance of specialized roles. Yet when job descriptions, the methodical division of labour, the careful definition of spheres of competence, the precise enumeration of responsibilities and prerogatives proved unable to cope with the exigencies of flexibility, of the diffusion of skills, of a sense of belonging, then cultural engineering was discovered as the last resort of social control through the social 'glue' of shared symbols.

When, in addition to the functions of ambiguous or univocal discourse in representing inner states, the languages of specialization and diffuseness are compared, one perceives that the former corresponds to a prosaic and affectively neutral language which conveys facts, techniques or expectations; the latter corresponds to ambiguous communication, which constitutes a powerful instrument for the expression of affectivity. When we allude to shared experiences and make verbal associations through sentiments and images, through jokes and double meanings, then emotionally rich responses are expressed and evoked.

The asceticism of technical and bureaucratic language forbids the aesthetic pleasure of nuances, of subtleties and indeterminacy, and condemns them as pointless self-indulgence. Thus, those who write or speak have a moral obligation to be overt and clear, to disclose their intentions, to be direct and transparent in compliance with universalist ethical standards. Egalitarian societies believe very strongly in the publicness of communication; yet simultaneously and in parallel there is a growing need for the maintenance of personal privacy. Ambiguous language shields what lies in our minds and hearts against prying eyes; it defends our privacy and our secrecy.

Unlike transparency, secrecy is favoured by those societies or situations organized along strongly hierarchical or authoritarian lines. In contexts of non-egalitarian power relationships, of repressive subordination and of social marginalization, the weaker culture protects itself by resorting to the obscurities of language.

Besides totalitarian societies themselves, strongly centralized organizations are those which most closely protect and value secrecy, the suppression of information, the esoteric knowledge of various occupational elites. These are the organizations which defend themselves most vigorously against outside intrusion. Within them, ambiguous and evasive communication is used as a defence against exploitation and against the asymmetry of power relationships. The occupational counter-cultures of manual workers have always been systems of defence against an intrusive management. Another example, in a very different context, is provided by the medieval witchcraft trials that sought to stamp out the secrets of folk medicine and to exert closer social control over women and female bodies.

There are many and good reasons for employing ambigous discourses when discussing gender. I am exploring here rich, complex and contradictory symbolic universes which arouse profound emotions and are rooted in a hierarchical order which ranks one as superior to the other. I am examining the male and the female as the co-presence of opposites, not as mutually exclusive entities; and this violates the principle of non-contradiction on which univocal language is founded.

Ambiguous discourse is therefore an instrument with high explanatory power in analysis of complex themes and multiple realities. Gender is one of the most powerful of symbols; indeed, the very word 'gender' encapsulates all the symbols that a culture elaborates to account for biological difference (Gherardi, 1991). Symbols signify what something is and what it is not, for it is the function of a symbol to express a polysemy, to contain and to convey ambiguity. I therefore believe that a symbolist approach is particularly able to grasp the ambiguity of gender relations.

The symbolic realm is a dimension of reality and a dimension of signification, but it does not replace other levels of reality, nor does it deny them. Indeed, as Mircea Eliade writes: 'There is no need to believe that symbolic implication annuls the concrete and specific value of an object or of an operation. Symbolism adds a new value to an object or an action without affecting its own, immediate or historical, values' (Eliade, 1952: 57).

Taking an example from Cirlot (1985: 7), and positing an analogy between an organization and the façade of a monastery, we can see in the latter: (a) the beauty of the whole; (b) the architectural technique used in its creation; (c) its architectural style and its geographical and historical implications; (d) its implicit or explicit cultural and religious values; but also (e) the symbolic significance of its shapes. The understanding of what is symbolized by an ogival arch beneath a rose window is a form of knowledge very different from the others listed above.

Likewise, we may possess aesthetic, technological, historical, cultural and symbolic knowledge of an organization: paradigm plurality is implicitly assumed by the symbolic approach.

Unlike science based on the dichotomous code of true/false, mythical expression is grounded on that of sacred/profane, which constitutes one of the ordering principles of social reality (Durkheim, 1912). This, according to Cassirer (1923), is the 'fundamental antithesis' which patterns reality according to a qualitative characterization. Cassirer (1923) described humans as symbolic animals in that symbols mediate between objective reality, the world or perception, and the knowing subject. Symbols are the medium between humankind and the world. Science is a specific form of expression of culture which employs signs to refer to things and universes of objects, and which performs a logical denotative function. Yet cultures are symbolic textures in which other expressive forms are at work, myth especially. Myth is a symbolic form in which the signifying function entails a relationship of reciprocal reference between signifier and signified. The symbolic medium

> thus assumes a density, a concreteness which the symbols of other expressive forms lack. Hence its structuring function of social experience: the values which regulate our behaviour, which indicate communalities and divergences in our systems of belonging, have this mythical cultural configuration. (Bolognini, 1986: 88)

For example, in Chinese culture the yin-yang symbol represents the dualistic distribution of forces between the active, masculine principle ('yang') and the passive, feminine one ('yin'). This distribution is symbolized by a circle divided by a sigmoid line indicating the dynamic interpenetration of the two principles. The light half of the figure is the 'yang' force and the dark one the 'yin' force, but each half contains a small circle of the opposite shade which symbolizes that each principle contains the germ of the other. This symbol is a cross-section of a helicoid structure which links opposites and generates constant movement; a metamorphosis through contrary positions and situations. The vertical axis at its centre constitutes the 'mystical centre' where there is neither turbulence, nor impulse, nor suffering. The three levels of signification are therefore present in this symbol, just as they are in Hindu or Hebrew symbols which elaborate sexual difference as separation and inseparability.

Symbolist theory is based on the following principles (Cirlot, 1985: 32):

a) There is nothing that does not matter. Everything expresses something and everything is meaningful.
b) No form of reality is independent: everything stands in relation to something else.
c) The quantitative is transformed into the qualitative at certain essential points which constitute the signification of quantity.
d) Everything is serial. Seriality includes both the physical world (the spectrum of colours, sounds, shapes, landscapes) and the spiritual world (virtues, vices, sentiments).
e) There are correlations of situation among different series, and of meaning among series and their constitutive elements.

If we take any particular symbol – the sword, for example – and analyse it, we first find the object in itself stripped of every relation, and then the object in its instrumental function. Finally we come to its symbolic function, which is the dynamic tendency of its quality equivalent to those located at the corresponding points in every analogous series. The symbolic function is to denote a general meaning, one which is often ambivalent and allusive. The multiplicity of which is never chaotic, however, because it moves to a shared rhythm. Thus the sword, iron, fire, the colour red, the god Mars, the Rocky Mountains, are interconnected and meet in a symbolic direction of equal significance: the desire for psychic determination and for physical destruction (Cirlot, 1985: 33). These symbols unite with each other, they call upon each other because of the inner affinity that unites them, the shared rhythm that enables connections to be established among the diverse levels of reality. For example, the ovoid shape, undulating rhythm, high sounds conjure up a female rhythm which projects itself on to nature by taking things and shapes and translating them into personages in the drama.

Returning to organizations, let us take one of these rhythms and examine what it is that ties the male to rationality, the female to emotionality and the organization to the male. Let us see what gender entails in the social construction of values that departs from that particular value which has been the structuring myth of the organization: rationality.

There is no doubt that in the dual hierarchical system of the representation of reality, the term rational/rationality is paramount: to the extent that its opposite or complementary term is defined as residual, marginal, that is, defined by default. 'Irrational' is usually the second term in the binary opposition, but it is a weak, improper term which signals a deficiency, a deviation, a lack; one which, thus defined, signals an absence rather than a presence. 'Irrational' is a word which covers several different concepts, ranging from the forms of rationality – which forced out by instrumental rationality have lost rationality with respect to a value – to litional rationality, to intuition, to the feelings, to the emotions; that is, hidden world where the body seems to contaminate the mind, where instinctive touches the cognitive. Consider the debate that still engages psychologists over the boundaries between the cognitive, the emotions and the sentiments. Thought (which implies rationality) is the legitimate boundary between cognition, choice and action, even when the complexity of everyday decisions induces the sentiments to revolt against their compartmentalization and marginalization. Therefore, instead of irrationality I prefer to use a second term – emotionality – which permits a less residual, more autonomous definition of the concept. Rationality and emotionality clearly belong to that continuum of symbolic values which delineates gender: the male, the rational, the public, activity, separation, thought, the mind, hardness, coldness, the vertical; as opposed to the female, the emotional, the private, receptivity, connection, sentiment, the body, softness, warmth, the horizontal.

Being rational has always been an ethical imperative in organizational thought, backed by the most grievous of threats visited upon human (i.e. finite) beings: the loss of life. Rational organizations go about their business, they intone the sacred texts of organization, on pain of death. Who dares to declare that they do not obey the principles of rationality and that, for example, they run a successful company on decisions prompted by the emotions? Were we to hear such an admission, we would assume that it was made by a female manager running some type of service or producing cosmetics, perhaps. Gender coherence would somehow be presented as a cultural continuity. 'True' organizations would continue to flex the muscles of rationality, to be business-oriented, optimizers, cold in their judgements and steadfast in their behaviour. Impassiveness would be stitched into their clothes as into their hearts. If they failed to be entirely rational, this would be bounded rationality, but they would still endeavour as much as possible to rationalize their activities. With a hint of irony I am suggesting that rationality is still the dream pursued by organizations, their myth of mediation (Abravanel, 1983) between the quotidian and the sublime. But the rationalization of past occurrences and the rhetoric of rationality are the two remedies (*a posteriori* and *a priori*) for breakdowns in rationality.

This latter statement allows me to propose two complementary readings of rationality: on the one hand, the rhetoric of rationality legitimizes and normalizes the attribution of a male character to most organizations; on the other, rationality as an organizing principle exerts control over emotionality.

Rationality as an organizing principle is the translation into structures of the thought that delimits, breaks down, analyses according to linear sequences, compares on the basis of utility criteria, and differentiates. Organizational structures by function are the concretization of a rational style of thought which decomposes the totality, hierarchizes functions, and establishes means–ends concatenations. The planning/execution distinction symbolizes the mind/body relationship; that is, the actuation of a separation and the establishment of a subordination relationship. For organizations, rationality was an efficient organizing principle as long as operational settings and socio-economic environments were relatively stable, and as long as conditions were almost certain. The onset of ambiguity required flexibility, a closer relation between conception and execution, custom with shifting boundaries, the emphasis on cooperation strategies and, ultimately, a distancing from the organizing principle of rationality (Berg, 1985).

Also sexual identity and its reflexive institutionalization could have been more clearly separated between female and male when the sexual division of labour gave rise to separate world experiences and life practices.

In contemporary society the symbolic fabric is much more fragmentary, complex and chaotic than it used to be in traditional societies. Bureaucracy has exalted legal-rational thought. It has institutionalized an organizational society (Perrow, 1991) and a 'rational, linear, denotative style of thought which thins out the symbolic density of cultural meaning arrays, which are then further fragmented by the prolific and sometimes incestuous transformations which we daily inflict upon all kinds of symbolic representations' (Turner, 1992: 63). It is not always easy to understand symbolic representations, nor to define the way in which they structure social experience. The difficulty stems from the nature itself of the symbol, which is so much the *significans* as to be indeterminate and constantly to defer its *significandum*, and which requires an indirect language, one which establishes relations and conserves transformative power. The invention of the symbol is a creative act which rests upon the ability to see a thing as what it is not (Casttoriadis, 1987: 137). Symbolic understanding is therefore generated on the borders of ambiguity, where being and non-being merge, where the indeterminate is about to transform itself into the determinate, and where possibilities are *in nuce*.

Is it possible to speak unambiguously about ambiguity, non-symbolically about symbols? Is it possible to identify a symbolist methodology and to specify symbolist research techniques? A radical answer would point to hermetic language and aesthetic experience as the only possibilities (indeed, for that matter, symbolism was born of the arts). However, linguistic mediation is possible if one wishes to remain in the field of organizational studies, even more so now that new metaphors taken from literary criticism are being used to rethink and rewrite the organization as a text.

I cannot offer recipes or prescriptions, but I shall try to describe what is meant by the 'symbolic perspective' and how this forms an independent strand of enquiry within the cultural approach. In the previous section I used the symbol of the dragon to illustrate the cultural approach, and the aim of this book is to give a symbolist reading of gender relations in organizations.

Let us look more closely at the distinction between these two forms of analysis in organizational studies; a distinction drawn with extreme clarity by Alvesson and Berg (1992: 118–26) and which can be summarized as follows:

(a) Symbolists do not start from the assumption that there is a culture in a company; instead they study organizations from a symbolic perspective.
(b) Symbolists also differ from many culture researchers in that they emphasize the aesthetic, ethical and emotional dimensions of human life, rather than simply examining its cognitive and axiological dimensions.
(c) Symbolists dissolve the difference between the subjective and the objective; they link symbols, images, metaphors, etc. together: 'the mythic mode of symbolling' (Witkin and Berg, 1984).
(d) Symbolists assume that there are clear and impassable parameters within which reality can be moulded. Despite considerable lack of agreement as to what these parameters actually are, they reflect the natural formation of meaning patterns resulting from historically-formed attitudes. These patterns have been communicated across generations and across cultural frontiers, and they express relationships with other human beings, the purpose of existence, of nature, etc.

In other words the symbolist has the following distinctive features:

- S/he is a qualitative researcher who prefers to see things through the eyes of the subject. S/he is interested in meanings, in the process of their attribution, in how they are sustained, in the way that some meanings prevail while others disappear.
- S/he is a participative researcher, who knows that s/he is part of the production of meaning and of the narration of stories, as both the narrating and the narrated subject.
- S/he is the product of contextual understanding of actions and symbols, not only because they are inseparable but because all symbols are value-laden and meaningful only in terms of their relationship to other symbols.
- S/he is a wanderer among the realms of knowledge seeking to reconstruct the links among the various levels of reality created by a symbol through individual symbolic production, the collective unconscious and artistic production: the immanent with the transcendent, the mental with the physical, with action, with transformation.

The symbolist is interested in three principal areas of enquiry (Turner, 1992):

- matters of style, the aesthetic qualities of a way of life, the generation and maintenance of identities, the symbolic construction of community;

- archetypes, allegories, myths, as the ways in which the collective unconscious – or the transpersonal production of culture – enter the phenomenal
  world of the organization and its processes;
- the imaginary capacity, as the mental and social ability to create symbols,
  evoke images, create a social imaginary as the context in which meanings,
  values and the prefigurations of will and action take shape. This is the locus
  of prospective symbols, those which create and develop a vision.

In the chapters that follow, these areas will be explored with reference to various organizational settings, but the logic used to propose a symbolic interpretation of gender will be different. I have chosen two symbols of gender relations – the sexual contract and the alchemic wedding – to denote respectively the opposition and the transformation that the gender relation may engender as the male and female reciprocally define each other.

The image of the contract and that of the wedding are symbolic representations of the separation and inseparability of the genders. It is the dialectic between these two images that produces the symbolic order of gender sustaining a specific cultural form. This symbolic order is produced, maintained and transformed within symbolic interactions among people who define themselves, or are defined, as belonging to one gender or the other. It is this classification process that structures social experiences in terms of opportunity, equality and justice. The symbolic construct of citizenship therefore comprises a plurality of social imaginaries which locate men and women differently according to their gender, class and race membership.

2

The Metaphor of the Sexual Contract

Among the various things – more or less reverent – that can be said about science is that it is a collection of stories about how the world is made, and that a number of these stories are nothing but scientific fairy tales. Take the egg and the sperm (Martin, 1991: 489):

> It is remarkable how 'femininely' the egg behaves and how 'masculinely' the sperm. The egg is seen as large and passive. It does not *move* or *journey*, but passively 'is transported', 'is swept', or even 'drifts' along the fallopian tube. In utter contrast, sperm are small, 'streamlined', and invariably active. They 'deliver' their genes to the egg, 'activate the developmental program of the egg', and have a 'velocity' that is often remarked upon. Their tails are 'strong' and efficiently powered. Together with the forces of ejaculation, they can 'propel the semen into the deepest recesses of the vagina'. For this they need 'energy', 'fuel', so that with a 'whiplashlike motion and strong lurches' they can 'burrow through the egg coat' and 'penetrate' it.
>
> At its extreme, the age-old relationship of the egg and the sperm takes on a royal or religious patina. The egg coat, its protective barrier, is sometimes called its 'vestments', a term usually reserved for sacred, religious dress. The egg is said to have a 'corona', a crown, and to be accompanied by 'attendant cells'. It is holy, set apart and above, the queen to the sperm's king. The egg is also passive, which means that it must depend on sperm for rescue.

This rhetoric, culturally constructed on anthropomorphic images, is a well-known story common to children's books, popular science and scientific textbooks. It is a rhetoric so diffuse that it has been left unscathed by recent scientific discoveries which demonstrate that, in actual fact, the sperm and the egg are mutually active partners. Martin's amusing article shows how the official language of biology has been unable to adapt itself to description of an 'encounter' between these equally but differently active partners, and how it has instead assimilated attempts to recast the description of scientific phenomena into its already-existing rhetoric. For example, the description of the egg which attracts the sperm, selects it, traps it with its micropyles and swallows it up, conveys an image which acknowledges the egg's active role but at the same time portrays it as a 'femme fatale' – a disturbingly aggressive image. The poor egg has no choice: it must either be the Sleeping Beauty waiting to be awoken and redeemed by the heroic sperm, or it is the spider-woman, the devouring mother. The attempt to describe its behaviour as interactive is thus thwarted.

Whenever the metaphors that lie dormant in scientific discourse are activated, ironic effects are produced which subvert the established order. Indeed, after I had read Martin's article, I could not forget her comment (Martin, 1991: 491) on describing a microscope photograph of an enormous egg and a tiny sperm bearing the title 'A Portrait of the Sperm': 'this is a little like showing a photo of a dog and calling it a picture of the fleas'.

Because an intentional act – a key feature in the construction of personal being in our culture – is attributed to the sperm, its importance to the egg is asserted to the point that it can be 'portrayed' and thereby acquire a 'personality' at the level of the individual cell. It is this social image-making on the representation of nature that attributes the creation of the persona to the moment of fertilization.

There is another aspect to the pervasiveness of the gendered imagery of production/reproduction, and therefore of organizational discourse, that I wish to stress, basing myself on Martin's article. The reproductive organs are a productive enterprise: this is one way of describing the romance of the egg and the sperm using the rhetoric of production. Both organs produce commodities endowed with value, but whereas the production of sperm is a constant process with an output of several hundred million items per day, the productive enterprise of the female organs is conditioned by the joyless reality of menstruation – interrupted production. Moreover, only a few follicles (400) reach maturity, and these are present from birth – an overstocked inventory which means wastage and the ineluctable destiny of monthly degeneration. Only the sperm – the corporate management – can change this destiny by embarking on a difficult voyage into the warm darkness of an exogenous environment. Many spermatozoa set off on this arduous journey, but only a few survive to launch their final assault and claim the prize. Their action is typified by autonomy, they operate independently and in isolation – for the sperm has only one mission: to search out the ovum.

Martin also refers to another popular account: the 'existential decision' taken by the sperm to penetrate the egg. Since these cells have only a limited behavioural repertoire, the language of 'executing decisions' is used to describe a situation of risk. What are the female organs doing in the meantime? They wait, prepare the nest, work together to protect the fragile and dependent egg.

The same social imagery is also used to describe the activity of the organization in male terms. Thus we have the heroic saga of the management as it sallies forth into a treacherous external environment, measuring its potency in figures, taking decisions and undertaking intentional acts. Production is the essence of the organization, and it is of paramount importance with respect to female reproductive activity. Like the fleas on the dog. The day-to-day activities of the organization as it reproduces the conditions for production – book-keeping, the cataloguing of information and its delivery, back-up activities, executive action and quality control, the maintenance of premises, machinery, interpersonal relations and feelings − may be invisible, but they are as important for the organization as the egg for the sperm.

The pervasiveness of gender resides in the seriality with which meanings are transferred from one province of meaning to another. Two cells are defined as male and female, they are attributed gender characteristics, they are personified to the point that human life stems from their first encounter (and Catholic morality posits the equation of abortion and murder).

Reproduction involves production. These two activities assume gender features and they are socially assigned to people with differently sexed bodies. All production activities acquire male characteristics, and vice versa, because it is thus inscribed in nature, in biological destiny. The symbolism of reproduction, based on the cultural elaboration of nature, extends to every sphere of the social division of nature. The production of knowledge, in its turn, a-critically imports the gender bias which, via scientific fairy tales, legitimizes a social order based on gender difference. And this gives rise to the inequality of social destiny.

The gendered features of organizational activities implicitly select people with matching gender features. The interaction of gendered activities and gendered people is inscribed in the social imaginary that projects the cultural elaboration of gender on to nature and then imports it back into the culture as natural difference.

Organization theory and biology have both developed a descriptive language of 'natural' phenomena which takes the tale of the egg and the sperm for granted, and presumes that women adhere to the egg and men to the sperm. Both languages resist the heresy of recent scientific 'discoveries': the sperm and the egg stick together because of adhesive molecules on their surfaces, the scientists of Johns Hopkins University tell us. But if science had conceptualized the romance of the egg and the sperm differently, might it not have discovered the interaction of the two cells earlier? Likewise, if the heroic language of the primacy of production (and of competition) had not obscured the ancillary language of reproduction (and of cooperation), might we not earlier have achieved the transition to a post-industrial and postmodern society of services, of interorganizational networks? These are questions to which there is no factual answer; they relate to the way we interrogate the relationship between the knowing subject and nature, and they relate to the gendered nature of the questions we ask and the descriptions we make.

The romance of the egg and the sperm is not the only example of a scientific fairy tale. I wish to examine another one, the social/sexual contract. This still concerns gender and power, but in the area of social behaviour.

The most influential political fairy tale of all is so-called social contract theory, which treats our democratic society as if it originated in a contract (the paradigm of free social relations) as opposed to status (the ascription of social positions, as in traditional societies). I shall use the concept of social contract – and in doing so refer to the book by Carole Pateman (1988) – to propose a metaphor for gender relationships. This metaphor is based on a notion of exchange which presupposes two free contractors.

In *The Sexual Contract* (1988: 1), Pateman declares that:

> The original contract is a sexual-social pact, but the story of the sexual contract has been repressed. Standard accounts of social contract theory do not discuss the whole story and contemporary contract theorists give no indication that half of the agreement is missing. The story of the social contract is also about the genesis of political right, and explains why exercise of the right is legitimate – but this story is about political right as patriarchical right or sex-right, the power that men exercise over women.

The hypothetical story of the birth of civil society displays a manifest paradox. It claims to be based on universal freedom, but simultaneously denies this attribute to women. One interpretation of the original contract is that those who lived in a state of nature exchanged the insecurity of natural freedom for equality and civil liberty protected by the state. In the new-found civil society all adults enjoyed civil liberty and replicated the original contract whenever, for example, they entered into a work contract or a marriage contract. Another interpretation views civil society as post-patriarchal because it was created by sons who rebelled against paternal authority and replaced the law of the father with civil government. Note how the story of the rebellion of the sons against the father is archetypical. It is found not only in Greek myths, in the struggle between the deities of the first and second generation, but also in other cosmogonies. The feature common to these narratives is that they omit to mention that the sons did not subvert the patriarchal order to establish universal civil liberty, but to get the women for themselves. The original contract came about after the political defeat of the father, after the sexual contract (i.e. equal access to women) had been established. Hence the social contract is a tale recounted by the modern fraternal patriarchy. The original contract envisaged both the freedom of men and the subjection of women.

The paradox is this: if women do not enjoy natural freedom they cannot be subject to a contract, nor can they possess the characteristics of an 'individual'. Moreover, the opposition between the state of nature and civil society creates a further paradox: between public and private, and between public-man and private-woman.

The history of patriarchal civil society recounts how the public sphere of civil freedom was created; yet it glosses over the other sphere, the private one, which it dismisses as largely irrelevant even though it is governed by the matrimonial contract. After the original contract, it was the antinomy between nature and civil society that constituted the sphere of civil society; subsequently, however, the term 'civil' applied only to the public sphere, not to the private one. Women were thus incorporated into civil society, but into an area of it that both was and was not civil society. As Pateman puts it (1988: 11): 'the private, womanly sphere (natural) and the public, masculine sphere (civil) are opposed but gain their meaning from each other, and the meaning of the civil freedom of public life is thrown into relief when counterposed to the natural rejection that characterizes the private realm'.

Critical analysis of the great thinkers of the social contract would continue at this point with direct reference to Pateman's book. For my present purposes, however, I shall only retain the image of the sexual contract as a metaphor for the incorporation of women into civil society by means of a story of subjection which parallels the tale of the egg and the sperm. Scientific and political fairy tales construct femininity as subjection, non-action. Moreover, it is the image of the contract which persuades people to subject themselves voluntarily to the state, to civil laws, to contractual obligations: freedom becomes obedience in exchange for protection.

By means of symbolic seriality I wish to maintain the ambiguity of the social construction of gender relationships: freedom and subjugation, the public and the private, sexual differences and sexualities.

Just as the sexual contract is the element left unsaid in the social contract, by analogy I wish to pursue this line of thought apropos of the sexual contract within the employment contract. I intend to show the sexual symbolism of organizational cultures, and sexuality as that dynamic of organizing which is left unsaid.

The sexuality of the employment contract

The employment contract is conventionally described as the economic exchange, more or less equal, of wages for labour. According to this economic fairy tale, the worker acts as though s/he is supplying his/her labour and ceding his/her command, within the limits of the contract, to the employer, who in turn acquires a series of rights over the worker's skills or services. What is left unsaid is that the employment contract also grants command over a body, which is utilized according to the times and in the manner stipulated; and bodies are sexually differentiated. When an organization creates a subordination relationship with a male or female body, it acquires rights of access which are differentiated according to the body's sexuality. In what follows, in fact, I propose to demonstrate that forms of subordination differ according to the body that enters into the employment contract.

First of all, when an organization hires a person, it hires not just a mind, but a body endowed with gender characteristics. Hence, in addition to the expectations associated with the work role there are those associated with the sex role. Nieva and Gutek (1981) use the term 'role spillover' to denote the carry-over of gender-based expectations into the workplace, and Benson (1986) describes it as the co-option of gender characteristics. In other words, organizations expect different behaviours from, for example, a male worker or office clerk than from a female one. Or again, the same work role has differing contents according to whether it is assigned to a man or a woman. An example is Teresa, an elderly woman who started working in a factory when the male workers had been enlisted into the armed forces during the Second World War. She stayed on in the factory even when the men had returned and most of her sister workers had gone back to housework:

> Because you're a woman you have to keep your work-bench clean and tidy. When we were all women we did it as a matter of course so that we would find everything in its place the next morning. There was only one man, and he didn't do it; the cleaning women did it for him, which was a bit of a privilege and a way of mollycoddling him. When the men came back and there were only a few of us women left, they didn't keep things tidy and the cleaning women did it for them. That was what they all expected of us. We had a row about this because cleaning used up our time and we were all on piecework. But there was nothing we could do. Everyone, workmates and cleaning women, said the same thing: you can't expect a man to clean up. (Teresa)

But not only gender characteristics are co-opted. Sexual skills, too, are acquired and incorporated into the organizational role. The organization acquires command over the sexuality of its employees, within certain limits. Women with jobs that require, implicitly or explicitly, an attractive appearance – hostesses, saleswomen, receptionists, secretaries – are duty-bound to be agreeable or seductive, and must be or pretend to be 'sexy' in their dealings with the public.

Traditionally, these demands were made of women because sexuality was symbolized by the female body and male desire; the commercialization and commodification of this was more explicit and widespread. More recently, however, the male body too has been caught up in the process, both in advertising and in the organizational demand for an 'attractive appearance' – or in the exploitation of sexual endowments to service a more economically independent female clientele, or a clientele with a different, less suppressed, sexual orientation. Sexuality is more and more a commodity, and as a commodity it colours the service that the organization delivers to its clientele. For their part, the customers (one thinks here of the tourist industry, the entertainment industry and personal services) ask to be seduced, to be inveigled into a trust relationship which massages their egos and fulfils their needs. Organizations deploy the sexual skills of their employees to flatter, to soothe, to satisfy, to ensnare the customer. Sexuality is brought on to the public stage in accordance with the social norms that regulate it.

The sexualization of the employment relationship is particularly evident in 'boundary roles' – those where the worker comes into contact with customers, with suppliers, or at any rate with significant areas of the environment external to the organization. But it is also an instrument for organizational control. It has been pointed out that women are very often used to socialize the group that comes into contact with the organization, especially when this group is particularly difficult, deviant, obstructive or does not readily accept authority. Clerical workers, sales and service staff – that is, two-thirds of the female labour force – perform tasks which Tancred-Sheriff (1989) and Grant and Tancred (1992) have called the 'adjunct control of the labour process'.

This form of control is exercised by female labour employed as: (a) clerical workers who exert control through the categorization of information about production, costs and the workforce; (b) sales workers who deliver goods, collect payments and socialize customers into correct behaviour as consumers; (c) service workers who, in producing services, socialize customers or users of the service in correct behaviour.

At work, therefore, women, 'seduced' by the power of others, act as the long arm of managerial, capitalist and patriarchal control.

One gender characteristic attributed to women is their scant personal authority compared with the power that attaches to their organizational roles. Hence it follows that, although they may be splendid Athenas (see Chapter 3) representing the authority of the father and reflecting his prestige, they have limited discretionary powers. They are 'there' to symbolize the authority of the organization and the sacredness of its rules. As the long arm of authority and of social control, they are credible because they are women; their lack of authority does not threaten their identity as women, and their being women may inhibit the hostility and resentment directed against the organization by its customers.

The same applies to the lower levels of management, where work consists more in the implementation of the authority wielded by others and in its representation than in the exercise of wider discretionary powers and control. Participating in the authority of others, representing it, exercising it vicariously, is seductive to the extent that the position of subordination is legitimate and psychologically acceptable. If the seductiveness of power, and the pleasure of intimacy with it, render these female or subordinate workers more closely attached to their tasks within the organization, they will be especially adept at socializing the groups that come into contact with it, and they will transmit their fascination with the organization to these groups. This is an example of control through sexuality and seduction. Not dissimilarly, in traditional family roles the mother's authority over the children was vicarious authority. It mediated between the exercise of control and assurance to the father that his children loved him by inhibiting their aggression towards him. Social workers, the majority of whom are women, act out the same script in protecting the state, just as secretaries act it out for their bosses, nurses for doctors, and front-desk workers for the rest of the organization.

Inscribed in the hierarchical relationship is not only the code of command/obedience, but also the eroticism of subordination and interdependence, as well as the fascination of delegated and vicarious power which, through the trappings of power, may give a hint of the sacred to those who do not possess it. The subject 'woman' is constructed within a dependence relationship, and being a 'spokesperson', acting as the envoy of authority that lies elsewhere, is a consistent characteristic of gender, to which corresponds a sexual pleasure also labelled 'female'.

That work roles are gendered and that organizations command not only bodies but also the sexuality of these bodies, is patently obvious. What is intriguing, though, is not the obviousness of the fact, but that organizational discourse should nevertheless assert that organizational roles are neutral, that there is no legitimate place for sexuality in the organization, and that pleasure belongs exclusively to the private sphere.

Starting from very different premises and intentions, both the organizational discourse that claims to desexualize the organization, and the feminist discourse that stresses the coercive aspects of sexuality, become unwitting allies in a form of social control which regards sex with prudish distaste.

A good example of the variety of discourses on sexuality is provided by the book edited by Hearn *et al.* (1989), *The Sexuality of Organization*, where the pervasiveness and ubiquity of sexualities is well illustrated by the diversity of views expressed by the authors. More in general, the desexualization of organizations and of organizational discourse (Burrell, 1984) is closely bound up with the valorization of rationality in the Weberian sense, of the principles of impersonality, specialization, authority, impartiality, and therefore of the separation of the public realm of rationality from the private one of emotionality and private feelings. Thus, in addition to the rationalization of all the areas of human activity, which already alarmed Weber, there is the supremacy of production over reproduction.

The organization, as the subject of discourse, is desexualized, and it desexualizes behaviours. The sexualization of behaviours, of languages and of the time devoted to profane matters is dismissed as irrelevant. It is in fact of little interest to the organization as long as it does not interfere with the sacred business of production. And yet it is of great interest if it eroticizes the workplace and weds control with pleasure.

Feminist discourse on male sexuality in organizations and on sexual harassment – to which almost two-thirds of the literature on sexuality in organizations is devoted (MacKinnon, 1979; Gutek, 1989) – also helps to desexualize the organization, because it constructs the woman as victim (that is, as a discourse object) and male sexuality as the sexuality only of males and only as heterosexual.

For example, if one reads Gutek's (1989) practical suggestions to managers for avoiding sexual harassment in their organizations, one realizes that this advice must be very welcome to managers, for it is part of the selfsame strategy for the social control of sexuality.

Gutek recommends five strategies (Gutek, 1989: 68–9), which can be summarized as follows:

1. Establish a policy on sexual harassment and a set of procedures to implement it.

2. Provide employees with knowledge about sexual harassment in special training sessions and in new employee orientation.
3. Vigorously pursue allegations of harassment and act on the basis of evidence gathered in an investigation.
4. Include sexual harassment in performance appraisals and act on those results.
5. Promote professional behaviour and a professional ambience throughout the organization. A sexualized workplace and an unprofessional ambience encourage sexual harassment.

I am not being insensitive to the gravity and extent of sexual harassment nor to sexual discrimination in the workplace. I wish merely to contest a unilateral and univocal way of defining sexuality and to urge the desexualization of workplaces, because power and pleasure are interrelated in a politics of the body and both are constituted as discourse relations.

To give an example of what I mean, I reproduce below the transcript of a conversation among a group of women discussing sexual harassment. I recorded this conversation in rather curious circumstances. For the purposes of research, I was interviewing the secretary of a university department. The interview had almost finished and we were waiting for the secretary from another department, with whom we had arranged to go out for lunch, to arrive. To stress the everyday, commonplace nature of the scene, I shall entitle it *Così fan tutte* (Like All the Others Do).

Imagine that you are watching a play.

Così fan tutte

The cast
– the first secretary, Daniela, a woman of about 35, married with two children, a trade union activist and an influential opinion leader;
– the interviewer, a university researcher, familiar with the environment because she has been conducting research there for about a month; she is the same age as the first secretary;
– the second secretary, Renata, a woman of pleasant and youthful appearance, presumably about 50 years old; a very energetic and forceful character who speaks with a high-pitched voice;
– the student: a young woman aged 23 or 24, extremely beautiful and outgoing; a student representative.

The scene
The first secretary (D) and the interviewer are seated at a desk. The second secretary (R) enters, followed by the student, who asks for the professor, a notorious 'ladies' man'. As she crosses the office and enters his room, the three women follow her with their eyes. They are all apparently thinking the same thing.

R (heaving a deep sigh): Those were the days! The older I get, the less I'm a sexual object!
[*All three laugh*]
D: Don't you think we should warn her?
R: It's a bit late, isn't it?
D: The deed's done by now. But we should have put her on her guard . . . then it was up to her to decide.
R: What gives us the right to interfere in her life, to tell her what she can and can't do, watch out for the big bad wolf? We're not her mother!
D: Yes, but we know what he's like. He tries it on with everyone, and he usually succeeds! [*Laughter*] And she's so young! Perhaps she won't even realize!
R: Yeah, you're right. It's a question of women's solidarity . . . [*long pause, exchange of glances; the women look at me: I shrug my shoulders*]
D: Yes, but who's going to tell her, and how? And if it's been done already, we're going to look stupid. He'll find out and we'll look like gossips.
R: If it's too late . . . well, hard luck! It'll only mean it was useless. But we won't feel guilty. And if that's not the case, it means that we warned her and then she did as she pleased.
D: It's easy for you to say that, but I have to work with him. And I don't want any more hassles than I've got.
R: Listen, we've all gone through these situations and we've been able to handle them. The same goes for her. And, anyway, being so pretty it won't be the first time she's been propositioned.
D: Yes, but in the workplace it's a different matter.
R [*shrugging her shoulders and looking at her watch*]: I don't know what to say. I think she has to go through it just like all of us.
D [*turning to me*]: Shall we go and eat?

I had inadvertently left my tape-recorder on when the interview was interrupted, and I was thus able to recover the exact sequence of this first conversation. At lunch, the discussion continued and other women were drawn into the argument. They took sides, advocating either intervention or non-interference: the latter, in fact, is what actually happened. Interestingly, those who took part in this second conversation could not agree on who should warn the girl student. One of them, a female trade union official, suggested that a female lecturer should warn her or, alternatively, threaten her colleague.

Let us look at what the above text tells us, at what it does. In what follows the italics represent my comments on the construction of the text and show the process of its deconstruction. As well as resolving the tension through laughter, Renata's initial joke shows that she knows this situation intimately: she has actually experienced what she calls 'being a sexual object'. Yet she plays down the drama by treating it as a joke and expressing apparent nostalgia ('Those were the days!') for a debatable sexual condition. She also minimizes her past as a sexual object by contextualizing it within the life cycle: these things only happen at a certain stage of a woman's life. The passage of time entails the waning of one's being a sexual object. *Is this therefore a natural phenomenon?*

Renata not only defines the situation with her joke, she also reveals her self-perception. She teases us about herself as a (still) attractive woman; a woman unafraid of sexual appreciation, and also one sufficiently sexually liberated to say so – even though her declaration takes the form of a joke. Daniela replies by expressing her worries, and indeed by describing the situation as dangerous. *Is it therefore a case of sexual harassment?* Simultaneously, however, she does not take the initiative but leaves it to us (two) to decide. She thus creates a collective subject (us three) for the action that she thinks should be taken.

Negotiation now begins over definition of the reality of the situation; negotiation which excludes me and gives me a chance to retreat to the sidelines, for I obviously do not belong to that particular action system even though I am part of the conversation. Renata, in fact, does not reply on the same discourse level. Instead she asks a question which insinuates scepticism over the girl student's identity, although overtly she only queries the temporal frame of the action.

Daniela takes up Renata's double insinuation. If it is too late, 'the deed has been done'. But what 'deed'? If it is not too late, then the girl student will decide. But what? The contraposition of the two frames of reference is thus acknowledged: is sexual harassment or free will at issue? Daniela reaffirms the presence of a collective subject as an ethical actor ('we should have. . .'). The ethical problem, therefore, is not the behaviour of the girl student but their own. This subtle distinction is fully grasped by Renata, who responds head-on by questioning the legitimacy of the action proposed. Within a frame of 'free will', a warning to the student would trigger the image of prohibition, of sexuality as danger (the bad wolf of the fairy tale also symbolizes sexuality in adult language), and of the adult as coercive authority. *Is this perhaps an act of rebellion? Does the girl enter the wolf's lair in order to breach certain social rules?*

Daniela now attempts to appease her interlocutor by making her laugh, but in doing so she confirms that the wolf is indeed bad, and she knows it! The girl student's role as the 'innocent' is further emphasized: she is young, perhaps she will not notice the 'sexual harassment'.

There is a momentary lull in the conversation, and agreement is apparently reached when Renata tells Daniela she is right. But she does so by redefining the situation in terms of women's solidarity. But among what women? The conflict of interpretations is still present: the 'sexual harassment' frame requires an innocent subject, and to create an innocent subject the girl student is ascribed the role of a minority; the 'free will' frame presupposes the ability to choose evil, to be a non-innocent subject. In order not to be a sexual object, therefore, one must be a non-innocent subject! And this initiates the second part of the story, when the organization enters the scene.

Having reached agreement over action, the problem of the agent now arises. Daniela suddenly seems to realize that she is in a setting of structured organizational relationships – and structured in such a way that the man in question is her superior. The girl student may not be so innocent; even worse, she might inform the man of the action taken against him. Daniela is worried that a possible audience would react by branding them as 'gossips'. This does not bother Renata, who offsets the possible failure of the action (at most useless) with relief from guilt. She drives home her point by reiterating her thesis of free choice.

Daniela now openly expresses her fear of reprisals, and emphasizes the difference between her and Renata in their organizational positions: the wolf is not just one of the many men in the organization; he is her boss. *Does loyalty to the boss therefore occupy a higher position in the scale of moral values than averting possible harassment?* Although the comparison is an extreme one, does it not frequently happen that mothers refuse to acknowledge the sexual abuse of their children because the men responsible are their husbands?

Renata appreciates Daniela's point and the value it expresses. She does not object, for example, that her boss is so well known in the organization as a Don Giovanni that they can talk freely about him in the presence of an outsider; hence the sanction of being labelled a 'gossip' is not a particularly severe one. Instead, Renata seeks to be reassuring. She lowers the pitch of her voice to invite intimacy and re-proposes a 'natural' version of the story: all attractive girls have experienced, experience, or are going to experience sexual advances. It is part of life. She thus deploys the conventional rhetoric that portrays man as the hunter and woman as the prey.

Daniela apparently accepts this rhetoric, but objects that it does not apply in the workplace. Does she thus presume that the workplace is a no-go area, some sort of sex-free zone where hunting is forbidden? *Or is it the lawfulness of bearing arms, the misappropriation of the organization's attributes and property – like organizational position, the office, time, work effort – at issue? Is this a case of unprofessional conduct?*

The conversation drew unsatisfactorily to a close. Left unresolved was both the conflict of interpretation between the two women and the strong emotionality and ethical tension that the problem had provoked. The subsequent discussion over lunch added the further issue of territoriality and its control by various organizational groups. Someone said that if the young 'innocent' had been an office worker, she would have been part of the community. Protecting her would not have been a problem and Daniela would have been safe because warnings would have reached her through everyday tittle-tattle. If necessary, the group could have erected a barrier of hostility in order to dissuade the academic staff from excessive prurience – even if affairs (or rumours of them) between the two groups were commonplace. The problem, therefore, was if and how to communicate with another group occupying an uncertain position in the organization (internal or external? customers or users?).

The female students belonged to another community, and it was the responsibility of that community's females, or its males, to look after them. Perhaps, indeed, they observed different sexual customs and rules. The symbology of the other tribe, clan, race, ethnic group is easily invoked; equality or sisterhood encounter invisible barriers, ones difficult to overcome even when the 'other' is not black or African, or at any rate not overtly different. The family marks out invisible boundaries around its children, wives and mothers, and occupational communities sometimes behave like extended families in caring only for their members.

Female students also occupy an ambigious position within the organizational hierarchy of the university, if they are deemed part of the organization. Consider what would have happened if a woman lecturer, a feminist, had either warned the student or taken action against Don Giovanni. In this case the woman lecturer would have become a member of another occupational community, but she would have occupied the one-up position in her relationship with the girl student. The secretary, by contrast, located herself in the weak (one-down) position. She did not consider herself entitled to establish any sort of relationship with the girl. As a feminist, the lecturer would have accepted the control of an outsider over her occupational community and might have exercised social control over her colleague. It is also probable that the power relationships within that particular community inhibited this kind of social control and blinded its members to sexual exploitation in highly asymmetric relationships such as those between lecturer and student, doctor and patient, boss and secretary, doctor and nurse. From the number of studies conducted on sexual harassment in universities (Crocker, 1983) one would say – whether this is fact or fiction – that they are organizations at risk!

The story, however, does not finish here: by a twist of fate it has a happy ending. A couple of years later I happened to meet the girl student again in my own university, where she had enrolled on the PhD programme. At a party one evening, I told her about the argument she had provoked, and how her case had become paradigmatic after my further discussion of it with my colleagues.

She seemed touched that so many people should have been worried about her, but she laughed until the tears came to her eyes. Predictably perhaps, there was no truth, no sexual harassment, no free will involved. Nor was she innocent. She told me that all the students were perfectly aware of how 'Don Giovanni' behaved, and also several other males in the faculty. The attractive girls would wear tight skirts and low-cut sweaters for their oral examinations, and this ensured them higher grades. This enraged the male students, who accused them of unfair competition. However, in the students' eyes the balance was redressed when a female lecturer was appointed who gave higher marks to attractive male students than to female ones.

If I were Aesop, the moral of the story would be a warning to would-be sexual harassers not to allow themselves to be sexually exploited: sexual harassment can be a two-edged sword. If, instead, one inspects this episode in terms of its sexual symbolism, one discovers the myth of Demeter and Persephone (which I explore in the next chapter). The desire to protect the maiden-daughter against possible rape by Hades, and the representation of female sexuality as innocence, are two components of the sexual imaginary in the relationship among women. And the reference to the life cycle, to oneself as a sexual object when a girl and presumably subject to sexuality when a woman, belongs to the myth of Persephone or Kore, the maiden.

This is the common organizational story of the sexual harassment which never actually took place but which could nevertheless always happen in a context in which women conduct their interrelationships problematically. The fantasy of protecting a young woman in a mother/daughter relation does not lead to any concrete action. The solidarity of sisterhood was demanded of women who did not accept it, and the 'virtue' of the young woman was in fact entrusted to the everyday gossip mill. Colluding with the system is easier than it seems, but the assertion that women may not be 'victims' implies, not that they are ingenuous, obtuse or innocent, but that they choose, they act or they do not act, that they are 'subject' and not just 'object'.

Central to this text is the concept of subordination, both in terms of a structural subordination relation between the professor and girl student, professor and secretary, and in the discourse collocation of girl student as object. I wish to explore further the link between subordination and sexuality by changing the setting and moving to the factory shop-floor – specifically, to the culture of male and female manual workers. In factories and in large-scale productive organizations, shop-floor workers symbolically occupy the lowest level of the hierarchy, and in an evident subordination relationship, even though the hierarchical scale defines many superordinate levels which are in turn subordinate to a higher one. Symbolically, workers are subjected to capitalism just as women are subjected to men. The social relationship of subordination is a symbolic threat to the virility of the (male) working class, and I shall show how this threat renders sexual identity central to the culture of male manual workers, and how collusion with shop-floor sexism is a cultural strategy to cope with the interaction of both class and gender.

Male sexual identity as a reaction to subordination

In this section I shall draw on my experience of teaching courses in further education to Italian women workers. For five years I met regularly with groups of women, most of whom worked in factories, to study and discuss topics of interest to them and which related to what in those years (1978–83) used to be called 'the woman's condition'. Sexuality was a constant theme, and classroom discussion of it taught me a great deal, especially about the relationship between class, gender and sexuality. These female manual workers were very sensitive to class differences, and they criticized bourgeois feminism by arguing that, apart from economic and social inequalities, there is also inequality in women's opportunities to construct/assert/discover their own femaleness.

Women office-workers and women shop-floor workers in the group very often found it difficult to understand each other. They gave different interpretations to the same episode, and drew on their respective class cultures for explanation of their conflict, which threatened their collective identity as woman. At moments of tension, the office-workers accused the shop-floor workers of colluding with the sexism of their male workmates, and were in turn accused of being bourgeois hypocrites who considered sex to be 'dirty'.

It is well known, of course, that the language, the jokes, the posters on the walls, the swearing on factory shop-floors are deeply imbued with male sexuality, which is expressed quite openly and according to cultural codes other than those of the 'genteel', middle-class and prudish office. Does the sexual imagination and the sexualization of organizational life differ only in the cultural code that it expresses and represents?

At the symbolic level, just as the secretary is conventionally a woman, so the blue-collar worker is a man, and in this case his work helps to create a sexual identity based simultaneously on the subordination of the female and resistance to capitalist exploitation of his body. His male body is designed for work: it can toil, drudge, do filthy work, sweat blood, with the eardrums bursting with the noise of the machines, and amid constant danger (Cockburn, 1985). All this is highly exciting and very physical. All this is inscribed in a poetic of the 'valiant warrior' and in the ethic of 'heroic masculinity'. Even when the same phenomena are framed as 'the capitalist exploitation of workers' bodies', the heroic rhetoric is secure: there is always trade unionization – resistance to subjugation – to portray the workers not as victims, but as fighters. When male workers size each other up in terms of skill, reputation, earnings, physical strength, or the women they have had or are going to have, they construct not just power relationships but sexual ones as well. The female body is absent, it is not glorified by dirt and sweat. Women working in the same environment as men are not heroes but victims. They are fundamentally out of place. Although present, they are virtually absent. Whether or not the women, the female workers, are present when this mutual male appraisal goes on is of no importance, for it is a sexual game played only among men and within the arena of work.

A woman worker described it as 'looking in the mirror': 'When they show off their muscles they're not doing it for us. They're like body-builders flaunting their bodies so that they can see them reflected in the eyes of the other.'

This woman expressed emotional detachment from this kind of male exhibitionism in the condescending terms of a mother criticizing her sons for excessively masculine behaviour when testing out their still uncertain sexual identity. Flaunted masculinity was not perceived as being exhibited *for* women nor, although sometimes distasteful, *against* them. The metaphor of the mirror expressed a narcissistic relation and the pleasure that derives from it.

This narcissistic relationship is expressed with great simplicity: work is constitutive of masculinity, and gratification of this sexuality can only be forthcoming from other men. Unemployment, in fact, threatens the identity of a man both as a worker and as a male. In white, European working-class culture, being male means being the economic mainstay of the family – something to be proud about and to boast about. I was told by an elderly woman that, in Italian working-class families during the 1960s, it was shameful for a man to be forced to send his wife out to work. Frequent expressions in working-class discourse were 'keeping the wife at home', 'sending her to work', 'taking her out'. The condition of non-subject, the absence of volition, obedience taken for granted, was offensive to many of the female workmates of these men. Yet what the men were exhibiting was their masculinity as heads of a household; their women were implicitly subsumed in discourse and reduced to silence. The masculinity of the strong and (sexually) potent man and 'man as breadwinner' appear to be values widespread in working-class culture – as one reads in Cockburn (1983), Hearn (1985), Wajcman (1991), Collinson and Collinson (1989), Collinson (1992).

Humour, jokes and language games are very important for the construction of masculinity (Collinson, 1988). The sexualization of language, smut and sexual insinuation were, I found, the forms of verbal violence that the women workers found most distressing. It is difficult and rather unpleasant to convey them in another language, for which reason I refer the reader to the above works and in particular to Hearn (1985), who identifies four types of male sexual behaviour in the workplace: horseplay, the exploitation of sexuality, sexual harassment, and mutual sexuality. Of these, I wish only to explore the topic of sexuality in language and verbal sexual aggression. I shall examine it in various contexts because, in my view, sexism in working-class cultures differs according to the extent to which female labour is segregated.

The need to display male sexuality as a reaction to subordination is an essential component of working-class identity, both in its aggressive form as male sexual power over the female body, and as the authority of the husband over his wife and children. It is a feature common both to gender-segregated work settings and to more mixed ones, although there are certain differences mediated by the hierarchy, by technology and by occupational competitiveness between men and women.

In prevalently female industries, like textiles or foodstuffs, and to some extent also the electronics industry, the gendered nature of blue-collar work overtly allocates tasks requiring precision and patience to women. The men are assigned control over the technology and supervision of the women's work. The sexualization of language, in the form of jokes and humour deployed in the vicinity of the female body, has the dual purpose of reaffirming the dependence of the women on the men, and of relieving the men's dependence on the managers. Yet, however unpleasant the situation may be to new arrivals, the female workers too exercise a form of control. As Anna, a textiles worker, told me:

When we women are together in a group, we can give as good as we get. We give them tit-for-tat, we make jokes about them to show that we can swear as well, that we're not shocked or that we plug our ears. We know the language too, and we can use it just as well, even better. Of course, it'd be better to stop this fooling around! Every so often someone is upset or offended. This need they have to show off their cock power is a hassle. But we enjoy it as well; it's a game, although it's not always fun.

A game that is not always fun seems to be the most suitable description of the women workers' resignation to a sexualized environment, and of their ability to act within it both defensively and offensively. This game was not the women's game; but it was apparently more irritating to them than really offensive, and none of them would have called it 'sexual harassment'. The most frequent explanation was that attachment of this label would attribute excessive importance to the game, and, in any case, the women were also its initiators. Both sides were quite clear about their gender relation: the women did women's work (i.e. jobs which the men would never accept); men exerted control which was either direct or mediated by technology, another component of male identity. The men's symbolic access to the bodies of these women was enshrined in a cultural code of dependence which concealed their dependence on the management. The solidarity among the men, in both their manhood and the reciprocal admiration of their masculinity, created a 'macho' collective identity which marked them off from the managers with their jackets and ties. They were 'real men', as their language was supposed to convey. The women knew that they were accomplices – more or less consenting – because there were other dimensions to the relation: the group and personal dimensions.

The sexism of *double entendres*, blue jokes and smutty stories was played by two actors – the men's group and the women's group – but the references were never personal. This arena of linguistic confrontation was also the symbolic construction site of their community. A manager, for example, could never have said to a woman what her workmate could have said. And, in an interpersonal relationship, her workmate could never have used the expressions which he employed to define women in general. Sexist language was used to affirm the superiority of men, but with a code that communicated non-aggression.

In interpersonal relationships in the factory, in the trade union, and externally in a community which, although not particularly small, was such that the workers frequently mixed outside work or met the wives or children of their workmates, things were different. In face-to-face relationships other roles intervened – those of the family, of the neighbourhood, of class solidarity. What was permitted within the frame of a 'sexual game' played by the men against the women – and vice versa – was no longer allowed, and was branded verbal aggression.

The sexual code of this type of working-class culture exalts the male definition of sexuality and of a sexuality imposed upon women. But it is mitigated by a traditional conception – or a patriarchical one if preferred

– of sexuality which protects the honour of one's 'own' wife and children. It is a traditional sexual code.

Different, however, is the sexual code of those working-class communities in which women's work is less clearly segregated and in which women perform the same tasks as the men, thereby threatening not so much their jobs as their sexual identity. Here the sexualization of the workplace takes the form of aggression, of reducing women to silence, of disciplining their behaviour. And it does so on both the levels of inter-personal relationship and of male community versus female community.

If the women do the same work as the men, this implies that it is not work for men, that 'they' are doing women's work. It is thus necessary either to differentiate the specific contents of the work or to persuade the women that it is not for them. To do this, the traditional methods of dissuasion are employed, those also used to socialize new arrivals, as well as sexual verbal aggression. The men try to break down the women's psychological resistance and to affirm their virility by humiliating them. Moreover, when there are few women present, or when those women that are present do not form a group, the situation becomes one of overt violence or of crude subjugation. Even when the display of masculinity is not explicitly directed towards the women present, they may be forced to join the men's sexual banter, which they usually interpret as violent rather than amusing. Being a spectator of masculine sexual culture and of men-only relationships was described to me thus, by Valeria, a shop-floor worker in an engineering company:

> They're like Martians. Sometimes they're like the little boys in Via Paal measuring who's got the longest one. Sometimes they frighten me, and I think that they could really rape someone instead of doing it in words.

Atavistic fears are activated in the women's sexual imagination, and those forms of exclusively male sociability based on an exclusively male code are viewed as threatening rather than excluding; they only become comprehensible when the woman can imagine herself as a mother and watch her sons as they clumsily invent their masculine identity. This alternative celebration of masculinity excludes her; it is not seductive and it is not even directed towards her. What is celebrated is the power of sexuality, not the pleasure. Celebrating the power of masculinity counteracts the woman's dependence and her lack of power in the organization.

A recurrent theme is contempt for any other form of sexuality; especially homosexuality, which is seen as threatening male identity. The sexual code of these working-class cultures is phallocentric to the extent that it almost entirely excises the female from the representation of the sexual. This is confirmed by the strategies employed by the women to defend themselves: firstly by avoiding, by not replying, by pretending not to hear; secondly by seeking the protection of a paternal/marital figure, for instance a supervisor, a shop steward, an older man or a foreman.

Unlike those working-class cultures in which female work is more markedly segregated, in this case the sexualization of language is much more threatening or punitive of female behaviour, and the celebration of the male is much more an exclusively male ritual. Both modalities communicate that women are intruders because they are doing male work and challenging male sexual identity. In more segregated cultures, men and women collude in the sexualization of verbal interaction in order to communicate and negotiate the fact that women are subordinate. Having social groups which are 'beneath', with all the significances that the term conveys, reassures the working man of his masculinity. The higher the position in the hierarchy, the more sexual symbols become sublimated into power symbols, and the more they are distanced from the symbology of the corporeal and the sexual.

Offices, too, are characterized by sexual banter, innuendo, teasing and jokes. The difference here is that the language is less explicit, and the level of admissible vulgarity and sexuality is lower. Both blue-collar and white-collar workers are subordinate in the organizational hierarchy. But control over their bodies takes different forms, and the body in work performance and in social imagery is of differential importance. Blue-collar workers work with their bodies, white-collar workers with their minds, and organizational control is more direct and visible in disciplining the mind than the body. For male manual workers, sexual identity is an attribute comprising strength and physical force, the social role as breadwinner, and the political stance of class resistance. In traditional working-class culture, with its sharp gender segregation of occupational opportunities, workplace sexuality is part of a language game in which both women and men participate collectively. Without denying its patronizing effect on women's subordination, the sexualization of the workplace is one form of workforce resistance against the boredom and exploitation of factory life. Paradoxically, occupational segregation shields women against discipline-through-sexuality by their male workmates. Male sexuality is aimed against women, is enacted jointly with women, and is deployed independently of women against the subordination imposed by the employment contract. Power, domination, pleasure and resistance are intertwined in complex practices and elaborated into ambiguous cultural codes. In my experience, these patterns are more evident in working-class cultures. Many similar ones are to be found in other occupational communities, but I am unable to say more on the joint effect of class and gender, just as I have no direct experience of the joint action of gender, class and race.

It is more difficult to give a succinct description of the sexual codes of occupational cultures at the intermediate organizational level. One would have to spell out the details of each organizational culture and of their different occupational cultures, each of which makes creative use of its technical vocabulary to imbue its instruments, procedures and everyday routines with sexuality. I also believe that it is extremely difficult to convey these subtleties from one language and national culture to another. English is a language in which only people have genders. The Romance languages, Italian in my case, construct the world in terms of masculine and feminine. Everything has a gender: people and things, adjectives and verbs, all must agree.

The fact is, when every object belongs to one symbolic universe or the other, there are infinite possibilities for imbuing discourse with sexuality and sensuality, and the boundaries between the virtuosity of mutual appreciation and the unfairness of the sexual power game can only be appreciated from within. This obviously holds for any culture which elaborates contingent definitions for its cultural facts. When sexuality is involved, the distinctions between what is acceptable and what is offensive are very subtle. I have conducted research in settings which I judged excessively sexualized but which were deemed 'fair' by those who lived in them; or, conversely, settings which I found extremely egalitarian but which were called 'bogus libertarian' because they only paid lip-service to emancipation.

Eros and organizational sexualities

There exists a specific form of sexuality which does not concern individuals, one which is not private but public: namely organizational sexuality, or better, organizational sexualities. Sexuality in organizations is not a residual phenomenon, nor can it be dismissed as folklore: sexuality is an extremely powerful and central impulse in the emotional structuring of work relations, and it is just as constitutive of gender as sexuality within the family. Studying gender while ignoring sex is to skirt round the embarrassing fact of sexual attraction, and, in particular, to deny the paradox of 'organizational sexuality' (Hearn and Parkin, 1987), which is a deliberately powerful and provocative term. Hearn and Parkin – a man and a woman – have explored the organization's construction of sexuality and the sexual construction of the organization. They have thus marked out an area of enquiry that warrants study in terms other than those of the over-constrictive framework of 'sexual harassment'.

Yet it is not enough merely to recognize the contextual processes of sexualization/desexualization in the workplace (Burrell, 1984); one must also make pleasure and eroticism overt. The concept of organizational sexuality is so powerful, I believe, because it signals an expressive form of sexuality which differs from that of both the private and the public sphere (i.e. such relatively unstructured meeting-places as the street). Organizational life stands on the borderline between these two territorial domains, and the rules of organizational sexuality are specific: sexual accessibility intersects with the hierarchical scale at various points, and the differential impact of sexual gossip reveals complex occupational hierarchies by role and by sex. Organizational sexuality is only permitted in certain settings and situations, and knowing when it can be implemented is part of competent organizational behaviour.

Organizational sexuality has its limits: it is not sex, and it requires the presence of an audience. It is not a private fact precisely because it interweaves with work, which distorts its ends and forces it to operate chiefly through myth and ritual. Organizational structures delimit and protect permissibile forms of sexuality: a secretary can flirt with a customer in ways that she would certainly eschew if she met him on the street. The sexual jokes and games permissible in a group of male and female colleagues at work would be entirely out of place in a supermarket. The organization therefore provides an extra-territorial arena for the expression of sexuality which (like humour) helps to relieve the boredom, the alienation, the burn-out and the depersonalization of the bureaucratic process. Once again the chief beneficiary is the organization itself, which allows sex in public!

Organizational sexualities are intrinsically ambiguous and contradictory because they are threefold: they are pleasure-driven because they allow people attracted to each other to meet in a safe environment; they are functional to the dependence relations created by work, to the survival of organizational boredom, a cooperative response designed to energize the life of the organization; and they are also instruments of corporate control or discipline over dissident behaviour. The sexualities that I have been able to identify personally are heterosexual attraction, according to the canons of courtship and flirtation, homosexual attraction in single-sex groups, and the pleasure of sado-masochism.

Sexual attraction affects people in their work in ways beyond their actual awareness of it. Organizational flirting is a dependency ritual (Konecki, 1990) in that it signals the direction of the dependence and the social distance between those who engage in it. It is the outcome of negotiation and mutual adjustment by those involved; a negotiation to which they bring different resources. The general terms of the sexual contract are obedience in exchange for protection, but the specific conditions of the trade-off are fixed by interaction.

Flirtation is a strategy for coping with the demands created by the structural dependence among occupational positions. Technological dependence among jobs, for example, generates patterns of interdependence among workers, and courtship is a 'soft' request ritual restricted to the task at hand and to the work setting. Flirting can function as a ritual which assigns women 'to their rightful place' when they manage an authority relationship, both when the subordinate belongs to the opposite sex and when a narcissistic relationship with other women or a subordinate woman is involved (Pringle, 1989b). For example, there are categories of workers – maintenance men and technicians, for instance – whose intervention is always solicited by a deferential display of courtship-like behaviour. Broadly speaking, when a worker has control over the time that he or she can wait before responding to a request made by a superior, the dependence relationship is reversed and it is the superior who – unable to impose his or her authority – resorts to seduction or flattery, ingratiating him or herself with the worker by exploiting a bond of intimacy and diffused sensuality. I am here using the term 'flirtation' in a very broad sense in order to relate it to behaviours between men and women as well as between people of the same sex, and also to stress the structural basis of flirting as organizational behaviour.

Organizational flirting is less an individual strategy than a cultural system developed by a group and among groups. Individuals are at liberty not to join in, but should they refrain from flirting they will lose face. This may harm their day-to-day relations with the group, since they may be ostracized and thereby forced to become outsiders (Konecki, 1990).

The amount of pleasure or eroticization in organizational flirtation depends on the people involved and on the extent to which it is overt, end-directed and lasting. Some forms of behaviour are explicit and taken for granted by both parties: for example when a woman clerk is asked to retrieve a file and the request is prefaced by a compliment, a brief chat about her private life, the more or less explicit signalling that she is found attractive (not necessarily sexually). Both parties are aware of the game being played, and the presence of an audience testifies to the innocence of the flirtation; a presence which may permit the exchange to acquire a highly parasexual character, which would assume quite different significance were it to take place in less secluded surroundings, or if it was less strictly codified as a 'work relationship'.

Other behaviours of this kind may structure themselves into enduring relationships, less overt in character and which lead to sexual outcomes. For example, the mentorship relation between people of different sexes seems frequently to generate organizational flirtation which subsequently develops into a sexual relationship (Noe, 1988). The eroticization, real or imagined, of the boss/secretary, doctor/nurse relationship (Pringle, 1989b) is another example, although it is governed by cultural codes which prescribe a reciprocity of behaviours.

Finally there are certain work alliances between men and women which are powerfully eroticized; work gives mutually attracted people the means, the motive and the excuse to spend time together. The interaction takes the form of amorous skirmishing, although the organizational nature of the relationship may prevent a sexual-private interpretation and permit enjoyment of the pleasure of being together.

I do not intend to present an idyllic vignette of the kind 'free love in a safe context'; nor do I intend to demonize eroticism as something wholly functional to something else. It is extremely difficult to decide when sexual exploitation is taking place (of people by the organization), who is exploiting whom (between organization and people, and among gendered persons), and for what purpose mutual attraction between people is being utilized. An ideological reading which ranges the 'bad girls' against the 'good girls' only glosses over the fact that work and pleasure are much more closely connected than might at first appear. We take it for granted that, for certain kinds of work to be successful, the people doing the work must like each other, understand each other, suit each other, make a good pair. Nor do we find it difficult to recognize the collective love affair that blossoms when a design group achieves a breakthrough: the team is enamoured of its creation, to the point that it uses the language of labour and childbirth to describe the process. There is an evident symbolic continuum between private eroticism and organizational sexuality; yet it embarrasses us to admit that eros is involved and follows the rules of organizational behaviour, and that our libidinous energies have been surrendered . . . but in exchange for what? This was a question that the Catholic or Marxist rhetoric of work was unable to answer, because work was pain, purgatory or, at most, the means to achieve redemption (personal for the Calvinists; of the working class for the socialists). Work was exploitation, and hence any connection between work and pleasure was impossible. The question becomes pressing, however, in a post-industrial, postmodern, and essentially narcissistic productive and cultural context. Let us admit, therefore, that we seek erotic gratification in our work, that organizations inhabit our sexual imaginations, and that we use organizations to fulfil our sexual fantasies.

This is not an attempt at intellectual provocation; I merely wish to propose a possible line of enquiry. First, however, I should explain the research context that first suggested this hypothesis. I was studying a number of work groups in a public organization; that is, in a setting where the levers of personnel management were structurally very constrained. I spent three months of research intervention in two offices which reacted with extreme hostility to my presence and in which things happened which I was unable to explain. My task was to find ways of increasing levels of work participation. My first impression was of what I called 'an authoritarian style of leadership', an impression confirmed by my inspection of the employment records of the section heads. Yet what struck me most forcefully was not the extent to which information and decision-making were centralized, nor the fact that no one in the office took any sort of initiative without the go-ahead of the boss. The most evident feature was the emotional intensity of the office atmosphere. The boss frequently indulged in violent temper tantrums which exceeded the bounds of acceptable behaviour: he abused the workers and belittled their professional competence and moral integrity. Those who worked in the office lived in fear of his daily moods: they never knew what to expect when he arrived in the morning, they worked as if he was breathing down their necks when he was present, and did absolutely nothing when he was absent. The boss's emotional outbursts, to which the personnel replied vigorously in kind, were followed by peaceful interludes of contrition. Excuses were made, personal reasons, sometimes very private, were given, and the boss often invited everyone to the bar in an act of contrition. But a few days later another storm would erupt, with the same melodramatic display of high emotion. The other offices were aware of what was happening, since they were often onlookers or called in as witnesses, but they explained the situation in personal terms as authoritarianism.

I was also struck by the fact that the office-workers did very little to change their procedures or routines in order to forestall their boss's violent outbursts. Indeed, although the clerks often seemed able to resolve problems by themselves and without the boss being aware that they were doing so, they deliberately brought them to his attention. This only served to reinforce the boss's opinion that he was dealing with 'cretins' (as he called them in public) and that his personal intervention was necessary. The situation was reflected in the rapid turnover of the office's personnel. The arrival of the boss had triggered an avalanche of transfer applications; new arrivals rarely lasted longer than the time necessary to submit their applications for transfer; and nobody was willing to be transferred into the office. Yet the boss seemed satisfied with his staff, he did not request extra workers, he did not ask for transfers, and he did not complain about his staff to the personnel office. For their part, the staff (almost all of whom were women) had been there for many years and said that they were used to their boss's rages, although at the beginning they regarded them as degrading to their dignity as workers. There was a complex mixture of personal relations among the women, frequent meetings outside work, and links through their children, all of which merged work and private life together. The women apparently had good reason to remain in the office and good reason not to change the situation. Their reaction to the threat of change posed by my presence was to minimize and dismiss as ridiculous a situation which they had initially described as unbearable. Organizational intervention was obviously a fiasco: no one was allowed to enter those dynamics, and no one was allowed to leave them.

The relationship between workers and boss called to mind the sexual fantasies of the slave/master. The language used in the office echoed the language and images of abuse. The physical poses struck by the boss mimicked stereotypical images of dominance, just as subjection and submission were displayed in response to his verbal onslaughts. The atmosphere was eroticized, the boss's tongue-lashings of one or other of the women workers were jokingly called sadism. But their reciprocal dependence and collusion were kept quiet.

When I discussed my hypothesis with colleagues and other people in the organization, many of them recognized this sado-masochistic relational model. They cited numerous other examples of slave/master bondings into which they themselves had been unwittingly drawn, and from which they had extricated themselves with difficulty: because the structure of organizational dependence reinforced the apparent legitimacy of the relationship, and because the nature itself of the organization, founded on hierarchy and dependence, lays the structural basis for various forms of sexuality, one of which is sado-masochism.

A relationship with sadistic and masochistic characteristics presupposes eroticization and a form of pleasure which, however questionable, involves presumably consenting adults. In the two offices that I studied, organizational sado-masochism was sustained not only by a power structure and its social legitimation, but also by an erotic bond of reciprocity which induced some to leave the office, but just as many others to stay. A situation of outright abuse would have prompted very different behaviour.

Organizational abuse is a metaphor, proposed by Bergin (1993), which draws a parallel between the abuse of children – that is, immature persons, who do not fully understand what is happening to them and are unable to give knowing assent – and the manner in which the organization treats its employees. The organizational literature frequently depicts the workforce as a minority, indulges in paternalism and ideologically legitimizes subordination. Drawing an analogy between organizational literature and the literature on child abuse, Bergin singles out four types of organizational abuse: physical abuse (for example when the work involves unjustified physical dangers); emotional abuse (by the egotistic leader); neglect (the opposite of human resources development, when human resources fail to thrive); and sexual abuse (as in sexual harassment).

I believe that this metaphor sheds fresh light on organizational sexuality. It reveals that men too are abused, and that – according to the literature on child abuse – the perpetrators are usually people who have been abused themselves. A weakness of the metaphor is that the parallel between children and employees risks perpetuating their minority status.

Research has very recently begun on the relationship between violence and organization (Hearn, 1994), in terms of both the conventional association between sexuality and obedience, and more generally the violence intrinsic to the organization, which depends on obedience to an unaccountable or unjustifiable authority. This research perspective is certain to develop in the near future. However, if it is not to give an excessively unidimensional account of violence, it must explore the ambiguous and uneasy relationship between violence and pleasure, between unjustified command and the complicity that encourages it, the seduction of violence sublimated in the ordinary enactment of authority.

The contradictoriness of pleasure, its negation, its exploitation, not only have cultural roots, they are imprinted in the organizational structure, above all in authority/dependence bonds, but also in the sexual segregation of work which creates and protects enclaves dominated by one of the two sexes. The pleasure of intimacy among women, or among men, cannot be labelled *tout court* as homosexual attraction – because it profoundly subverts the moral order of heterosexuality based on the homo/hetero dichotomy which constructs homosexuality as inherently 'other'. We can, however, conceive of a more or less sexualized continuum of attraction to people of the same sex, and a sexual repertoire in which both fear of and attraction towards self-equals are expressed. The organizational segregation of occupations also structures the time and space inhabited by one gender. Yet the search for places and times shielded against scrutiny and interference by the other sex is evident in almost all mixed occupational communities. It is well known that the communicative codes, the discourse topics, the intimacies of speech, and even the proxemics of single-sex groups, differ from those of mixed ones, where the two genders exercise a form of reciprocal control.

The intimacy – chosen or imposed – of single-gender groups is ambivalent: the spectre of homosexuality is exorcized by jokes and the insinuation of its presence, through the construction of a collective sexual identity; but at the same time the pleasure of mirror imagery and ambiguity provide a safe haven above every suspicion.

Physical contact or other forms of shared intimacy are given freer rein because they occur within public space. There is greater tolerance for the proximity of female bodies, and also for expressions of mutual affection (which among males often takes the form of mock wrestling). For example, the taboo on touching another person's genitals without permission is flouted when this act changes code, becomes a sign of conquest and the expression of the victor's prerogative. This example was provided by Lucia, a worker on a farm cooperative:

> The men were all quite young, and one of their games was to pretend to fight when they argued. One of them always asked: 'Are you jerking my dick?' The other one then tried to show that he really could do it because he was tougher. Apparently this trial of strength was what they enjoyed most, but I think the joke was obscene.

When this behaviour was discussed in class, the women agreed about the obscenity, and they were particularly worried about what they called the expropriated right of access to another person's body. They identified the eroticism of the trial of strength, the subjugation of the weaker, as typical of male sexuality among men. And the women expressed the fear that this relational model might be extended to female bodies as well. The male interpretation of their behaviour might be different. Proper analysis would therefore require descriptions of the intimacy patterns of single-gender groups provided by both genders.

Intimacy among women is usually highly idealized (when it is perceived). Differences are denied and the relationship with the mother's body as well as (more or less) reciprocal mothering is the dominant relational pattern. Yet there is oppression in this idyllic representation, too, for those who wish to affirm their own diversity or who seek to define a femaleness which is not exclusively maternal. The social control of the definition of femaleness passes not solely through male discourse, but through female discourse as well. There is a female version of the feminine mystique which confines women to the women-only group, within the womb of the mother, and which culturally intimidates those who break free to pursue a career, to follow a mentor, to explore the dark planet of power or money; that is, to enter the male cultural world. The eroticism of the mother's body is threatened by separation and by diversity; its pleasure lies in the fusion of the indistinct: protection (pleasure) is given in exchange for obedience.

The pleasures of working life have been little studied. Working people themselves seem to have scant awareness of what gives them pleasure in performing an activity with its own intrinsic physicality. Garson (1975) reports the experience of a female worker who spent her work-day gutting fish and described the experience as sensual. Many activities involve direct manipulation of other people's bodies, many of them are occasions for covert exhibitionism (from the fashion model who displays his/her body, from the university lecturer who displays his/her brain). Many activities establish and allow eroticism *à la* Pygmalion in that they involve prolonged and close intimacy between people of very different generations. Finally, the public nature of work offers infinite possibilities for voyeurism.

Not only may work be eroticized, but the encounter itself between sexed bodies that the organization requires and imposes is an opportunity to express that physicality – non-culturally mediated – which embarrasses us because it belongs to the symbolic realm of the private, of the body, of 'below', of the impure, of animality, of the instincts. Public discourse on gender also runs the risk of cancelling pleasure and the attraction and repulsion of sexed bodies.

When the category 'gender' enters scientific and political discourse it is counterposed to 'sex', a word too strongly connoted with biological determinism and which sustains a dichotomous logic based on the opposition between male and female. The concept of gender proposes a relational mode of thought which, as an implicative relation, culturally and socially constructs the male and female: there is never one without the other. The message, and the political change that it brings about, is that sex is not destiny. Gendered social experiences, and the system of social inequality that rests upon them, are the products of history. They vary over space and time, and according to the specific social settings in which men and women meet and produce the meanings and structures of gender experiences. The forcefulness of this message has obscured and silenced the term which gender has replaced. 'Sex' denotes a social and mainly organizational process whereby every newborn infant is attributed sexual membership and is issued with an official certificate which will accompany him or her for the rest of his/her life. This certificate implicitly assumes that biological sex (determined on sight) corresponds to a sexual orientation, and that this is 'naturally' towards persons of the opposite sex. In this case too, sexuality is biologicized through a cultural process which establishes a coherent system of sex, gender characteristics and sexual orientation. This system sustains a political process of social control over sexuality and pleasure. Foucault's history of sexuality (1984) is a classic analysis of how sexuality, power and politics closely interweave. Likewise Elias (1978) is a masterly study of how the civilizing process is based on the repression of instincts and therefore also of the sexual instinct.

I am not proposing a simple solution to the complex relation between gender and sexuality. But I wish to stress that the complexity of the relationship between sexed bodies, sexuality and gender also derives from coercion by the symbolic system which imposes continuity between woman's body, heterosexuality and femaleness.

I have posited the relation between heterosexuality and sexuality because, paradoxically, male sexuality has been identified with heterosexuality, and this latter with the sexuality that punishes and exploits women, even by the texts that reflect critically on the phenomenon. Is it perhaps that 'compulsory heterosexuality' (Rich, 1984) has been imposed on both men and women, just as both are caught in the gender trap? This is the same system of thought which asserts that there are only people of one or the other gender, and declares that they are 'naturally' attracted to each other and that establishes one and only one 'healthy' type of sexuality while others are pathologies or perversions.

The paradox arises because no analytical distinction is drawn between sexuality and dominance based on sexuality. This induces the misunderstandings like that committed, for example, by Witz and Savage (1992), who object to studies of what they call the 'sexuality of organization' by such authors as Burrell (1984), Hearn and Parkin (1987), Pringle (1989b), Mills (1989), Collinson and Collinson (1989) and Hearn et al. (1989). Witz and Savage criticize the fact that this line of research was initiated by male theorists, not least of whom was Foucault, and that 'whereas the use of the term "gender"' usefully counteracted an 'oversexualized version of womanhood', the use of the term "sexuality" ambiguously counteracts an "overgenderized" version of womanhood' (Witz and Savage, 1992: 54). Is there no place for those men who wish to criticize the social construction of masculinity and gender? Are women the only political actors entitled to represent the interests of a movement for emancipation, liberation and democratization?

However problematic and elusive the relationship between gender and sexuality, and however much male sexuality becomes a way to discipline behaviour and to keep women 'in their place', desexualizing gender or identifying heterosexuality with the practice and symbolism of a male sexuality amounts to eliminating one of the two problematic terms by concealing it. The discourse on sexuality which constructs women as victims, as forced to desexualize themselves to enter organizations, as the sole bearers of gender, is a discourse which continues to construct women as objects and which keeps silent on female sexuality and on women's capacity to be the subject of pleasure. A position overtly in favour of sexuality as a political resource and a liberating force is taken up by Pringle (1989a), who argues that 'sexual pleasure might be used to disrupt male rationality and to empower women' (Pringle, 1989a: 166). The danger of studying gender from the utopian perspective of a genderless or de-gendered solution is that it suppresses sexuality. Consequently, sexuality is only seen in terms of its relationship with power and domination, while its relationship with pleasure is ignored. Heterosexuality is singled out as the only legitimate and 'natural' sexuality. By adopting this analytical perspective, the literature on gender, too, helps to encourage the civilizing process which confines the body, pleasure and sexuality to the private, while only talking heads meet in public and the impure is ruled out of bounds. An alternative to the de-gendering process is that of 'differently-gendering', where gender and inequality stand in a different relationship.

I conclude by summarizing what the metaphor of the sexual contract reveals to us of the gendered life of the organization. First of all, the organization's claim that it is 'alien' to sexuality is yet another of the many scientific fairy tales intended both to desexualize our knowledge of organizations and to have the gendered nature of this knowledge taken for granted. By means of the employment contract, the organization purchases the right to command, within certain limits, differently sexed bodies and to structure the ways in which they express their sexuality: exploiting this sexuality when it has value (for the organization) and repressing it when it proves useless to the organization or impedes production.

Workers enter an organization with bodies, with instincts, with passions and with sexual urges. They like, attract or repulse each other according to a pre-verbal biological code constituted by odours and flavours. They also work with this body; but sexuality and work intermesh in various forms, for various purposes and in paradoxical ways.

The contract – the paradigm of freedom – obscures the fact that the subject 'woman' is constructed within a dependence relation which denies her status as an individual endowed with free will and with a 'subject' sexuality. As the paradigm of free exchange, it conceals the fact that what is exchanged is primarily obedience for protection. The sexual employment contract regulates access to different structurings of organizational sexualities. Organizational sexuality/ies is/are specific forms of sexual expression, neither private nor public. They obey organizational norms; they are permitted within the walls of the organization; they do not have explicitly sexual ends; they require an audience which ensures that limits are respected; they are learnt as part of the socialization process whereby the individual becomes a member of the organization.

Organizational sexualities are an organizational fact; they are principally strategies devised to cope with the demands of a dependence relationship and with the ambiguous erotic links that bind power and authority, dependence and obedience, together. Organizations *qua* formal organizations contain a curious paradox. Today they are predominantly masculine because they institutionalize the interests of men (as the economically dominant group) and masculine values (as the expression of a cultural hegemony which devalues the female). Simultaneously, however, their use of female resources has helped to liberate women from the private. Thus, willy-nilly, organizations have changed the status of women in society and have become the 'public' arena in which gender relations between men and women are negotiated.

3

Jerosgamos: The Metaphor of the Alchemic Wedding

In the Middle Ages hundreds of treatises were written in an attempt to unravel a celebrated mystery: the cryptic inscription on a tombstone in the Italian city of Bologna which became known as the *Enigma of Bologna*. The epitaph was later quoted by Jung (1963: 56–7) in his *Mysterium Coniunctionis*:

> *Aelia Laelia Crispis*, neither man nor woman, nor mongrel, nor maid, nor boy, nor crone, nor chaste, nor whore, nor virtuous, but all.
> Carried away neither by hunger, nor by sword, nor by poison, but by all.
> Neither in heaven, nor in earth, nor in water, but everywhere is her resting place.
> *Lucius Agatho Priscius*, neither husband, nor lover, nor kinsman, neither mourning, nor rejoicing, nor weeping, (raised up) neither mound, nor pyramid, nor tomb, but all.
> He knows and knows not (what) he raised up to whom.
> (This is a tomb that has no body in it.
> This is a body that has no tomb round it.
> But body and tomb are the same.)

The epitaph for Aelia Laelia Crispis is based upon a negation of the male–female dichotomy which, in some obscure manner, disobeys the principle of non-contradiction to talk of an inextricable conjunction. The Bologna enigma is paradigmatic of what is impossible to understand and can only be expressed by impenetrable paradoxes.

Male and female symbolize contraries; as contraries they are separate, and as separate they may be parties to the sexual contract. Male and female as contraries are symbols of the binary logic of either/or, of the Aristotelian rationality of the *tertium non datum*. They express the principle of non-contradiction on which the logic of identification is based: the One in opposition to the Other. Distinction, as the separation of contraries, of being from non-being, is the foundation of univocal language, of the language of science.

Male and female also paradoxically symbolize the union of contraries, and the sexual encounter is the image most commonly used to represent the attraction, tension and union of opposites. Like Uroboros, the snake biting its own tail, sexual encounter is heterosexual encounter. The union of irreconcilables may also be represented by the embracing man and woman (each with four hands to symbolize their multiple capacities) in the painting described by Jung (1966a) which symbolizes the marriage of fire and water. The wedding is the symbol of the union of contraries, and the union of male and female is the symbol of transformation, of creation, of creativity. Cosmogonic symbols – which denote features recurrent in even very distant cultures – are elaborations of genesis as units of male and female principles, as metamorphosis.

The inseparability of male and female is founded on a conception of nature in which contraries seek each other out – *les extrèmes se touchent* – because they are mutually attractive, because they are tied together by creative tension, by a bond of implication. Just as distinction is deemed *contra naturam* because it separates contraries, so implication relaxes the tension and unifies what was separate to restore the 'natural' union.

The Bologna enigma enables me to frame the metaphor of the alchemic wedding as a relation of both/and, neither/nor between the genders. In what follows I shall continue to cite Jung, and in particular his *Psychology and Alchemy* (1966a), not because I propose a psychoanalytical reading of gender but because Jung conducted a cultural analysis of alchemy whose masterly insight has never been equalled and because his psychological reading lends itself well to the cultural approach.

The marriage, the union of male and female, is the archetype of unity. It is a symbol also to be found in Jung's depth-psychology as a symbol of the self, of the union of animus and anima within each individual. More recent criticism of the unity of the self and the interpretative proposal of the multiple self employs the discourse structure 'self' to describe identity as unitariness. And yet the one contains the many. The tension between the one as the suppression of diversity and multiplicity and the other as the principle of multiplicity is constantly reborn in our society as the protean dragon.

The epitaph to Aelia Laelia Crispis repeatedly uses the disjunction neither/nor, neither man, nor woman . . . but all, and suggests an image of unity through the non-distinction of content from container – body and tomb – which 'are the same'.

Sameness and diversity, unity and multiplicity, are tensions of thought and language inscribed in the symbol of the wedding, just as body and tomb, body and spirit are united in the matrimony which is the union of matter and spirit.

I propose the metaphor of the alchemic wedding, together with the metaphor of the sexual contract, to indicate a different route for exploration of gender in organizations. These two metaphors encapsulate two ways of thinking about gender: in terms of separation in the former case, in terms of union in the latter. Both develop a metaphor-sustained similarity up to a certain point, after which difference predominates. Hence neither of them is more complete than the other, and both rely on the other for support.

The alchemic wedding symbolizes the union of supreme contraries in the form of male and female (as in the Chinese yin and yang) which fuse into a unity that admits of no further oppositions. The wedding takes place in the last act of the Opera, when the process of transformation begins.

Alchemy is a twofold body of knowledge as both the forerunner of modern chemistry on the one hand, and a philosophical system on the other. The alchemist in his laboratory sought to transmute base metals into gold, but chemical matter and its transformation constituted the Opera, the transformation of the spirit. Yet chemical transmutation is not simply an allegory for the process of spiritual transformation, because the interior transformation of the alchemist derived from doing and from learning-by-doing. The alchemists coined the ironic dictum *obscurum per obscurius* (towards the obscure via the even more obscure) about themselves to stress that their texts were anything but clear and unambiguous, that they transmitted knowledge by means of symbols instead of models. Symbols served two principal purposes in alchemy. The obscure symbolism and ambiguous language of the alchemic texts protected their writers against persecution by the Church, which regarded alchemy on a par with heresy. However, the texts and their symbols were obscure to the alchemist himself, who, as he worked in solitude and privation, gave his own interpretation to them. The symbols touched and stimulated his unconscious, freeing it to obey the promptings of his spirit and mind. Alchemy was inimical to Christianity because it filled the gaps that the tension of contraries had created in the official religion and in the doctrine that resolved this tension into the synthesis arising from the fusion of thesis and antithesis. Since antiquity, odd numbers have been considered to be male and even numbers female. In the Holy Trinity of Christianity the three is one and the divinity is a male divinity. In the alchemic axiom of Maria Prophetissa, the One becomes Two, Two becomes Three, and by means of the Third, the Fourth attains Unity. The quaternary element provides the basis for the symbology of the square. The squaring of the circle is illustrated (Jung, 1966a: 130) by a female and male figure depicted in a circle containing a square: the circle represents unity, the square represents the four elements (fire, earth, air and water). The One is produced from the Four by a process of distillation known as quintessence, one of the many names for the One which is eternally sought but never attained. It has, said the alchemists, 'one thousand names'.

The circle (the symbol of unity) contains the male and the female which are separable and inseparable, and the relationship between them is one of compensation, not of complementarity. The female element of unconsciousness has historically compensated for the evolution of 'male' consciousness, Jung argues in his analysis of the psychological significance of alchemy. The unconscious is not simply the antithesis of consciousness; it accompanies and to some extent modifies it. The unconscious retrieves and recycles that which consciousness has cancelled or discarded. Unconsiousness and consciousness, female and male, are not complementary as the conventional image of the two halves of a shell would suggest; an image constructed on the separation of male and female whose union is simply the summation of two self-standing parts. Instead, the conception of male and female as both separate and inseparable principles expresses a logic of compensation, a dynamic process of constant union and transformation in which whatever is momentarily crushed is endlessly revived and renewed.

The alchemists identified this pattern of dynamic transformation in the relationship between matter and spirit; the depth-psychologists in the relationship between unconsciousness and consciousness; the post-structuralists in the coexistence of terms, the fact that every term is necessarily inhabited by its opposite and hence possesses the potential for its own corruption. The alchemists also talked of corruption and incorruptibility!

The metaphor of the alchemic wedding can be used to explore the archetypical models of femaleness and the way in which a certain type of femaleness elicits and/or activates a corresponding type of maleness. My thesis is that research on women has implicitly defined gender in oppositional terms, and that this definition has given rise to a literature which minimizes the differences among women and unintentionally reinforces the image of gender uniformity. The political purpose of this literature has been to construct a collective subject and a system of interests representation to which uniformity and separation are functional. Only recently has the diversity of women – and not just the difference between men and women – become a matter of feminist debate. This multiplicity of gender may be more fruitfully explored, I contend, if we examine the ancient archetypes of femaleness that still imbue our culture.

The word 'typos' derives from 'stroke', 'imprint'; and the archetype is that which preserves this imprint and conveys it into the multiplicity of contingent forms. Hence, beneath ideas and images which differ from one culture to another, from one historical period to another, the original matrix can still be discerned. Archetypes are cultural patterns which recur in myths, in dreams, in art, in the individual and collective imaginary, in folklore, in the literatures of peoples, races and cultures.

I am interested in archetypes as forms of cultural expression and forms of consciousness. This should not be taken to imply, however, that I accept the Jungian interpretation of archetypes or the theory of personality that it entails.

Caution is required, in fact, in talking about male *and* female, and when one does so in reference to Jung. Here I am not discussing psychological androgyny or a fundamental and essential difference between the male and the female nature. There is a feminism (Singer, 1976) which uses the concept of androgyny to criticize male epistemology and to advocate a new unified being: the androgyne. This position has been extensively criticized (Trebilcot, 1982; Elshtain, 1987; Raymond, 1981), although the debate has been marred by shaky understanding of the symbology of the androgynous. Entering into this argument here would be too much of a digression, but I must stress that what the alchemic wedding emphasizes is not union, but inseparability and separation: male and female are symbolic universes of meaning which are socially constructed according to a dichotomous modality, and yet they are inseparable because what is affirmed by the one is denied by the other. Defining the female as passive, emotional, irrational and dependent is to deny that the male possesses these characteristics. Hence, according to how one gender is defined, the other is defined by default. This is not a matter, therefore, of attacking the stereotypical definitions of male and female that have penalized the female for millennia, or of specifying the diversity of the female. Instead, the problem is how to avoid thought and language based on antithesis and dichotomy (based, that is, on the Aristotelean principle of non-contradiction), on the univocality of the meaning of male *or* female.

Archetypes of femaleness

As an instrument of knowledge and experience, the archetype enables us to evade the restrictions of positivism and enter the collective imaginary. According to Jung (1966a: 24), the archetype confronts the individual with the abyssal contradictoriness of human nature and provides us with absolutely immediate experience of light and dark, of Christ and the Devil. Archetypes are forms of apprehension which give rise to ways of thinking, feeling, imagining and experiencing. Hillman (1975: 118) maintains that 'archetypal ideas are primarily speculative ideas, that is they encourage speculation, a word which means mirroring, reflecting, visioning'. The contents of archetypes are both personal and supra-personal because they vary according to both individual experience and the history and culture of a society. Although potentially of limitless number, they reflect typical life-experiences and therefore represent humanity's most immediate realities: motherhood, fatherhood, childhood, heroism, wisdom (Bowles, 1993).

The archetype therefore outwardly projects inner experience and replicates the history of knowledge in general. Science began with the stars; the stars with which humankind identified the gods while attributing mental qualities to the zodiac. This projective process is repeated whenever a void is filled with living figurations and the active imagination (Jung, 1966b) comes into play. Analogic processes in scientific enquiry and the metaphors of science continue the alchemist tradition.

In the world of work and organizations, as in other spheres of social life, cultural models of femaleness can be identified which, as regards their archetypical features, fashion different patterns of womanhood and structure different relationships, each with its corresponding model of maleness and relations in public. In order to stress the archetypical and transcultural nature of these models, I shall refer to Greek mythology and its female and male divinities. I shall show how these goddesses and gods correspond to specific embodiments of femaleness and maleness in modern organizational cultures (Bolen, 1984, 1989; Bowles, 1993).

The Jungian psychologist Jean Bolen (1984) has explored the presence of Greek deities within the female psyche. Her work has been a major stimulus to my enquiry into the deepest roots of forms of work behaviour – forms that constitute typologies of which an appropriate definition previously eluded me.

It was, in fact, while I was examining the data from interviews carried out during a survey of women at work and drawing up a typology for which I was unable to find labels that did not stigmatize behaviours, that I stumbled across Bolen's book and discovered a surprising correspondence between her archetypes of the female and my typology. In my subsequent discussion with groups of men and women interviewees of the archetypes that I had identified, further insights emerged. Nevertheless I wish to make it clear that archetypes are suggested by empirical observation, not derived from it. I shall be discussing cultural models which, in a certain sense, are 'pre-packaged' categories used to represent certain types of performance; they are not the elements of the individual psyche, nor are they behavioural prescriptions for 'discovering goddesses within yourself'.

In constructing the models presented below, I have drawn on case studies conducted in the following organizations: a large printing company, in which I studied the technical staff (38 interviewees, eight of whom were women); three offices in a large government department (49 interviewees, 31 women); three university departments (67 interviewees, 18 women); and nine cooperatives of various sizes (four with fewer than 20 workers, three with 50–100 workers, and two with 250–500 workers). In the cooperatives I was the participant observer of decision-making processes, and the women involved varied greatly from case to case. Finally, I shall refer to a number of voluntary associations, in which, however, I conducted only collective interviews.

We can view organizations as constituting so many small Olympuses, each populated by gods and goddesses who engage in great battles, form alliances, wage vicious vendettas and achieve idyllic peace. Strong emotions and stable affective bonds tie this large and quarrelsome family together.

I shall first illustrate the femaleness of the organization-Olympus and then compare it with the kind of maleness with which it is most intimately acquainted, and with the dynamics that femaleness/maleness pairings generate in social life.

Greek female deities divide roughly between the virgin goddesses (Artemis, Athena, Hestia) and the vulnerable goddesses (Hera, Demeter, Persephone). The virgin deities represent a femaleness that has not been manipulated either by social and cultural expectations or by the judgement of a man. They are the female-as-separate with no relationship with the male: in Greek mythology they are the only female deities not to have been abducted or raped. The virgin goddesses represent a femaleness which pursues its own goals and accomplishes them regardless of the expectations and discouragement of others.

The vulnerable goddesses are ready to engage in relationships, and they find their identity and well-being in relations. Whereas the virgin deities embody the female need for independence, the vulnerable deities express the need for affiliation. All three of the vulnerable goddesses were raped and dominated by male deities, and suffered on account of the love relationship.

The model of femaleness as displayed by the virgin and vulnerable goddess can be used to analyse gendered work in organizations. Its characteristics are set out in Figure 3.1 at the end of this section (p. 83).

The female Artemis, or the 'sister'

Artemis, whom the Romans called Diana, was the goddess of the hunt and of the moon, who dwelt in the forest in the company of a flock of attendant nymphs. She was the twin sister of Apollo, the god of the sun. I found the female Artemis in organizations with offices staffed only by women – women who had formed themselves into a peer group and allowed themselves to be led by one of their number who acted as their mentor, protector and champion against the rest of the organization. Offices of this kind were apparently most frequent in the civil service: they were often accounts offices, or at any rate ones with routine administrative functions and in which everyone knew the work of everyone else. Within them, a model of participative management had been implicitly established, for Artemis is *una inter pares*. Thus communication, the exchange of experiences, mutual help and the interchangeability of tasks were part of the management style of this organizational culture. Group solidarity had even effectively invalidated formal job classifications, so that women with higher qualifications performed simpler tasks because they found them more congenial. Conversely, women with lower qualifications enjoyed the challenge of more complex tasks. The motto of the office could have been 'one for all and all for one', except that no one doubted that the leader was Artemis and that she demanded unswerving loyalty. The flock of nymphs had gradually formed over time; and if there had been men in the office, they would either have left quickly or accepted a role as 'one of the girls'. Had other Artemises arrived, their challenge would have been beaten off – the loser either withdrawing or venting her malice from the margins of the nymph flock.

Artemis marks out and defends her organizational territory. Her professional sphere of competence, and the authority that this endows her with, are recognized and respected; her determination to defend her organizational space frightens off potential rivals. The Artemis of mythology was merciless to intruders, as the legend of her savage punishment of Actaeon graphically shows. When Actaeon was out hunting with his dogs he came across Artemis and her nymphs bathing naked in a hidden pool. He stood and watched. Angered by Actaeon's effrontery, Artemis splashed water into his face and transformed him into a stag. He was then hunted down by his hounds and torn to pieces.

Artemis is a leader who defends her charges against outside interference with drawn sword. She helps them in their work, but demands loyalty and reciprocity, especially when she decides to embark upon a new venture.

Constituting the dark side of this cultural model of female independence is competition. The image of Artemis is the huntress as she strains to take aim with her bow. Her pose announces 'I know how to look after myself': she has no need of male approval, she focuses unerringly on her objective, and she relishes the competitiveness of the 'hunt'.

The only man that Artemis ever loved fell victim to her competitiveness. According to the legend, Orion was swimming far out to sea. Apollo pointed to the faint object moving through the water and challenged Artemis to strike it with an arrow. Not knowing that the distant target was Orion, Artemis accepted the challenge, let fly her arrow and killed him.

Sisterly and compassionate in her dealings with her nymphs, ruthlessly competitive in the world of men, the Artemis of organizations is a committed individualist who pursues her goals without seeking the support of either men or women.

The female Athena, or the 'father's girl'.

Athena, called Minerva by the Romans, the goddess of wisdom and of the arts, was the offspring of a single parent, Zeus. As Zeus' most trusted companion, she was the only goddess to whom he would entrust his thunderbolt and shield, the twin symbols of his power. The birth of Athena was spectacular: she emerged from Zeus' head as a fully-formed woman, sheathed in golden armour, with a spear in her hand and uttering a fierce battle cry. She thereafter became the protector, counsellor and ally of heroes and men of valour.

Athena represents the woman who takes sides with the patriarchy. During the trial of Orestes – accused of killing his mother Clytemnestra in revenge for the murder of his father Agamemnon – Athena cast the deciding vote for his acquittal. In doing so, she bowed to the arguments of Apollo, who maintained that the mother was merely the container for the seed planted by the father and proclaimed the supremacy of the male over the female, citing as an example the birth of Athena herself.

Athena as a cultural model is widespread and pervasive in organizations, both in her role as the trusted accomplice of leaders and as the spokeswoman for the established order.

The cultural model of the woman as 'right-hand man' does not necessarily require her to conceal herself or to become invisible. Athena is the goddess of wisdom. She presides over battle strategy in times of war, and over the domestic arts in times of peace. She therefore stands resolutely at the side of a dauntless leader who relies on her advice. For the attributes of her power are a gift from her father, and they reflect his potency.

It is Athena's proximity to power that justifies her identification with men and sanctions her participation in their activities, as either a peer or a superior aware of what is happening behind the scenes and able to make dispassionate assessment of possible strategies. To the 'great man' who has chosen Athena, whose trust she has won with her devotion and tireless work, and to whom she is by now indispensable, she gives advice that although certainly useful is at times merciless. Athena scorns weakness, she has time only for men who emanate the aura of power, she loves the astute and the victorious. For her only heroes matter.

I have encountered the Athena cultural model most frequently in productive organizations which revel in the epic of conquest and whose culture therefore exalts the virtues of victory. But also in trade unions, with their strong commitment to a culture of conflictuality, there emerge models of Athena-like femaleness: women who take pride in their strategic talents and in their respected positions as 'seconds-in-command'. Whether as 'the boss's indispensable secretary', as the exemplary pupil launched on a career by her mentor, as assistant to a manager more or less high in the hierarchy, these women speak with their master's voice.

The mythical Athena, goddess of the arts, was challenged by Arachne, a weaver of great skill and presumption, to a contest of tapestry-weaving. On viewing the completed tapestries, Athena admired Arachne's talents, but then flew into a rage when she saw that Arachne had dared to depict the treacheries of Zeus. As punishment, she transformed Arachne into a spider and forced her to weave for eternity. Athena, in fact, was not enraged because of the impudence of Arachne's challenge, but because she had brought the perfidious behaviour of her father into the public domain.

The Athena of organizations is the cultural model who also conceals the flaws of her patron, defends his public image and is angered by other women who gossip, complain or declare themselves victims of situations which they themselves have created. This model of femaleness normally rules out sisterhood, and the professional success of an Athena rarely prompts other women to follow in her footsteps.

By representing the patriarchical order, the Athena model of femaleness defends the status quo. It demonstrates acceptance of established norms and of 'professional' behaviour; that is, self-control, objectivity, impersonality, logical thought, and the development of specific skills.

Athena is especially well equipped for her role. Born wearing a splendid cuirass of gold (unlike Artemis and her short tunic for running and competing) she is armoured against sentiment; she coldly analyses situations and devises winning strategies which enable her to concentrate on her objective while remaining impervious to the needs of others. The standards of professional behaviour in highly femalized occupations are generally drawn up according to the Athena model of femaleness:

organization, expertise, efficiency, manual skills, confidence with technology, clearness of thought, colleagueship with men.

Hestia, or the 'spinster aunt'

Hestia (Vesta in Roman mythology) was the goddess of the hearth
and custodian of the fire which burned on a round stone in the *megaron*
(hall). She was a goddess of the first Olympian generation, the first-born
daughter of Rhea and Chronos, and therefore the unmarried aunt of the
deities of the second generation, the children of Zeus. She was the least
personalized of the Olympians, and was portrayed not in human guise, but
in the symbolic form of the circle. Little is known of Hestia, since she was
involved neither in wars nor in romance.

The distinctive feature of Hestia was that she was set apart by men, she
went unnoticed and kept her own counsel. Unlike the other goddesses, she
never ventured into the outside world, but tended the hearth within the
innermost room of the house or at the temple. Her presence outside was
only required when she was called upon to consecrate the dwellings of
newly-wed couples, so that their houses could become hearths.

The Hestia of organizations is, accordingly, invisible. If anyone happens
to notice her, she is then rapidly forgotten and her work dismissed as
unimportant. The Hestia model is exemplified by those women adept at
making others feel at home, at transforming a workplace into an intimate
and familiar setting, at creating a warm and comfortable atmosphere
without being noticed.

Hestia-like femaleness produces this halo effect because it concentrates
upon what is done. It is as though the organizational Hestia follows a
ritual – as though her routine is a ceremonial whose significance lies in its
faithful repetition of gestures and precedents.

One striking feature of Hestia's femaleness is its apparent timelessness.
She works as if she has all the time in the world; she listens as though she
is participating with her whole being. One gains the impression that she,
the custodian of the hearth, will always be there, and that she is forgotten
because she is taken for granted; her presence is only noticed when she
retires or is absent for a long periods. Because Hestia is not normally
ambitious, she neglects her career. She tends to remain for long periods
in the same physical environment, and ends up as a 'pillar' of the
organization, a sort of historical memory.

Set apart from the outside world, Hestia is isolated from the rumours
that flow through the organization. She usually stands aloof from disputes,
or refuses to take sides in arguments because she finds them uninteresting.
Although this behaviour marginalizes her from the social life of the
organization, it is of no great concern to her.

As in the extended family, where the maiden aunts live in the household
and participate obliquely in family life, the organization's Hestia watches,
with the clarity of detachment, its goings-on. When necessary, her

workmates (nephews and nieces) seek her out as a source of wisdom and advice.

The custodians of the hearth may be valuable collaborators, if the right balance has been struck between them and the organization. They tend to occupy a protected niche in the organization far from the clamour of battle and the shifting tides of fashion, and thus provide a dependable and welcoming refuge in times of conflict or stress.

I found custodians of the hearth in all the organizations I studied, and perhaps most frequently in non-profit or voluntary ones – where they could more freely indulge a certain relish for the ritualization of the everyday and the sacredness of gestures. Many of the elderly women I met were indeed spinsters and married to their work, even though they did not aspire to a career. Retirement was unthinkable to them; or else, once they had retired, they would soon look for another job as essential for their psychological well-being.

I am still unable to resolve my moral doubt as to whether organizations exploit the discretion and the willingness of this kind of femaleness, or whether they provide a safe and hospitable refuge where it can express a range of talents and values which are undoubtedly central to our culture but profoundly spiritual in nature. I admit that I feel more empathy for a partnership involving Hestia and an Athena or an Artemis as boss, since this kind of working relationship seems to yield a warmer femaleness, one beneficial to the organizations that I studied. When the boss was a man, I noted a traditional separateness of sexual roles with reciprocal satisfaction and non-interference. More often, however, I found that custodians of the hearth were simply treated as one of the office staff, and that they were not directly involved in the dyadic relationship. The Hestia cultural model is indifferent to power, self-affirmation and competitiveness. It is easily dismissed as a 'loser' model because of its passivity; yet if one thinks carefully about the values that conventionally define a 'winner' model, one recognizes the clash between the values of materialism and domination of the world on the one hand, and those of receptiveness to the world on the other. Only religious organizations or those of humanitarian inspiration are ready to acknowledge the value of spirituality and detachment from the world; all other organizations normally undervalue the role and the contribution of their vestal virgins.

I have described the three virgin goddesses who either chose to live apart from men (Artemis), or identified with them (Athena), or were marginalized by them (Hestia). I now turn to the three female deities who suffered from, but also rejoiced in, their relationships with men – relationships which motivated them more profoundly than accomplishing an objective, autonomy or pleasurable experience. In Greek mythology, Hera represented the desire to provide companionship, Demeter attention to household chores, and Persephone dependence: all three sought approval, love and attention.

Hera, or the 'wife'

Hera, whom the Romans called Juno, was the goddess of matrimony, the consort of Zeus. She wreaked terrible vengeance on the women with whom her husband betrayed her (an occurrence of some frequency), and also on their children. In his courtship of Hera, Zeus transformed himself into a fragile and trembling bird. Her pity aroused, Hera pressed the bird to her breast in order to give it warmth, whereupon Zeus promptly abandoned his disguise and tried to rape her. Hera resisted his amorous advances until she had extracted his promise to marry her. Their honeymoon lasted three hundred years. However, on their return Zeus resumed his reprobate ways, provoking the furious jealousy of Hera, who did not take revenge on him, however, but on 'the others' and their children.

The Hera model of femaleness expresses the desire to be first and foremost a wife, and thus enjoy the social status deriving from being one half of a couple. But she also embodies the rage and pain of being deprived of this status. Not only, therefore, does Hera represent the desire for the prestige, respect and honour that marriage provides, she expresses the ability to forge a bond, to be faithful and loyal to a companion, and to derive pleasure from coping jointly with difficulties. When Hera femaleness is wedded to someone or something, the woman undertakes a sacred marriage in which she finds either complete self-realization or suffering and anger, according to the 'husband' that she has taken.

Unless her spouse is the organization itself, or the ideal that it represents, or the organization in the mediated form of some male working within it (as in the case of the office secretary/wife), the Hera cultural model regards work as a secondary aspect of life. Work is something that one does, perhaps successfully and satisfyingly; but 'life is elsewhere'. Hera's true career is her marriage and her devotion to a husband who recognizes Hera femaleness. According to this cultural model, an unmarried woman who works is waiting to find a husband; if she is married, she subordinates her career and the demands of her work to those of her husband. She announces that she has married, and that she has married well, by taking her husband's surname. She conducts her relational life in the company of other 'super-married' couples and proclaims the fact at work. She engages in intense communicative activity. In the work environment of a Hera, whatever social class she may belong to, her colleagues are better informed of her husband's difficulties at work than her own. Her married life is a romance which she narrates by herself. Her unmarried female colleagues often accuse her of devaluing women without steady male companions in their lives, and of maintaining only superficial relationships with other women.

A classic example of the woman-wife dedicated exclusively to her husband's career is the American First Lady. In Europe the role of 'important man's wife' is less constrictive; yet, at both the symbolic and practical levels, the woman who devotes her labour to her husband's success is an extremely widespread cultural model, the legitimacy of which is not called into question.

When Hera's devotion is focused on her boss, we encounter the office wife, who supplies both emotional support as well as her effective labour, and is willing to follow a boss through his career and to dedicate her female talents and her intelligence to his success.

Many excellent secretaries, of course, have assumed the guise of workplace wives. But many male protégés, too, have served as the longstanding wives of a patron before acquiring their personal independence (although this happens less frequently when the boss is also a woman).

Demeter, or 'the mother'

Demeter, worshipped by the Romans as Ceres, was the goddess of harvests and abundant crops. She was the mother of Persephone, the girl who, as she gathered flowers in a meadow, was seized by Hades and taken to the underworld to become his wife. Persephone's abduction and rape was implicitly condoned by Zeus, who stood idly by as Demeter, for nine days and nights without eating, sleeping or washing, searched desperately for her daughter. Only when Demeter refused to fulfil her task of bringing forth the crops, and mankind was on the brink of starvation, did Zeus intervene by sending Hermes to recover Persephone, who thereafter spent two-thirds of the year with her mother and the remaining third with Hades.

The archetype of Demeter femaleness represents the maternal instinct, and self-realization through the provision of physical, psychological and moral nourishment to others. Demeter is the 'nurturer' *par excellence* and she symbolizes the joy and the pain that the caring instinct can bring.

One frequently encounters an 'earth mother' of this kind in offices, and also in other private and public settings. She devotes great energy to helping others, concerns herself with both their private and working lives, and organizes outings and social events with the same enthusiasm that she devotes to her children's birthday parties. With a perseverance equal to that of Demeter in search of her daughter, the colleague-nurturer attends to the psycho-physical well-being of her office. She also shows great generosity in welcoming and socializing new colleagues (especially if they are young women), in substituting for colleagues on sick leave, in covering up inefficiency or mistakes, in giving moral support to colleagues in distress, and in being generally understanding.

We have perhaps all benefited at some point in our working lives from the warmth and generosity of a Demeter. And perhaps many of us have also experienced the subsequent difficulty of extricating ourselves from her over-affectionate embrace without making her feel rejected. In fact, when a position of authority combines with a Demeter model of femaleness, one may encounter a 'mother-hen' manager who tries to gather the young women in the office (or if not young, then in subordinate positions) under her protective wing, or even male workers if they are willing to be 'mothered'. This may confront these workers with the problem of emancipating themselves from a too-oppressive parental figure, with the consequence that the behaviour of the 'earth mother' may prove counterproductive for organizations.

I can illustrate this last point more clearly by describing the example of a voluntary organization which I studied. I should first point out that women greatly outnumber men in the Italian non-profit sector. Since, therefore, there are numerous women responsible for the creation of these organizations and who now act as their charismatic leaders, one frequently encounters models of Demeter femaleness. In this particular case, the founder of the association was a woman of great energy and resourcefulness who, in the space of seven years, had built up an organization that gave steady employment to twelve people (of whom nine were women) and utilized sixty volunteers, as well as deploying considerable financial resources. This woman was liked and respected by everyone and, even after a number of years, during which many of the founders had left and the association had diminished notably in size, almost nobody blamed her for the organization's failure to take off and consolidate. In short, what had happened was that the founder became totally absorbed by her work and by her relationships with her colleagues, who referred to her, and discussed with her, every aspect of the organization's work.

Although she was still indispensable, her ability to be present always and everywhere was being severely tested by the increasing complexity of the organization's activities. Simultaneously, her colleagues had grown in experience and were pressing for more efficient distribution of tasks and for greater autonomy. Moreover, they were seriously worried about her health. The organizational literature abounds with examples of the growth pattern of small democratic organizations whose initial success is compromised by their failure to introduce more complex management methods with sufficient rapidity. In this case the organization's inability to consolidate was due to an interpersonal dynamic: the generous leader felt that her solicitude for others was being rejected, and her reaction took the same form as Demeter's when she threatened humankind with starvation. Consequently the coordination of information and action began to break down. And the routine activities of everyone who worked for the organization grew increasingly confused – which engendered obvious overlaps or failures to respond. Her co-workers were unable independently to elaborate a collegiate system of decision-making and blamed themselves for their failure to do so. This was inevitable, because the most important – indeed the only – point of contact between the association and the external environment was the founder, as the sole channel for all incoming information.

Many years later, the leader recounted the experience by comparing it to her sense of loss when her only son moved abroad and to the depression that his decision provoked. The group dynamic that had arisen in the meantime was not, in fact, particularly conflictual. Little by little, members had left the association, its activities had declined, numerous minor 'critical events' had come to dominate discussion, until an air of resignation prevailed.

In my studies of organizations I frequently encountered working women who embodied the Demeter model, whose generosity was plainly exploited by both the organization and their workmates. I also frequently met the Demeter who considered the product of her work to be her own 'creature', something that she had created and brought up, and the loss of which she felt as a grave privation. And by no means rare was the 'mother-hen' version of Demeter who inveigled others into dependence upon her.

I have dwelt on Demeter because the 'maternal instinct' and maternity is a resource from which organizations derive both benefits and disadvantages. I conclude by pointing out that this model of femaleness, with its readiness to care for others, to show concern for their problems, to sacrifice free time for them, and so forth, is ultimately counterproductive and leads to symptoms of burn-out: a feeling of being emptied, sucked dry, of constant fatigue or apathy.

Persephone, or 'mummy's little girl'

Persephone, known as Proserpina in Roman mythology, was worshipped in two forms: as a maiden before her abduction by Hades, and then as queen of the dead, a mature woman who guided the living through the underworld and took whatever she wanted. The cyclical pattern of her life, spent partly among the living and partly in Hell, symbolizes the mystery of life after death, or the return of springtime.

In her guise as Kore (the Maiden), Persephone is an archetypal symbol of the season in a woman's life when she is still young, uncertain, ingenuous, full of promise. She also symbolizes the wait for something to happen, for someone to come and give shape to life. She is therefore receptivity and passivity, the ability to be open and flexible.

Persephone is the maiden in Botticelli's *Primavera*; but at first sight she is comparatively rare in organizations, or perhaps our perception of her changes when she dons her work clothes.

The Persephone model can perhaps be more readily understood if we think back to our first experience of work – as we approached it with the curiosity, ingenuousness and enthusiasm of the neophyte and felt that our entire lives stretched before us. Perhaps we were already interrogating ourselves on what we would do as adults – no matter what we actually became – or perhaps we were determined not to stay more than three months in the job, but now, more than twenty years hence, are still doing it.

The Persephone model is not to the liking of all work groups or individuals in organizations. There are some who look indulgently on the young Persephone, who are willing to listen and help when she declares herself ready to do anything asked of her, but instead proves careless of deadlines, heedless of commitments and utterly disorganized. But there are others who are ferociously dismissive of 'today's young women'.

The work trajectories of young Persephones are diversified: there are those who constantly and recklessly change jobs, thus failing to accumulate any sort of experience or to develop any interest in one kind of work rather than another. There are others who adapt well to jobs which require no initiative, responsibility or autonomy, and consequently turn into the office mascot, protected and coddled by everybody. There are finally those who develop both work experience and other aspects of their individuality within a 'career' path in the broad sense of the term. In fact the Persephone model may represent both a woman in a transitional phase of her working life and the eternal 'little girl' metaphorically clinging to her mother's apron-strings (i.e to whoever takes her decisions for her). Or else Persephone's working life languishes in suspended animation as she waits for something to happen, as she abandons herself to the flow of events and allows circumstances to take her decisions for her.

Work is certainly not a significant experience in the Persephone model of femaleness. It represents the time spent with a mother – that is, the time of girlhood, of minority, of bowing to the will of others – whereas other spheres of activity represent the time and place where Persephone is queen of hell and a woman.

The three vulnerable goddesses embody three parallel forms of femaleness expressed through relationships with others: wifehood, motherhood and daughterhood. The three virgin goddesses, instead, express themselves in relation to their goals (Figure 3.1). Greek mythology therefore propounds a distinction that is nothing new to organization studies: the distinction between task-oriented and relation-oriented individuals. But it adds the warning that the former are not to be identified with maleness or the latter with femaleness.

We may now enquire how the various archetypes of femaleness stand in relation to each other, and how their presence evokes or activates corresponding archetypes of maleness in everyday relations within organizations.

Organizing as family dynamics

In the previous section I illustrated a set of archetypal types of femaleness and stressed their correlation to roles within the family. I now intend to explore the work environment further, and in terms of the alliances that form between archetypal figures of femaleness and maleness as family dynamics. I wish to stress once again, however, that it is not my intention to propose stereotypes which classify individuals as one deity or another, or as family roles; I merely point out that there is a set of gendered

THE VIRGIN GODDESSES:	FEMALE-AS-SEPARATE IN FAMILY DYNAMICS	
ARTEMIS	female independence: those women who have chosen to live apart from men	sisterhood to other women
ATHENA	female rational thought: those women who identify with men	daughterhood to the father
HESTIA	female self-autonomy: those women who live at the margins	the aunt
THE VULNERABLE GODDESSES:	FEMALE-AS-INSEPARABLE	
HERA	female companionship	wifehood
DEMETER	female nurturer	motherhood
PERSEPHONE	female dependence and the cyclical force of renewal	daughterhood to the mother

Figure 3.1   *Archetypal types of femaleness*

cultural models which constantly recur, and specific associations between a model of femaleness and another of maleness which reciprocally evoke each other.

The patterns of gender relation that we learn in infancy, and which we recognize principally by analogy in others in social situations, are family patterns. Anthropology also teaches us that the kinship system is variable. I used two symbolic systems which were (and are) easily accessible to my research subjects. Roman mythology is part of my country's cultural heritage and is well known to anyone who has completed compulsory schooling. I have preferred, however, to refer to Greek mythology in order to address an international readership. Secondly, the family is the paramount symbolic locus of the construction of the patriarchal system.

These two symbolic systems enable me to explore ground which has been neglected by the dominant discourse on gender. Foregrounding the opposition between the genders has not only led us to think in terms of two genders but it has also emphasized the uniformity of gender while ignoring the diversity, the plurality and the ambiguity of the gender relation. Femaleness is not unitary, the goddesses tell us, and maleness is multiform. Having described these gods I shall not dwell on them further, both because I have not studied them specifically and because others have done so for purposes other than mine (Bolen, 1989; Bowles, 1993). I wish to stress that my research was conducted within the framework of 'women's studies'. I was therefore interested in understanding the plurality of models of femaleness and how these operate in the workplace. It was through my observation of women's interactions with men, and how a

Hera was frequently found in attendance on a Zeus, that I came to hypothesize their reciprocal construction. Today I would direct my research immediately to the gender relation, but I want neither to overinterpret my data nor to present them with the wisdom of hindsight

My analysis draws principally on notes taken during participant observation of decision processes in (mainly) cooperatives; that is, in democratic organizations typified by decision-making involving a large number of people, some of whom were women. When I wrote my study (Gherardi and Masiero, 1987), I was not addressing the problematic of female participation, and only subsequently, upon re-reading my field notes, did I give more systematic formulation to the hypothesis that I develop below. When possible, I returned to the organizations concerned in order to interview the women whom I felt to be key informants.

I begin by illustrating an emblematic case of an alliance relation: that of the Hera-as-wife model of femaleness when it encounters a corresponding Zeus-as-husband. I was able to interview the person concerned on more than one occasion, because, by sheer coincidence, I met her in two different organizations and at two different stages of her career. I then identified similar features in other informant biographies – features which, taken jointly, yielded a composite portrait of the ideal Hera.

I met Hera, not in a cooperative, but in the boardroom of an important organization. The board consisted of around thirty people, of whom only three were women. I had previously encountered Hera while conducting action research in a local government service employing around forty people and run in a highly participative manner by the professionals who worked therein. Only ten women were employed by the service, and of these only Hera had high-ranking status. Her transfer from one organization to another was due to recognition of her outstanding professionalism. It crowned a brilliant career and, as Hera entered her fifties, it was her due reward for her many years of sacrifice and hard work. As a pioneer, she had testified to female ability in a professional field dominated by males, and she was also known to the public as one of the first feminists. She was married to a colleague and had two adolescent children.

The crowning point of her career came with her three-year appointment to the vice-presidency of the board of directors, flanking a president some ten years older than she was, with a different occupational background and of notoriously conservative views.

The older members of the board expected a tough stand-off between the two, given their conflicting personalities and their already well-known divergences of opinion in public. Yet many were surprised by the rapport that developed between them – to the extent that they came to be known as 'the couple', the king and the royal consort, the 'magnificent two'. No closer interpersonal relationship was insinuated, but a set of events invited the label of a 'court' and a gendered division of tasks.

For example, my notes on discourse turn-taking showed that almost all opening exchanges at board meetings followed a pattern in which Hera spoke immediately after the president, and that many of her subsequent interventions were explicit offers of mediation between a challenger and the president. The search for an honourable compromise was accompanied by situations in which Hera interceded in favour of a weaker subject or something that required protection. Had the conflict failed to materialize or had it been only imagined? As in the best families, the most awkward questions were discussed away from indiscreet ears, when the children had gone to bed. Traces of previous arguments lingered, but there was a special place for private discussion, a parents' room to which access by anyone else was barred.

The older members were also able to compare the management style of the previous board, in which the vice-president had been distinctly ineffectual and had contributed very little, and the present one under Hera's vice-presidency. The members were unanimous that this was a more relaxed style (some also called it more polite) and that the level of conflictuality had diminished; and many of them declared that Hera exerted a beneficent influence on the president. Hera's interpretation of matters was rather different, however. When invited to talk openly about the situation, she described it in terms of 'a struggle', a great effort to be understood, diplomacy, a filter to shield her against his negative reactions. She attributed the more serene atmosphere in the boardroom to respect for ceremonial, not as an end in itself but as due to the sacredness of the rules of the game. Extremely significantly, a year after the experience, Hera remembered the critical decisions taken by the board as occasions when she had failed to reach agreement with the president and lost her temper: she had lost control of the situation and hence of herself. On these occasions, though, I did not observe a genuine alliance between Hera and other members of the board; nor did I observe any particularly intense or meaningful relationship among the three women present. In that context, being in the minority was of no significance.

I was able to observe similar work-couples in other settings, but I shall concentrate on this particular woman because I had already met her at a previous stage in her career: a phase when she embodied various femaleness archetypes (also in relation to other men and women). In different life-periods, in different contexts, and with different people, different patterns of femaleness may be activated: archetypes are of help in interpreting the multiplicity of relations, not in fixing stereotypes or personalities.

In this previous organizational situation, the boss was an old man frequently absent, hanging on for his pension and therefore with very little authority. Hera had been the oldest and highest-ranking woman. There were also a number of men of her age and seniority, one of whom held moral ascendancy over the others, but not to the extent that he obscured Hera. For many years they both acted as – gendered – reference figures, the one (she) providing emotional leadership, the other (he) goal-oriented leadership, thereby constituting a clearly defined pair of complementary points of reference.

Had we been on Olympus, we would have been in the company of a first-generation god, Chronos, a female daughter and several male sons. However, in contrast to the mythological account, Chronos was a good father, perhaps a little distracted because he was not greatly preoccupied with family matters and was hoping to leave. The children were not eager to take power because they had apparently established some sort of democracy centred on the brother/sister pairing. They were vaguely aware that on the natural 'death' of Chronos one of them would be elected to the throne by the other siblings. Whether each of them secretly believed him/herself to be the successor, and whether there was latent rivalry between them, we cannot tell, because what the visitor to Olympus observed was more a pacific division of tasks and spheres of influence than a covert struggle for succession. Indeed, in many respects the brother/sister couple resembled Zeus-as-father and Demeter-as-mother. Both exercised parental functions over younger people, and brother/sister incest was acknowledged by Greek mythology although it did not occur in this particular Olympus.

Hera also acted as Demeter because she had gathered all the other women under her protection and preferred to work only with them. She had also sought to extend her influence over the younger men, although they generally preferred the guidance of other males, to whom they overtly attributed more power. Nor were all the young women ready to accept Hera-Demeter's protection. Some of them obviously regarded her feminist stance to be incoherent with her hierarchical position in the organization. This, they believed, conflicted with the message of sisterhood she conveyed. Demeter was nevertheless solicitous towards all the other women, and they took pride in her successes because – as a woman – these successes were also their own. Yet this woman had raised a brood of Persephones who were destined to remain little girls for as long as they stayed by her side.

The sibling group was also closely knit. They placed great value in the fact that they had grown up together (they had all entered the organization at practically the same time, and being of the same age they shared the same generational culture) and they also mixed socially outside work. Hera, moreover, was confidante to the other men of her age, who, to varying extents, were her career companions. As the cleverest, Demeter dispensed career advice, she shared her knowledge with them, she was generous and ready to help, she exchanged invitations with her colleagues' wives and their children (of the same age as her own).

However, Hera's ascent to Mount Olympus entered a critical phase – which was also an organizational crisis – when the head of the service retired, and her colleagues appointed their operational leader to take his place. Despite similar service records, seniority and work performance, the appointment had gone to a man. Hera refused to 'make the best of a bad job': feeling betrayed, she resigned and left the service. All her colleagues were stunned, albeit to different extents: her male colleagues maintained that the man's promotion was legitimate and deserved because, in their opinion, his curriculum vitae was slightly better. Note that the woman's professional competence was universally recognized and that she could not have attained a position of leadership if she had been less than professionally outstanding. Yet this constituted only one prerequisite, necessary but not sufficient, for her success.

Nevertheless the woman's male colleagues denied any gender bias and defended their behaviour, although they were sorry that they had provoked an 'excessive reaction' and surprised that the woman cared so deeply. Since the other women had not directly influenced the decision, they saw it as yet another example of women's lot as women. They criticized what had happened but were substantially resigned to the situation. The young men, who had been equally marginal to the decision, shrugged their shoulders and refused to pronounce on the matter. The winner felt embarrassed, slightly guilty and effectively delegitimized. The activities of the service came to a standstill. Research with outside consultants was halted, so that my subsequent information came to me only second-hand: it depicted an atmosphere of demoralization and distrust which lasted until the incident had been forgotten and morale revived.

I have made explicit reference to an individual case in order to illustrate how distinct models of femaleness can arise at different stages and in different situations of the same person's life-span. The woman in question was involved in a brother/sister relationship, and the balance of organizational power relations expressed a division of leadership (which reflected a separation of powers along gender lines). She was also a Demeter who fulfilled the mothering needs of other people and based her authority on an ability to manage the emotionality of a particular social structure in the role of nurturer. And when organizational equilibrium rested on a power pattern narrowly centred on one particular person in the guise of an 'elder' symbolizing the power of the father, then this woman assumed a Hera behavioural model whose ascendancy over the group was based on its ability to handle relations with authority and to mediate these relations between the group and the higher decision-maker.

The two partners personified, in their turn, two distinct models of maleness: the brother, in order to sustain the gendered division of labour, embodied the values of rationality, activity and technique as opposed to those of emotionality; the husband embodied the world of command and prohibition as attributes of authority – also over the wife.

When the social structure which ties decision-makers together has several decisional loci, it is probable that sibling relations will come into operation. Both the Artemis and Athena models frequently ally themselves with male figures occupying intermediate positions in the hierarchy. But they do so in very different ways, just as their alliances with other women take very different forms.

In Greek mythology, the newborn Artemis assisted her mother Leto in giving birth to her twin brother Apollo. In archetypal relations, Artemis' active feature is solidarity with other women, combined with her competitiveness against men. Characteristic of the Artemis–Apollo pair is the fact that sister and brother pursue cross-gendered interests: Apollo (associated with rationality and the law) also had an explicit relationship with the irrational as the god of prophecy. Artemis was the goddess of hunting, which is a male pursuit. The Artemis–Apollo twinship symbolizes an equality relationship with respect to a separation of realms: Apollo was the sun, Artemis the moon; his kingdom was the city, hers the forest; to him belonged domestic animals, to her belonged wild ones.

Generally speaking, women constitute the minority in decision-making settings, and like all minorities they show a tendency to develop internal solidarity, to constitute one 'voice', to merge into one decisional pole. In such cases, it is highly likely that the spokesperson for the group of women will be an Artemis who has explicitly created a system of alliances with her colleagues. She sets out to enhance their capacities or to form a team which she can lead in an assault on the male power establishment. And to achieve her ends, she may forge tactical alliances with the Apollo model of maleness.

Many of these alliances – which the other members of the group call 'historic' – display this pattern of complementariness between an Artemis–Apollo pair of twins and a group of sisters or brothers who give them emotional support as well as acting as a pressure group. It may happen, however, that competition breaks out between the members of the couple so that each of them launches a challenge against the other. It is in this sense that these alliances are tactical, because they incorporate a dynamic principle which renders them unstable. Personal conflicts may arise which, although they have nothing to do with the decisions in question, obstruct them by imposing a series of cross-vetoes. Likewise, ferocious conflicts may be followed by the restoration of former alliances. Many other decision-makers are drawn into the conflict and forced to take sides, even though they are extraneous to the situation which first gave origin to it. It is difficult for Artemis' companions to withdraw their support, for such action might undermine the internal cohesion of the group and therefore threaten its identity. The independence of Artemis, her rages and her competitiveness, may jeopardize her ability to create, maintain and develop a solidarist group of women.

In the Athena behavioural model, the relationship with other women is very different: quite simply, they do not exist, nor does the problem of collectively furthering the cause. Athena is not part of a female genealogy and therefore has relationships with neither a mother nor with sisters; she has only her daughters to empathize with because they are identical to her. Consequently, she is frequently the target of the vindictiveness of other women who do not regard her successes as enhancing women in general; instead, they dismiss her as some sort of 'queen bee'. She is often the protégée of an elderly Pygmalion who, through her, fulfils his dream of reproducing himself and transmitting his knowledge and experience to a docile and intelligent human artefact. When the 'father's girl' has sufficient power in decision processes, she bestows her patronage on young heroes – or at any rate she tends to associate herself with those for whom she foresees victory. With the authority and the attributes of her father, her heroism is that of her children, even though in the case of conflict between fathers and sons Athena takes the side of the former.

I have often discerned the Artemis and Athena archetypes in decision-making processes involving both men and women, most strikingly in the case of a manufacturing cooperative (Gherardi and Masiero, 1987) in which all decision-makers were women. On re-reading my field notes, I was able to interpret events in the light of these archetypes with great ease.

Following fierce conflict among the members of the cooperative, two anatagonistic groups had formed, with shop-floor workers ranged on one side and office clerks on the other. The first administrative board consisted of one worker and eight clerks. However, following a dispute over which markets the cooperative should enter, the members decided to disband the administrative board and to elect a new one. The second board consisted of one clerk and eight shop-floor workers. Conflict continued, and in order to reach an agreement, the board decided to set up a discussion seminar, which drew up the following decision-making model. A technical group (three workers) was appointed to take responsibility for management, to monitor productivity, and to identify important issues which were then submitted to the board of administration at its fortnightly meetings. If disagreements arose over objectives, the decision was referred to the factory assembly (Gherardi and Masiero, 1987: 339). To understand how these decision rules were arrived at, one must know the power dynamics internal to this group of sisters.

The workers and the clerks each constituted a group of sisters with bonds of mutual support and a dynamic of reciprocal valorization. But at the beginning of the process, when the decision had been taken to form a cooperative, differences in expertise, in social background and of aspirations for the future had been concealed and minimized, both because of the need to cope with economic problems and because of the idealistic principle that the founders were all equal because they were all women. Only subsequently, and gradually, did the two groups begin to split apart from each other. In both groups an Artemis figure emerged, each focused on the goal of equality and yet suspicious of the other because each possessed a different vision of equality and the means to achieve it. Each Artemis gathered a certain number of comrades around her, and every fortnight a meeting was held to take strategic decisions. In the meantime, operational decisions were taken by a technical directoress – an Athena who had remained extraneous to the polarization and was firmly convinced that the cooperative should maintain internal order, respond to the market, and preserve close contacts with the outside agent promoting the initiative – namely the trade union delegate, a male, who had first suggested that the cooperative should be formed.

This situation had taken some time to develop because the initial antagonism between the two Artemises had gradually evolved into a division between their spheres of influence and thence into mutual esteem. Although Athena acted as the fulcrum in a situation of precarious balance, both groups placed its trust in her 'technical' and non-political role because each regarded her as extraneous to it and as a guarantor of order. However, this situation comprised another figure who acted as an emotional reference: a Hestia, to whom all those concerned resorted for advice or simply in order to discuss what was happening. She was an elderly unmarried woman who had worked in the factory since it opened, and now accepted the passage from collective ownership with equanimity; indeed it was a matter of comparative indifference to her. In this marginal role she provided a stable point of reference for Athena and the two Artemises, and also for the men, trade unionists or local politicians who had supported the women's struggle to save their jobs. These latter were male presences who came into contact only on public occasions or through Athena who incarnated her father's will. These men standing at the threshold symbolized Hermes, the pillar that stood at the door to the house, the hinges of the door, the link between the interior and the exterior.

The example of this cooperative prompts a number of considerations concerning both dynamics among women and the alleged specificity of women's organizations.

The sisterhood bond, explicitly called such by feminism, symbolizes solidarity among women, and, in the name of solidarity, similarity has been exalted above difference. This threatens the cohesion of a group of women because it lays bare the problems of power and leadership. It is also a threat to the collective identity that more easily comes about when everyone is equal; that is, when uniformity is the rule. The tension between separation and inseparability, between equality and difference, also arises among sisters. The archetypes of Athena, Artemis, Hera and the other goddesses body forth the differences internal to the female and the shifting boundaries between the genders.

A second point, which I shall only deal with briefly, is whether it is enough to create a women-only organization for a new mode of organizing to be born. *Women Organizing* is the title of a book by Brown (1991) which denotes the organizing experiences of women's centres and by extension a non-hierarchical, participative organizational modality with diffused leadership. Unlike formal and hierarchical ones – those 'normal' in the sense that they constitute the model of organizational theory – these women's organizations stand at the opposite extreme of a hypothetical continuum where, according to Rothschild (1990), one finds 'a tendency in negotiating to seek equitable agreements rather than self-advantage, a preference for involving others rather than a unilateral style, a habit of cultivating others' talents and crediting them, a sense of responsibility for others' well-being and a desire for relationships at work that are valued in themselves'. I conclude from my experience of research on cooperatives of various sizes and voluntary organizations (so-called 'proximity services') – conducted from a European perspective and therefore in comparison with studies by other colleagues (Paton *et al.*, 1989; Laville, 1992; Macfarlane and Laville, 1992) – that the constitutive values of democratic organizations give rise to an organizational culture which expresses rules of behaviour and patterns of organizing which are also evident in women's organizations or in organizations formed by women alone. I am puzzled by such statements as: 'women's socialization makes them better equipped than men to perform the skills necessary for the creation of democratic and non-hierarchical organization' (Brown, 1991: 192), although the author warns against transforming this assertion into a new (alternative) determinism. In my opinion the socialization of women to extra-domestic work, to organizational life, to organizing, does not come about in a context 'separate' from that of men; and socialization to the private, to care, to nurturing does not create a protective sheath around values which constitute the dowry that women bring with them when they enter the public sphere. Otherwise how can we understand all those men who prefer to work in or to found democratic organizations, so many of which are to be found in the tertiary sector? The traps of either/or language, of oppositionism in thought, induce us to deny of the Other what we affirm for the One. The comparison can be drawn between democratic/non-democratic organizations and not between women/men organizations.

When we think gender, not in terms of relation but of opposition, who is contrasted against whom, what is counterposed or complementary to what? Men and women? But men in what position with respect to women in what position? Are we contrasting a husband and a wife, a father and a mother, a lover and the beloved? In this case, the One is defined by its relation with the Other, and vice versa. We first learn gender relations in the family, where the male is the father, the husband, the brother, the uncle, the brother-in-law, and the female is the mother, the wife, the sister, the aunt, and so on. The reproduction of such relations in organizational Olympuses has been noted by the organizational literature, which talks of kinship (Grafton-Small and Linstead, 1985) and clan systems. The archetypes of family gender relations replicate the ambivalence and ambiguity of the family: the locus of solidarity, of profound affections and of psychological growth, but also of dominance, of abuse and of mental breakdown. The gender relations which activate the family archetypes are a rich resource for organizations, which in exalting the positive face of the family conceal its patriarchical and oppressive one. Consider how gender learnt in the family develops into an organizing principle. When organizations intend to solicit cooperation and incite commitment, the metaphor most frequently used is that of the large family; the metaphor also most widely used to convey the image of democracy and to hide that of hierarchy. When management or leadership wants to legitimize itself as responsible, as a good administrator and the curator of the public good, it summons up the archetype of the paterfamilias. The family discipline which teaches the subordination of the woman to the male head of the household, and the obedience of the children to the father, is the archetypal pattern of exchange regulation in many complementary work roles (boss/secretary, doctor/nurse), as well as in organizational gerontocracy and the mentor relationship that reproduces the *puer/senex* archetype.

Mentorship is one of the fundamental socialization processes. The reproduction of many organizations (e.g. universities), and the recruitment of many components qualitatively critical to an organization (executives or highly skilled personnel), are based on the master/pupil relationship. This in turn has its roots in the code of family discipline and is as emotionally intense as the relationship between parents and children. Organizations draw on the family for manpower socialized into the subordination of the woman to men, of the young to the old, of those with few resources to those who have them in abundance. In doing so, however, organizations not only make a saving; they create a symbolic reservoir from which they may tap emotional resources to exploit. These resources are both invested and used to control the workforce.

The association of masculinity with authority, with the (relative) abundance of resources, is a gender relation model which organizations reproduce through the allocation of jobs, careers and wages, and through their authority structure, as a specifically organizational form of mobilization with a masculine bias (Burton, 1992). They allocate resources among men and women according to a 'taste for discrimination' rooted in family archetypes of gender relations. But the ambiguity and ambivalence of the imagery activated by symbols tells us that the family is also made up of relations between brother and sister, and among brothers and sisters, and that these relations are among equals: solidarist, incestuous, patricidal and matricidal relations.

The image of the family also enables us to adopt an intergenerational perspective and to examine gender relations in the course of the life cycle. An example of this approach is provided by Kvande and Rasmussen's (1994) study of the way in which engineers culturally elaborate the presence of women intruders in a traditionally male environment.

After studying men in six large Norwegian companies, Kvande and Rasmussen identified four patterns of reaction to women intruders:

The cavaliers are older managers with wide experience who do not understand women who work. They are the old guard, their wives stay at home or work part-time. They feel unsure about their female colleagues and are far less familiar with them than they are with other men.

The competitors are at the beginning of their careers in the company and have women as colleagues at the same level and with the same education. They are not receptive to the ideal of improved opportunities for women in the engineering profession and think in terms of formal equality. They construct active concepts about women in order to justify their subordinate status: motherhood, family and lack of motivation inhibit women's careers.

The comrades are mainly young graduate engineers who are not yet in competition with their women colleagues. They like having female colleagues and enjoy a working environment in which there are colleagues of both sexes, because with only men there is a 'stag environment'. They are used to having female co-mates at university, are positive towards female professional skills. They see a common interest in learning the profession. Their wives are often working women too with professional careers, and this gives them a more favourable attitude to equality.

The comets are a small group who have carved out their own careers. Fairly young, they are satisfied with what they have attained. They have demonstrated their competence, and they feel wanted and not threatened by women. They are positive towards the idea of more women being taken into the organization, and acknowledge that women do not have equal opportunities with men. Like the cavaliers, they approach the problem of equal opportunity from a position of superiority.

I too have noticed that in the course of their professional careers and lifecycle men and women change their perception of gender. Those younger in age and with less professional experience are like children who find enjoyment in each other's company. They have been brought up to obey the same rules. Competition arises later as a claim for equality in the distribution of resources (the family's assets, for example), while there can be no competition either with members of another generation or with those who have left the peer group (siblings) some time previously.

The dual presence

I am intrigued by the *Enigma of Bologna* because it simultaneously suggests a critique of oppositionism – the habit of thinking in opposites – and implies that it is possible to shift oppositions so that we are less conditioned by them and better able to utilize them.

Oppositionism is so deeply inculcated in Western culture – from Aristotle, through the Judaeo-Christian tradition, to information theory – that it is extremely difficult to free ourselves of it. It is the logic of opposites which holds that the pair of terms completes the relation. Thus sexual difference is represented by the contraries male/female, people by men/women, personal traits by masculine/feminine. And these two symbolic universes predicated on continuity and coherence are founded on the nature/culture opposition. Dualism is also a consequence of the religions which supplanted the polytheism of the Greek world and create the polarization between body/mind, superior/inferior, terrestrial/celestial. The Greek gods and goddesses persist in our collective imaginary as cultural models of a pluralist principle of maleness and femaleness where monotheism has fashioned the triad of father/mother/child.

The oppositional universe draws its strength from its weakness. Since it is only able to abstract what is simple, and therefore simplifies what it abstracts, it creates distinctions by going to extremes and hence extremizes everything that it distinguishes (Hillman, 1979). The greatest danger of oppositionism is that it mistakes form for substance, that it takes as constitutive of things what is in fact an epistemological procedure for setting them in order, a way of talking about them, of drawing distinctions between them. Oppositionism also comes in a romantic version in which opposites manifest a single phenomenon through opposing forces or opposites united by a mystic bond. In their mystic union, male and female became archetypes of transformation *qua* transcendence, conjunction, the union of opposites. Besides the conjunction of opposites there is the further modality of their displacement and coincidence. Here the opposite is already present and compensation is the transformation of one into the other, of the restoration of what has been set aside, of juxtaposition without arrangement into pairs or polarities. This is the holistic vision.

The compensation principle is an ancient strand of Western thought. It can be traced back to Heraclitus and has recently reappeared in post-structuralism. Heraclitus declared that 'the way up and the way down are one and the same'. Jung considered compensation to be a psychic process of the regulation of oppositions because understanding always requires the other term in the pair: when this is denied or displaced, it reappears to compensate for unilaterality. Derrida argues that the erased (*sous rature*) term reappears in the text through contradictions, disjunctions and silences.

Shifting oppositions is no easy matter, for they are deeply embedded in thought and in language. Nevertheless, as Hillman (1979) suggests, we may think of opposition as an extreme metaphor, as a radical way of saying one thing as if it were two quite different ones, locked in a fierce struggle which the intrepid ego must literally imagine and confront as a challenge. Gender may therefore be the extreme metaphor for the difference which, to be comprehensible, must be represented by male and female as paired contraries and antagonists. Its meaning, however, is not static because it cannot be harnessed by the simplification and extremism of oppositionism. It is instead dynamic because it results from the compensation relation between opposites.

The feminist literature has treated the complexity created by the shifting of opposites in two different ways, which here I only examine briefly. First, complexity has been handled by developing the implication of male *and* female, as for example in the concept of the dual presence. Second, it has been addressed by developing the disjunction of neither male nor female into the multiple signification implicit to post-structuralist feminism. Leaving discussion of this latter modality to subsequent chapters, I introduce here the concept of dual presence.

The 'dual presence' (Balbo, 1979; Zanuso, 1987) is a category invented by Italian feminists in the 1970s to indicate cross-gender experiences and the simultaneous presence (in the consciousness and experience of women) of public and private, of home and work, of the personal and the political. The expression 'dual presence' denotes a frame of mind which, midway through the 1970s, came to typify a growing number of adult women who thought of themselves in a 'crosswise' manner with respect to different worlds – material and symbolic – conceived as different and in opposition to each other and, not coincidentally, pertaining to one or the other of the sexes: public/private, the family/the labour market, the personal/the political, the places of production/the places of reproduction (Zanuso, 1987:43). In social practices, more and more women found themselves operating in a plurality of arenas, they broke with traditional role models, they created a space which was practical *and* mental, structural *and* projectural, adaptive to given constraints *and* productive of new personal and social arrangements. In short, the boundaries between the symbolic universes of male and female became fluid, negotiable: they intersected and they merged.

The expression 'dual presence' aptly sums up the changes in industrial and post-industrial society. It conveys the greater presence of women in the public sphere, their different role in the private one. It denotes their different behaviour in public, in terms of the inclusion or exclusion of men from such social experiences as reproduction, child-rearing, the expression of feelings, subordinate work. Gender-ordered social experiences are phenomenologically changing, and this may give rise to new alliances aimed at the common representation of interests, but also to the cultural production of gender ideals or utopias which break with gender stereotypes deriving from social arrangements which no longer exist.

The dual presence is therefore a material and mental space in which the genders are blurred, in which the signification of women's experience in the male symbolic universe (female rationality, female independence) is invented, and vice versa the signification of the male (male dependence, compliance, emotionality), and in which the everyday relations of cooperation and conflict that innovate gender relations are established.

The dual presence enables us to think and to do gender differently (Gherardi, 1994).

4

The Symbolic Order of Gender in Organizations

The Caterpillar and Alice looked at each other for some time in silence: at last the Caterpillar took the hookah out of its mouth, and addressed her in a languid, sleepy voice.
'Who are *you?*' said the Caterpillar.
This was not an encouraging opening for a conversation.
Alice replied, rather shyly, 'I – I hardly know, Sir, just at present – at least I know who I *was* when I got up this morning, but I think I must have been changed several times since then'. (Carroll, 1980: 120)

The Caterpillar insists on knowing who and what Alice is and on extracting an explanation from her. But, 'I can't explain *myself*, I'm afraid, Sir,' says Alice, 'because I'm not myself, you see.'

Alice is a child and has a problematic relationship with her identity. She is confused after changing size so many times in a day; her relationship with a body which she fails to recognize as her own is a source of anxiety. She tries to break off the conversation with the Caterpillar when it tells her that it has something important to say: 'Keep your temper.'

On several occasions in the book, Alice meets curious animals and people who, in various ways, ask her the same question and give her the same advice. The Caterpillar, like the Dog or the Crab or the Duchess, represents the mature adult who admonishes the child not to lose her temper, not to abandon herself to her impulses.

Alice's identity is problematic because she is a child. But what, enquires Deleuze (1969), is a child? Carroll's book is entirely devoted not to answering this question, but to evoking and ordering the sole event that makes it a question.

Empson (1935) points out the symbolic completeness of Alice's experience: she is the father when she falls down the rabbit hole; she becomes the foetus when she finds herself at the bottom; but the foetus can be born only by becoming a mother and by secreting its own amniotic fluid. The whole gamut of sex is therefore enclosed in a girl, in a being with a concealed sex. In some obscure way, identity and sexuality closely interweave in this initiation to the adult world. But it is a world which speaks with a confused voice, or better, it speaks with several voices at once: the language of the unconscious is play, transgression and creativity, but also madness. Alice's language displays the typical patterns of schizophrenia – which manifests itself in 'nonsense', in puns that break words down and restructure them into speech fraught with anxiety, anguish and aggression. At the same time this is the precondition, in linguistic transgression, for the creation of text. Poems, lullabies and children's stories are subjected to parody which assails adults for the imbecility of their moralizing pedagogy. The sabotaging of language from within conjures up a different vision of the world; irony assaults the presumptuous dictates of adulthood and undermines the alleged universal order of all things.

Alice, as Virginia Woolf argued, is a text for adults, an opportunity to rediscover the pleasure of regression and transgression. Alice unmasks the apparent order of language and discourse; she is a subversive who exposes the construction and breakdown of communication, the acquisition of language and its loss of meaning, the boorishness of institutions (Victorian or otherwise) and the lucid creativity of language.

'Everything's got a moral, if only you can find it' (Carroll, 1980: 214) and 'Take care of the sense, and the sounds will take care of themselves' (ibid.: 216): these could be the maxims with which to attack the stability of meaning and the authoritativeness of those who claim to interpret it.

Today, a postmodern reading can be made of *Alice's Adventures in Wonderland*, for it is not difficult to identify in the Victorian text many of the problematics raised by the critique of modernity: the problem of subjectivity, the weakness of reason, the discourse-based nature of social relations, irony as a destabilizing phenomenon. I want to use Alice as a metaphor for a schizogenic condition: that is, the dual presence in organizations and the difficult construction of gender identity at work.

I contend that the condition of women working in organizations and who interrogate themselves on the gendered nature of work relationships is similar to Alice's: they must answer the painful question of what *their* identity is, they have interlocutors who do not listen or who fail to give satisfactory answers, and they invariably receive contradictory messages, often in the prescriptive form: 'Be equal but at the same time different!' Women entering the public sphere can be compared to children entering the world of adults. They must assume a role, and every role has its own inflexible etiquette, the principal rule of which – implicit, of course – is that questions must not be asked as to the etiquette's meaning. But Alice's initiation is back-to-front: crossing the threshold takes her to a subterranean world where everything takes on the opposite meaning. Growing larger or smaller is a strategy to escape from every preordained role, including physical development and temporal order.

Alice, the symbol of problematic identity, is caught between two voices: in her left ear she hears the voice of transcendence, which invites her to immerse herself in the sea of non-distinction, where Female and Male have always been and always will be. In her right ear she hears the voice of separation, of immanence and of the war between the sexes. The voice of transcendence, of finding oblivion in the collectivity and merging with a mystic body, has been symbolized by the alchemic wedding; the voice of immanence, of exchange and of negotiated individuality by the sexual contract. The two metaphors are different paradigms with which to understand gender relationships; relationships which can all too easily be set in opposition to each other and intrepreted as antagonistic. But this is to obscure the intimate relation that unites them and which generates the ambiguity, the ambivalence or the schizophrenia of two co-present and mutually exclusive 'truths'.

When Alice hears the voice of the alchemic wedding, it is the voice of society that resonates in her being, the call to be an a-historical and a-temporal Woman and Man with innately female and male characteristics. It is the voice of collective culture which speaks to the individual, it is the ontogenesis that repeats phylogenesis. It is a symbolic order that transcends the individual, which harbours his or her capacity to be an agent, but which in its complexity reproduces itself as different from and equal to itself, overwhelming the individual agent's capacities for change. The fascination of this voice lies in its invitation to unite with a mystical body, to become part of the sacredness and mystery of the Eternal Female and Male; an invitation to yield to the seduction of already-existing narratives awaiting someone to take possession of them and to reinterpret them, just as in the past other millions of interpreters created the Greek myths. The fascination of difference lies in the desire for otherness, for absence.

Murmuring in Alice's right ear, however, is another voice which echoes a negotiative process, one of exchange, bargaining and contextual action, a voice which speaks the language of immanence. It is the call of the body, of carnal seduction, of the perpetually disintegrating seat of passion, of desires, of loves. In the postmodern interpretation of the body, it is the organ of difference (Foucault, 1966).

The voice that speaks of the sexual contract speaks of a patriarchical structure of a domination which is first and foremost command over a sexed body, a discourse on the body and sexuality. The allure of the sexual contract is that of presence, of being subject and actor in the process whereby meanings are negotiated. Here the symbolic order springs from interaction.

Is Alice caught between these two identity-threatening voices, or is a positive definition of the female possible? Or again, is Alice's existence only possible as the existence of liminarity, the suspension between being and becoming? Let us explore Alice's possible responses.

Women's standpoint versus positionality

Gender is one of the traditional categories of self-identification. But if biological differences and sexual preferences are not enough to ascribe gender to persons, and if societal practices for drawing gender distinctions and marking social experiences are blurring the boundaries between symbolic universes of male and female, how can the assumption of self-identity be accomplished?

The questions of who is the female subject and what is a subject revolve around the centrality of language. The use of language by definition involves separation and differentiation, but also power. Male and female stand in a dichotomous and hierarchical relation: the first term is defined in positive as the One, the second is defined by difference, by default, as the non-One, that is, the Other. This was the lesson taught by Simone de Beauvoir (1949), from whom we have inherited the concept of second sex; an extremely useful analytical category both to describe female experiences of subordination and, by extension as in Ferguson (1984), to describe the clients of the bureaucracy, who are second-sexed whether they are men or women. When, immediately after the Second World War, de Beauvoir described the woman as the Other, the problem of language was not yet paramount, although the ontological problem was. Subsequently both issues were to be radically problematized by feminism and by other currents of thought which came under the label of 'postmodern'.

It is not my intention, nor do I possess the expertise, to review the long debate on language conducted by feminism, and how it was revitalized by the impact of French post-structuralism, crossed the Atlantic and thence returned to the centre of European debate. What is certain is that the feminist critique of language, and through it of the concept of person, of selfhood and of subjectivity, rapidly and importantly developed a wide range of themes over a period of around twenty years.

Language was denounced for a masculine bias which underpinned a form of 'power over' others and expressed the experiences of the oppressors and their construction of reality. In parallel with this assault on language as a form of domination, the question arose as to whether a language of liberation could be created. French feminism was closely involved in this linguistic enterprise, for example in the wide-ranging work of Irigaray (1974), who examined the concept of woman as Other from a psychoanalytic perspective and proposed the body as a writing instrument. Research at the end of the 1970s sought to create space for a *relecture interpretante* (interpretative re-reading) of theory on the female subject, where women could 'speak female' (*parler femme*) and speak to each other without the interference of men (Irigaray, 1977; Marks and de Courtivron, 1980).

Another point of view, which argued against the project of a feminist discourse, described language users as hiding behind a variety of irremovable masks. Some of these masks are (Elshtain, 1982): the mask of purity (presuming the victim's language to be untainted by her world), the mask of orthodox Marxism (presuming that discourse is nothing but rationalization of exploitative relations), the mask of militancy (the language of grim personal renunciation), the mask of systematic know-it-allism, or of unquestioned inner authenticity based on claims to the ontological superiority of the female being-in-itself. This latter point is particularly important because it leads directly to the trap of language as the grammar constitutive of human experience. If male and female stand in an oppositional and hierarchical relationship, and if they constitute the One and the Other, can the Other be defined without running the risk of reversing the relation while failing to resolve the contradiction? The question is anything but grammatical, for as soon as the political project predicated on difference – as opposed to the project in pursuit of equality – seeks to define difference, to valorize the female, to empower women with assertiveness and pride in female principles, it is in danger of re-proposing the selfsame relation by defining man as non-woman. It may be politically useful to reverse the relation in order to redress the balance of power, but theoretically it does not provide a way out of the gender trap. One way to reframe the question is to accept the position aptly expressed by Kristeva (1981) as 'women can never be defined'.

In the 1980s, French feminism continued its critique of language in semiological terms, adopting a position coherent with the school of thought that launched the attack on structuralism – Lacan, Derrida, Foucault – and called itself post-structuralist. Its essential thesis was that all social practices, including the meaning of subject and subjectivity, are not simply mediated by language but are constituted in and through language. Hence it follows that one must examine the tradition by which language has been understood, and deconstruct that tradition in order to understand how persons are constituted in social and linguistic practice. The self as the centre of consciousness, the person as a distinctive whole and as a bounded and integrated unity, are linguistic inventions, artifices with which to give spatial and temporal location to the self which speaks and has one body.

Social psychology joined this current of critical thought by dissolving the boundaries between individual and society and analysing the role of language in sustaining self-construction and the social construction of personhood (Gergen, 1982, 1991; Harré, 1984, 1987; Shotter and Gergen, 1989; Gergen and Davis, 1985). Concepts such as the multiple self (Elster, 1986), the saturated and populated self (Gergen, 1991), the masquerade or pastiche personality, completed the decentralization of subjectivity, and the postmodern revolution was therefore accomplished. The autonomous self of the romantic and modernist tradition, the centre of consciousness, the agent *par excellence*, was relativized and dismissed as conviction, a way of talking and a product of conversation. Language was a form of relatedness, sense derived only from coordinated effort among people, and meaning was born of interdependence. In Baudrillard's (1981) words, 'we are terminals of multiple networks'. Our potential is realized because there are others who sustain it, who possess an identity deriving from the social processes in which we participate, and who are the type of person that the linguistic games we play enable them to be.

Several currents of thought were involved in the project to deconstruct the self and to create a relational self (Sampson, 1989). Alongside feminism, social constructionism contributed analysis of the individual as a social and historical construction; systems theory contributed the ontological primacy granted to relations rather than to individual entities; critical theory – the Frankfurt School – contributed its unmasking of the ideology of advanced capitalism; and deconstructionism contributed a perspective internal to post-structuralism.

Although these approaches belonged to very different disciplinary traditions, they converge on a conception of subjectivity in which 'the subjects are constituted in and through a symbolic system that fixes the subject in place while remaining beyond the subject's full mastery. In other words, persons are not at the centre [. . .] but have been decentred by these relations to the symbolic order' (Sampson, 1989: 14).

The symbolic order of gender that separates the symbolic universes of the female and the male sanctions a difference whereby what is affirmed by the One is denied by the Other. The One and the Other draw meaning from this binary opposition, which forms a contrast created *ad hoc* and which maintains a hierarchical interdependence (Derrida, 1967, 1971).

The interdependence-based symbolic order is a relational order which rests upon difference and the impossibility of its definition. Male and female are undecidable, their meaning is indeterminate and constantly deferred.

The origins of the widely used concept of '*différance*' (Derrida, 1971) warrant examination. By '*différance*' is meant a form of self-reference 'in which terms contain their own opposites and thus refuse any singular grasp of their meanings' (Cooper and Burrell, 1988). In order to stress the processual nature of difference, Derrida invented the term *différance*, which in French is pronounced the same as *différence* and incorporates the two meanings of the verb *différer*: defer in time, and differ in space. Male and female are not only different from each other (static difference) but they constantly defer each other (processual difference), in the sense that the latter, the momentarily deferred term, is waiting to return because, at a profound level, it is united with the former. The difference separates, but it also unites because it represents the unity of the process of division. Alice therefore has two ways of conceiving gender difference: as two separate terms – male and female – and as a process of reciprocal deferral where the presence of one term depends on the absence of the other. Derrida calls these two modes of thought 'logic of identity' and 'logic of the supplement' respectively.

Alice's distress springs from the fact that she stands at the point of intersection between the voice of static difference and the voice of processual difference. Because of their multi-individual dimension and supra-individual duration, male and female as symbolic systems possess a static aspect, which creates a social perception of immutability, of social structure and institution. But male and female is also a dynamic social relation whereby meaning is processually enucleated within society and individual and collective phenomena. The symbolic order of gender is static difference and processual difference. Put better, it is the product of their interdependence: the impossibility of fixing meaning once and for all sanctions the transitoriness of every interpretation and exposes the political nature of every discourse on gender. Feminism is a discourse on gender, but internally to it there exist many different voices.

The theoretical debate on the relationship between modernism/postmodernism and feminism on the one hand, and a postmodern approach to feminism on the other, has been well described by Hekman (1990). The crucial theoretical issue is whether a male epistemology can/must be replaced by a female one, or whether the concept itself of epistemology must/can be replaced by an explanation of the discourse processes by which human beings acquire understanding of their common world. Another key issue is the relationship between knowledge and political action, where feminism posits the ambiguity of Enlightenment discourse, while postmodernism seemingly excludes the possibility of action. Whence derive various proposals for the maintenance of ambiguity (e.g. Harding, 1986a) and instability in the analytical categories of feminism (Ferguson, 1991). Ferguson compares the hermeneutic account, to which she attributes an ontology of discovery in order to interpret the patriarchal domination of women, with the deconstructionist account based on genealogy, i.e. a posture of subversion towards fixed meaning claims. Interpretation, as a project which articulates the voice of women, and genealogy must be taken with a pinch of pragmatic irony, because 'affirmations are always tied to ambiguity and resolutions to endless deferral' (Ferguson, 1991: 339).

It is not my intention to draw a map of feminism, but I believe I should specify to which area of theoretical enquiry my analysis of gender belongs. In order to do this briefly, and I hope with due respect to positions other than my own, I shall compare two very broad views, both of which contain further articulations but which can nevertheless be used to illustrate static difference. The first view I have called 'women's standpoint'; the second, which is my own, I call 'positionality'.

It may appear contradictory to resort to a binary structure of thought when I have attacked the system of opposites that underlies language. For heuristic purposes, and at the cost of a certain amount of simplification, I shall contrast two approaches to gender in order to argue the following thesis: there is one way of thinking gender relations that belongs to a postmodern condition – what I have called 'positionality' – which breaks with the school of thought that seeks to articulate a specifically female point of view. This I shall call 'women's standpoint'.

Early feminism addressed what were distinctly feminist issues: the condition of women and the forms of patriarchal dominance. This was an endeavour to enhance the experience of women and to bring political change that would reduce male power and restore a female perspective to all areas of the social. It was this perspective that gave women a voice, which made them visible, which narrated them in history (her/story) and literature, and which revealed the male bias in the construction of science. The articulation of a specific women's standpoint took it for granted that the categories of male and female were mutually exclusive, and hence that there was a male and a female experience of the world. The word 'gender' came to be synonymous with women, or else it was apparently only women who possessed a gender.

This account is opposed by a relational conception of gender which seeks to deconstruct gender and which rejects the male/female dualism. Male and female, the argument runs, are indivisible positions of reciprocal relation. Both men and women are prisoners of gender, albeit in different ways, in asymmetrical situations of power, and in an interrelated manner. Gender relations are problematized thus: the rigidity of categories which create two and only two types of human character, the presupposed rigidity of these categories which obscures the variability of experiences over time and among different cultures. Hence it follows that differences must be articulated and contextualized.

The women's standpoint, by contrast, searched for a common denominator and extolled the condition of sameness. Equality of condition was varyingly founded on sexuality, reproduction, child-rearing, the sexual division of labour: the body, the mind or production relations were the foundation of communality. This desire to discover a common male/ female bedrock led to the undervaluation of a plurality of differences: class, gender and race modulate women's voices in different ways (Lugones and Spelman, 1983). Perhaps gender is not the principal difference, or perhaps it is not always. The overvaluation of sameness had a further consequence. Gender relations were based on a normative order which reproduced femaleness and maleness through socialization. By contrast, positionality presupposes a discursive order where gender relations are the outcome of discourse practices; that is, they derive from the way in which people actively produce social and psychological realities. The scientific and political account that sustains positionality is a postmodern project in the sense that it aims to problematize knowledge, to delegitimize all beliefs concerning truth, power, the self, language, and everything that is taken for granted. Conversely, the inscribing of a female perspective in knowledge, in power, in the truth system, in subjectivity, can be called a modernist project which constructs a definitive subjectivity. For example, the project that gave rise to equal opportunity programmes in organizations is inscribed in modernity, in a conception of equality as assimilation and similarity. Quite different is the project that seeks to deconstruct subjectivity into a plurality of variously positioned selves.

These two strategies – to articulate the women's standpoint on the one hand, and to position the discursive production of gender on the other – are compared in Figure 4.1.

However, the concept of positionality still requires clarification as regards the conversational production of subjectivity, or its positioning in a symbolic order of gender. I use the concept because I need to account

WOMEN'S STANDPOINT VERSUS POSITIONALITY

sees male and female as mutually exclusive	sees male and female as indivisible positions of reciprocal relation
stresses sameness	stresses difference
presupposes a normative order	presupposes a discursive order
recalls a modern project	envisions a postmodern project
emphasizes subjectivity	deconstructs subjectivity

Figure 4.1   *The 'woman's standpoint' approach compared to the 'positionality' approach*

for the dynamic that unites the production of gender relations at the level of interaction with the cultural structures that transcend concrete behaviour. This dynamic both produces and is produced by a symbolic order of gender. The concept of positionality recognizes the constitutive force of a symbolic order of gender which shapes discourse practices and also people's ability to exercise choice in relation to those practices.

I have borrowed the concept of positionality from two works (Davies and Harré, 1990; Alcoff, 1988) which, although they have concerns different from mine, nevertheless examine the problem of the production of subjectivity. For Davies and Harré, the concept of positioning belongs to social psychology, and their use of the term 'positioning' contrasts with the concept of human agency as role player. It is therefore useful for the analysis of the production of self as a linguistic practice within the dynamic occasions of encounters. A discourse is an institutionalized use of language and of other similar sign systems, and it is within a particular discourse that a subject (the position of a subject) is constructed as a compound of knowledge and power into a more or less coercive structure which ties it to an identity.

A subject position incorporates both a conceptual repertoire and a location for persons within the structure of the rights pertaining to those who use the repertoire. A position is what is created in and through conversations as speakers and hearers construct themselves as persons: it creates a location in which social relations and actions are mediated by symbolic forms and modes of being. And part of my conception of positionality is the production of the positions of women and men as a discursive construction of an interpersonal relation in a multi-faceted public process by which gender meanings are progressively and dynamically achieved, transformed and institutionalized.

Whereas Davies and Harré employ the concept of positioning to illuminate the social level of interaction, Alcoff uses it to shed light on a politics of identity understood as the choice from among a plurality of selves and as positionality in a social context. Alcoff's concern is to steer a middle course through the aporia of, on the one hand, cultural feminism as a movement which arrogates to itself the right to give a positive answer to Simone de Beauvoir's classic question 'Are there women?', and therefore to contrast the male definition of women with a female one, and, on the other, the post-structuralism which answers in the negative and attacks the category and concept of women by problematizing subjectivity. Alcoff therefore proposes a positional definition of woman which 'makes her identity relative to a constantly shifting context, to a situation that includes a network of elements involving others, the objective economic conditions, cultural and political institutions and ideologies, and so on' (Alcoff, 1988: 433).

It is not easy to understand whether Alcoff's concept of positionality is to be considered as still part of a conception which seeks to found a women's point of view, or whether it belongs to a postmodern conception of gender and subjectivity. Alcoff's concern is to distance herself from cultural feminism (which she accuses of essentialism) and from post-structuralism (which she accuses of nominalism). But, however much one sympathizes with her need to mark out her position, post-structuralism can hardly be regarded as nominalist. Alcoff gives a twofold definition of positionality: (a) the concept of woman is a relational term identifiable only within a (constantly shifting) context; (b) the position that women find themselves in can be actively utilized (rather than transcended) as a site for the construction of meaning, a place where meaning is constructed, rather than simply the place where a meaning can be discovered (Alcoff, 1988: 434). As I understand her concept of positionality, it is historical and relational, but not postmodern, and it is intended more to establish a women's standpoint than to problematize the social construction of the subjectivity of women and men through language.

Put in my terms, the concept of positionality reveals how women define themselves and are defined within a contingently determined context, but at the same time it rejects any answer that seeks to transcend the *hic et nunc*. The answer to de Beauvoir's question would be 'yes and no'. This definition comes closest to Kristeva's position when she says 'that's not it; that's still not it': meaning the transitoriness, the instrumentality and the instability of every definition that does not seek an essentialist answer. Negative feminism *à la* Kristeva alarms feminists with a political background because, in my view, they underestimate the destabilizing character of postmodern criticism, which, although it does not propose positive actions, corrodes the legitimacy of every claim to truth from within. Put otherwise, it is as though it does not forgo definition of us and affirmation of our (their) existence, but with the self-deprecation necessary for us not to take ourselves too seriously and to develop the game in an attitude of continuous creativity. Positioning gender is an approach which does not seek to posit a subjectivity of women or men in oppositional terms. It is instead an approach which reflects the essential indeterminacy of the symbolic order of gender, governed as it is by the endless process of the difference and deferral of the meaning of male and female. Positioning gender introduces a concept of subjectivity in which the subject is open ended and indeterminate except when it is fixed in place by the culturally constituted symbolic order of gender.

Before using the concept of positionality to show how the symbolic order of gender structures work cultures, I shall briefly review other contributions to organizational study which, in a manner more or less similar to mine, have posited a difference between postmodern feminism and its previous versions.

For example, Calás and Smircich (1992b) distinguish between two strands of feminist theorizing in order to question the production of knowledge in the organizational sciences and to examine its social consequences. The first of these strands goes by the name of women's voice/women's experience and attempts to demonstrate 'the differences between male and female experiences and then position "the different" as another valid form of representing human experience' (Calás and Smircich, 1992b: 225). The second is the post-structuralist feminism which questions the stability itself of such cultural categories as gender and 'points instead to how these purportedly "natural" oppositions are culturally constituted categories, products, and producers of particular social and material relations' (Calás and Smircich, 1992b: 226).

In organizational studies, the feminist perspectives of the first and second strand have addressed the question: how is organization (male) gendered, and with what consequences? (Calás and Smircich, 1992a), which it has answered by means of three epistemological activities: re-vising, re-flecting, and re-writing. The first activity has completed/corrected the record (accounting for women's absence), assessed gender bias in current knowledge, and conducted 'new' organizational theorizing. The second activity is an analysis of the subjects of knowledge which reveals that revising the discipline has not produced a single and coherent 'feminist perspective' but instead fragmented feminist theorizing. Which account, therefore, is the best? What is the meaning of epistemological multiplicity in feminism? Calás and Smircich thus propose the activity of re-writing as a form of political engagement beyond the limits of 'knowledge-making'. In post-structuralism and post-structuralist feminism, writing is the metaphor for knowledge, the mode of constructing the 'general text' of our society in which cultural conditions are inscribed via our modes of signification. Thus organization theory (meaning by this term a number of texts well known and affirmed in the discipline) are re-written (Calás and Smircich, 1991, 1992a) to reveal their politics by calling attention to strategies of 'truth-making' while leaving the original text 'under erasure' (*sous rature* as in Spivak, 1974), where if the word is inaccurate it is crossed out, if it is necessary it remains legible.

I would stress that Calás and Smircich conceive the two strands of feminist theorizing as two terms in constant tension. They believe that the women's voices position is a necessary step towards a post-structuralist feminist analysis because women's voices revise the 'historical text' by inverting oppositional constructions. Once these oppositions have been destablilized by post-structuralist feminism, it will be impossible to reinscribe them in their original form.

Within post-structuralism, deconstructionism is an analytic strategy which exposes the manifold ways in which a text can be interpreted. Martin (1990) offers a good example of deconstructive methodology within organization studies. Apparently well-intentioned organizational practices may reify rather than alleviate gender inequalities, Martin argues. She recounts the story of a young woman for whom the organization arranged a closed-circuit television so that she could watch the launching of a new product while she was in bed recovering from a Caesarean birth, deliberately timed so that she could follow the event.

Martin deconstructs this story in order to reveal the suppressed gender conflicts behind the lines of the text. She lists the following nine deconstruction strategies:

1. dismantling a dichotomy, exposing it as a false distinction;
2. examining silences – what is not said;
3. attending to disruptions and contradictions, places where the text fails to make sense;
4. focusing on the element that is most alien to a text or a context as a means of deciphering implicit taboos – the limits to what is conceivable or permissible;
5. interpreting metaphors as a rich source of multiple meanings;
6. analysing *double-entendres* that may point to an unconscious subtext, often sexual in content;
7. separating group-specific and more general sources of bias by 'reconstructing' the text with iterative substitution of phrases;
8. exploring, with careful 'reconstructions', the unexpected ramifications and inherent limitations of minor policy changes;
9. using the limitations exposed by 'reconstruction' to explain the persistence of the status quo and the need for more ambitious change programmes.

Deconstruction and post-structuralist feminism have greatly helped to shift attention from the subject 'woman' to the gender relation, to how this is constituted in and by language, and to the relationship between discourses and institutional forms which create forms of power backed by knowledge claims.

This is not to imply, however, that only these approaches have brought about this shift; nor, even less, that they have become the new orthodoxy, or that the only way to produce knowledge is to deconstruct one text after another. On the contrary, what I find so interesting in the passage from modernity to a postmodern culture is the multiplicity of competing voices which create plurality of perspectives and blur boundaries, so that from an assumption of 'things or persons in themselves' one passes to reconstruction of things and persons as 'relation'. Self-definition and the erosion of self-definition is threatening but it is also challenging: 'a once obdurate and unquestionable fact of biological life – that there are two sexes, male and female – now moves slowly toward mythology' (Gergen, 1991: 143). How then can one construct a politics of identity (De Lauretis, 1984) and represent the interests of those subjects who are still disadvantaged? Perhaps it is better to leave this question aside and reflect on changes in terms such as 'subjectivity' and 'politics' in a postmodern context, and analyse how subjectivity is produced in everyday interactions.

Narratives of travellers in a male world

I have always been fascinated by the experiences of women pioneers in male occupations, those women who have been the first to join a group of male colleagues. These women often have a story to tell and often, with the same experience in academia, I have found myself reflecting together with them on how the encounter between a male world and an 'embarrassing' presence comes about. I began to collect these spontaneous stories when I realized that most of them share the same plot – the outsider who enters an alien culture – and that they showed very clearly how organizational culture positions the male and the female in a reciprocal relation. The outsider, the journey, the unexpected encounter with the different are symbolic constructs which sustain both the narrative of the everyday and anthropological and sociological story-telling. Persons are constructed through talk (Harré, 1984), and in assuming their multiple social roles they narrate themselves, they are narrated, they negotiate their multiple subjectivities and position them within a social order. Our experience of life depends on the narrative structures that we impose upon experience.

The experience of being an outsider and entering a 'non-natural' culture entails, as brilliantly shown by Schutz (1971), the suspension of normal thought patterns, and it provides the outsider with insights into the culture that elude its natives. The insiders have different modes of accepting, assimilating and respecting the diversity of the outsider. Being an outsider may therefore, depending on the encounter, signify very different things (Levine, 1985), from being a guest to being a 'marginal'. In my terms, the way in which the (male-gendered) host culture positions the Other (the woman traveller), and the way in which this Other positions itself (the narrative self), constitutes the symbolic order of gender in that culture. For this reason, I have preserved the sequence of the recounted experience in order to expose the construction of conversational identity; a process which pivots on a paradox: women are rightful members of the organization in which they work, but in actual fact, to use Judi Marshall's words (1984), they are 'travellers in a male world'. And as travellers they acquire different identities in differently structured relational and cultural

Table 4.1 *Women travellers in a male world and their discursive positionality*

Male positioning	Women reciprocal positioning		
	ACCEPTED	CONTESTED	IMPOSED
Friendly	*The guest* a cooperative position	*The holidaymaker* a mismatched position	*The newcomer* an open-ended position
Hostile	*The marginal* a stigmatized position	*The snake in the grass* a contested position	*The intruder* a unilaterally imposed position

contexts. In this imaginary realm our travellers, like Alice, are trapped within the narratives of culturally pre-existing femalenesses (the Greek goddesses are ready to lend them their clothing). But they also use these narratives to reinvent themselves, to present themselves, and to affirm themselves in a negotiative process. Let us look at some examples.

Table 4.1 sets out the narrative structure that I shall follow in telling these stories, and it shows why I alternate between the narrative self's encounters with a friendly culture and a hostile one.

This distinction between friendly and hostile cultures is part of the description of the context in which the various self-narratives operate. I have omitted it in order not to over-encumber the descriptions. The successive distinctions refer to the fact that the discourse construction of the traveller arises from a positioning in which both subjects agree on defining and being defined or not, as the case may be. Consider by analogy an invitation to 'take one's place'. The invitation may be accepted more or less gratefully, and this is the case in which the traveller is a guest or a marginal. The invitation may be misunderstood or rejected, in which case the traveller believes s/he is a member of the community while instead s/he is only a visitor and possibly regarded as a 'snake in the grass'. Finally, the invitation may be taken to be obligatory and unilateral, leaving margins for redefinition, as in the case of the newcomer who is required to integrate, or instead precluding any such possibility, as in the case of the intruder.

My aim in recounting the stories of Giovanna, Angelina and the other women is to show the crucial role of narrative in interpreting the world, especially when it is sensitive to the context, and to demonstrate how a story relates to the social order that allows us to progress beyond the individualistic account of narrative construction (Murray, 1989). My stories are arranged in the following order:

a friendly culture and the position of the guest;
a hostile culture and the position of marginality;
a friendly culture and the position of the holiday maker;

a hostile culture and the position of the snake in the grass;

a friendly culture and the position of newcomer;

a hostile culture and the position of the intruder.

A friendly culture and the position of the guest

The host and the guest is a story in which the roles are well known, and in which the assumption of a role entails seeing the world from the vantage point of that position and in terms of the particular images, story lines and concepts made relevant within the particular discursive practice in which they are positioned (Davies and Harré, 1990).

The story of Giovanna shows how these positions are taken up over time. Giovanna was the first female graduate from a school of graphic design to join a group of male technicians. She found an office occupied by fifteen men, most of them over 50, and almost all of whom had moved up the firm's internal career ladder from the shop-floor to the office. Only two of the men had diplomas in graphic design. This was Giovanna's first 'real' job: previously she had only managed to find casual work unsuited to her qualifications and she was, moreover, married with two small children.

In her early thirties and full of enthusiasm, she threw herself headlong into her new job and her new work environment. She still remembers her initial satisfaction at finding herself able to cope with challenges:

> I wasn't worried about joining a group of men. I was already used to being the only woman at school, or one of the very few. I thought I could handle myself very well, indeed I was happy to be with men. I couldn't foresee any problems. And then I was welcomed with such enthusiasm; everyone was friendly, ready to teach me and help me. I didn't have any difficulties with the job, or with combining work and looking after a family. Everybody was very understanding, including the boss, when I took my holidays because one of my children was ill, or when I couldn't do overtime because I had problems at home.

As time passed, other women came to work in the office, replacing the older men as they retired. And they too were given a friendly welcome. Giovanna felt comforted by the presence of other women, but a subtle sense of unease, of inexplicable discontent began to take hold of her. She had nothing to complain about; indeed, she was lucky because she was certainly not discriminated against. But there was something which, after seven years in the job, she found disquieting:

> I felt as if I was a guest. Just as a guest is placed at the head of the table, treated politely, and never allowed to wash the dishes, so I was surrounded by a web of polite but invisible restraints. I began to suspect something when I saw the other women when they arrived and were, so to speak, 'integrated'. For example, I almost never go into the production department to talk with the workers. My older male colleagues go because they like it. They go and see their friends, and then they pretend that they are protecting me from the 'uncouthness' of the working class. So I find myself constantly on the phone dealing with the editorial office, the commercial office, the administration. I'm almost always in the office. It's as if I'm at home and they're always out. It's true that they are

better at what they do, and I'm better at what I do, or we women are, but constantly being their guest is getting me down.

Giovanna's feelings were complex. Her gratitude at her friendly welcome induced her to be compliant. And this – together with a confused feeling that she had exploited her colleagues' helpfulness when she had to cope with both children and work – prevented her from taking the initiative in changing matters. Her clumsy (in her opinion) attempts to talk about the problem with colleagues rebounded on her. Now she felt that she was ungrateful, troublesome, or discontented for no reason.

Playing the host and extending a friendly and solicitious welcome to the guest was a ruse employed by the men to maintain a structure of rights, and to extend it by means of accepted practices of labour division to the other men who later joined the office. Her status as guest invested Giovanna with a set of rights which assigned her a position of privilege; but it prevented her from achieving equality. This was formally present in the promise of reciprocity but was denied to Giovanna because, as a guest, she could never become the host. And if she wanted to repay her debt, she could only do it from a subordinate position, the position that had been assigned to her. In Giovanna's story the territories were clearly marked out: the men patrolled the organization, while the women stayed at home and answered the phone. The symbolic order of gender emerged when positions of reciprocal protection and dependence had been taken up: public men and private women is a very well-known story.

A hostile culture and the position of marginality

There are so many reasons that explain, and dynamics responsible for, social centrality or marginality that gender is just part of this particular process of social differentiation in which the different are marginalized merely because they are different.

Fiorella is a young executive employed by the local government of one of the largest and richest of the Italian provinces. She now runs the accountancy section, after a relatively rapid career which brought her to a job in top management at the age of 45. She is the first woman to occupy the position, and the youngest of all the executives in the province's administration. Local government positions in Italy are awarded by public examination, and Fiorella found posts falling vacant one after the other at just the right moments in her professional career:

I felt as though I was moving along a conveyor belt. I must admit that I was never stretched until I got this job. And I never had to make sacrifices for my family life. It was good luck as well as historical accident. When I entered the civil service, increasing numbers of women were being recruited, mainly because a lot of men were moving to the private sector for better pay and more prestige. And it was also a time when women's mentalities were changing and they were deciding not to take early retirement at 35. So now, twenty years later, half the people in this organization are women, if not more. But not so the management, although things will have to change in a few years' time when new jobs are created and the old managers retire. So it was my good luck and bad luck to be a guinea pig.

Fiorella's explanation of what being a guinea pig meant to her was dry and laconic, as was her manner of getting right to the heart of the issue:

> I felt I'd become invisible, I thought I was transparent. There's no point in recounting individual episodes or blaming things on hostility. Formally, everything was as it should be, and they treated me politely, like gentlemen, but I counted for nothing. I discovered this little by little and it was tough admitting it to myself. What had I got to complain about? The situations were quite clear, the solutions were reasonable; indeed they were the only ones feasible. Everything was already decided and all I had to do was agree and implement. There was no need to open my mouth at meetings. I realized I had been pushed to one side even though my expertise was publicly praised.

Fiorella dwelt long on her doubts and on the reasons why she felt marginalized, and on the dynamics that had led to her isolation in a group of equals. At first she thought that this was a natural initiation process, that she had to conquer a place in a pre-existing group. Then she blamed the condescension shown to her on differences in age, experience and seniority. Then again she thought that her colleagues doubted her professional capabilities because she was a woman.

> I'm sure now that all these things were mixed together. My feelings were mixed too. I am sorry that I felt so resentful, but being ignored is horrible. On the other hand, I understand that they don't know how to relate to me. They veer between paternalism and a genuine desire to help me and to let me know that they respect me. But they seem more worried about ensuring that I obey, that I keep my place and that I don't do anything unpredictable, than about really putting me at my ease. My presence upsets them, and they try to reduce the nuisance to the minimum, to anticipate it and control it. If I'm not a nuisance then they accept me, but they'll never be able to treat me as an equal. For that matter, I don't feel that I'm one of them. That would be awful, and I set great store by being different. We are not equal, and it would be absurd to pretend that we are. It's true that I'm resigned to the situation, and to these see-saw emotions. But it's because I've made my calculations and I know that there's going to be a large intake in the next few years. Whether men or women arrive, the climate will change and this 'old country gentleman' style will end up in the attic along with the old guard.

Fiorella imagines a large attic used to store unused objects, old clothes, broken-down gadgets and furniture replaced because tastes have changed and things once useful and valued are now rejected. But perhaps one day our grandchildren will open the attic and rediscover our antiquities with glee!

Fiorella's story illuminates a symbolic order of gender in which the presence of women is tolerated because it is one of the rules of the game, although writing the rules of the game is a male activity. The bureaucracy displays all its ambivalence here: the private sector is male because it is more prestigious; the public sector is for the Cinderellas of the labour market. But it also happens that open competition for jobs brings Cinderellas into the control room. They cannot touch the levers of power, however, and wait for the not too distant day – so the statistics on the feminization of the bureaucracy assure us – when other Cinderellas will join them. Will they be able to pull the levers?

A friendly culture and the position of the holidaymaker

Perhaps the mass tourism of today (or the services culture) has changed the experience of leaving home to spend a long period, usually the summer, in another place, where one returns for several years and where one feels partly a guest and partly a seasonal resident. Those who live in tourist areas know the two faces of the season, or better, the difference between the high and low season. The high and the low. During the season, holidaymakers are the actors; out of season, the townspeople return to centre stage and exact some sort of moral revenge on the 'foolish' holidaymakers. But the two experiences are separate even when residents and tourists both occupy the town square.

The holidaymaker is in any case only passing through, as was Rita before she took possession of her territory.

Rita was, so to speak, born into the trade. Her father had worked for the same company for forty years. And he was still one of its most influential and popular managers when Rita returned from the United States, armed with a master's in business studies and a degree in computer science, and ready to embark upon her career. All doors were apparently open to her, or they would have been as soon as she knocked. After a job as a technician, which she left after a year, she was appointed manager of a branch office and set off to assume responsibility for a staff of around forty people. She found a cooperative atmosphere and was welcomed warmly, with neither surprise at her rapid promotion nor resentment at her youth or sex. Some of her colleagues had been at university with her, and the general climate in the branch-office was youthful, easygoing and cordial. High productivity was expected, but since the market was flourishing in those years, production targets were regarded as a stimulating challenge rather than a constraint.

Rita had noticed that, with the exception of the secretaries, there were very few women among the specialized staff. She was therefore extremely pleased to find she had a female assistant manager: Elsa, a woman older than herself but who apparently harboured no resentment at being passed over for promotion. Nevertheless, working relationships between the two women were not easy:

> There was a time when I thought I would have her transferred. I came to see her as a real gloom-monger. She was always warning me, pointing out conflict, envy and malice where I could only see joshing and high-spiritedness among people of the same age. She maintained that there weren't any women in the organization because of a male culture that excluded them, when I was living proof of exactly the opposite. I thought to myself that I had met the usual feminist ball-breaker who in the name of ideology would deny even the self-evident truth.

Rita felt perfectly at ease. She was satisfied with her work, she felt that she was learning a great deal, and she was proud of the spirit of comradeship and professional equality that she had established with her fellow-workers. The only drawback was that she felt obliged to adopt the same managerial style as her predecessor. She would have preferred to stamp her own personality on her work, involve the staff in more genuine cooperation, in more effective communication; things that she felt were lacking or were only superficial in her work environment. Rita's relationship with her assistant also suffered from this absence of close rapport, this subtle remoteness. Four years passed in this manner when, in a moment of relaxation and finding herself alone with the other woman, Rita began to tell Elsa about her doubts and her feelings:

> I never imagined that it would end in a stand-up row, in one of those slanging matches we had criticized for so long. At a certain point Elsa told me brutally that everyone thought I was just 'passing through'. That I would go and work at company headquarters after I had served my apprenticeship in the branch-office, and that the battle for my job was already going on behind my back. I was literally struck dumb, my world collapsed around my ears. Strangely, an image of the countryside popped into my mind. I saw the little village in the mountains where my family used to spend every summer. Everyone knew us, they admired my father, and it was one big party when we arrived in the summer after the schools closed. For years I was convinced that this was the 'real' world, where everything was as genuine as fresh cow's milk, as home-baked bread. Human relationships, too, were 'real', not like in the city. But as I grew older I realized that these were two worlds which met only for a few months of the year. Then the visitors returned to the city while the villagers remained. These two separate worlds were only apparently one.

This was a critical moment for the two women, and it marked the beginning of a different working relationship between them. Rita had no plans for a rapid career; she did not want to exploit her father's position, but to prove her managerial skills on her own. When I interviewed her, eight years had passed since the fracas with Elsa, and, given the usual stages of career development in the company, Rita staying in the branch-office was a deliberate decision not to progress any further up the career ladder.

The two women told me with great amusement how they had embarked on their own 'equal discrimination' programme. They had more or less overtly favoured female graduates, until they had substantially increased the number of women technicians and formed work groups which were collectively responsible for their results. They had reduced the number of secretaries by persuading them to retrain. And they were proud that their branch-office was the only one in which the receptionists were both men and women.

This narrative well illustrates how reciprocal positionings can coexist in a sort of ostensible dialogue: the boss positions him/herself as democratic and his/her subordinates as willing partners in the same game. Yet as these latter play the game they are waiting for the holidaymaker to go home.

Rita and her colleagues each continued with their own story. The game changed when Rita symbolically took possession of her territory, changed the rules and positioned herself as the 'boss' who exercised discretionary powers. The power structure of which she was part permitted her to do this, but this alone did not guarantee that she would or could have done this.

Rita's story first constructs a narrative self in terms of the emancipated woman, a person who obtains a job because of her abilities and who presumes that all women could do the same if – individually – they had the chance. As an emancipated woman she describes an equally emancipated symbolic order of gender: brothers and sisters (albeit only a few of them, as sometimes happens in a family) or old schoolfriends. Later, after the crisis, a new narrative self emerged which contested this way of being positioned, which created a new alliance, and which combated the demarcation of the territory as a male domain. Symbolically, she began her quest for the hidden treasure.

The symbolic order of gender was sustained by Rita's colleagues through their expectation that she would conform with the behaviour of her predecessor (a man), that she would not change the rules of the game, and that she would run the business on behalf of her father; indeed, that precisely because of her father's influence she would rapidly advance up the career ladder and vacate her post. As losers or winners, women do not upset the symbolic order of gender as women but as persons who alter the power relationships in gender management.

A hostile culture and the position of the snake in the grass

The internal enemy and the coalition of friends which comes together for self-protection is another well-known plot. The outsider who does not understand and refuses to conform to local traditions, who asks embarrassing questions and who raises a potential threat against the safety of the group, soon becomes an enemy to liquidate.

Fiammetta is a woman of about 50, of plain appearance and a reserved, even self-effacing, demeanour. On meeting her in the corridor of the town hall where she works, one would never suspect that she is head of personnel, and indeed she herself still finds it somewhat strange:

> I first came to work in the town hall as an accountant when I was 20 years old. And I always had a simple life in this office. I got on well with my colleagues, and the boss was a good man. He took care of everything, and we just attended to wages, pensions, and so on. I had all the time I needed to get married, study for a degree in economics, and have two children. I never thought that one day I would become section head and personnel manager.

She still laughs at her younger self, and is not at all embarrassed to describe herself as an 'accidental' director. The accident that brought her to this position was a mixture of various independent stories:

> My boss had taken early retirement. Perhaps he was tired or perhaps he was persuaded to leave. In any case, his job was advertised and everyone in the office was asking who would take his place. It began as a joke when a colleague and then all the office asked me why I didn't apply. My husband was decisive, though. I think he was worried about me at that time. I was a bit depressed, I saw my children growing up. I felt as though I was losing something, but I didn't know what I wanted. I sent in my application and began to study for the exam − but mostly so that I wouldn't make a fool of myself, not to win. I knew that to get to the top someone had to pull strings for you.

It was also by chance that a programme of local government reform had got under way at the same time. Among the various changes introduced, the regulations governing public appointment procedures were altered. Politicians were excluded from appointment boards and greater power was given to board members extraneous to the organization concerned. The outcome was as much a surprise for Fiammetta as for her future colleagues.

Fiammetta never suspected that her life would change so dramatically. Nor did she suspect that, for the first time in her working life, she would encounter open hostility:

> They greeted me like a bad smell, and they treated me like the book-keeper they had always known. They thought that I would continue to take orders and be obedient.

This was not merely an initial reaction or some sort of initiation ritual within a tight-knit community. Matters continued to deteriorate as Fiammetta began to discover the real reasons for the alarm she provoked among the other section heads. In her new position she uncovered the mechanisms used by local councillors and the other section heads to exert total control over personnel recruitment and management, while it was the task of her section to make things perfectly legal and formally irreproachable. This style of management Fiammetta called 'traditional' and she intended to replace it with a 'transparent' style in line with the wind of change then blowing through local government. It was not easy, of course:

> It took me a long time to get a complete picture of the situation and when and how I could start to change things. And it also took a long time to persuade my town councillor to back me up. I didn't want to play Joan of Arc, I had to move cautiously. The more I dug my heels in with the other section heads, the more they treated me as an enemy and the more they saw me as a 'snake in the grass'. I was a mistake, I had slipped through the net. Most of all, I apparently didn't understand what they thought 'normal' but I thought bordered on the illegal.

Fiammetta was the first to admit that a man in her situation would also have had a tough time of it. She knew that she had not been socialized to management in previous years, but she thought that she was paying an extra price for being the only woman manager. She blamed this on a gender relation and on her colleagues' assumption that she would be obedient, that she would conform 'like a good little girl':

They would have granted a man the right to disagree, even to be an enemy, because he was their equal. But they expected me as a woman to understand quickly without asking questions, and not to bother anyone.

Fiammetta reproached herself for being extremely ingenuous, for not having suspected earlier what she later discovered. But if she had not been ingenuous, she would not have applied for the job: she would have excluded herself. On looking back on her experience she began to reflect on the absence of women in top management posts, even in local government where rules are more universalistic. In her organization, for example, there were numerous women with managerial qualifications; but none of them competed for vacant jobs in top management. Fiammetta had talked to a number of these women managers, those whom she believed could have competed and won. She discovered that they found high-level jobs distasteful because of the working relationships among top managers, because they would have to collaborate with (or obey?) politicians, and because of the loss of what they called 'a real job', i.e. with well-defined responsibilities and as part of a group of people working together as a team. Fiammetta wanted to introduce women's training courses based on the 'women empowerment' model. Yet, at bottom, she knew that what was wrong was the type of work involved at the top level, and she was reluctant to blame those who withdrew from the game because they didn't feel it worth the candle.

Fiammetta's positioning as an internal enemy was the product of a conflictual discourse in which she had presented herself as the dissenter, in which she was partly acknowledged to be both a full member of the group and partly excluded from it; a discourse in which both parties rapidly came to realize that their positions were irreconcilable. It is worth noting the symbolic order of gender ingrained in the expectations with which the male colleagues assimilated the outsider: the status of belonging to top management, in the form of access to/sharing 'secrets', the conformity required of a weak subject (woman, new arrival, the error or accident of her presence), the group pressure applied to obtain her silence. The strategy designed to render her inoffensive would certainly have worked if the political context had not been in crisis and if organizational change had not weakened the local culture, both by altering the rules that ensured its reproduction as a closed clan, and by delegitimizing paternalism as an organizational value. Fiammetta's very presence was a living symbol of the transparency that another organizational actor – the politicians – wanted to introduce in order to counteract the local managerial culture. Fiammetta's positioning as the 'enemy within' acquired significance for both group interactions and the context within which this positioning took place.

A friendly culture and the position of the newcomer

A newcomer arouses curiosity, interest. He or she is unilaterally positioned as a potential friend or enemy; he or she may bring change, may possibly become a pupil or 'one of us' – perhaps after the appropriate initiation ritual. The 'diversity' of the new arrival may provoke anxiety, and the archetype of the *femme fatale* contains all the elements of fear and attraction that men attribute to women. But it is not necessary to be or appear to be a *femme fatale* to encounter the anxiety that femininity, represented by its outward trappings of different clothing, provokes. Is it, perhaps, that a non-feminine woman is reassuring? Or that the defeminized woman can be more easily accepted? Many work cultures force women to cancel the diversity of their external guise of femaleness.

Alessandra had a degree in chemistry and, at the beginning of the 1980s, was one of the first women to be hired by the R&D department of a leading Italian chemicals group. In actual fact, however, this honour entailed working in an outlying factory and in a laboratory which treated research as a routine like any other. Alessandra is not particularly tall, she is heavily built, with short hair and huge blue eyes that light up her face.

When I met her she was on the point of leaving her job to become a schoolteacher. She stressed, however, that this was a deliberate choice:

> It's not a defeat. I've spent ten years here and I've never had any problems. But I want to change my job and do something that makes sense. I'm not interested in studying and doing research so that others can get rich. Chemicals are extremely profitable compared with the cost of the raw materials, and research is not very stimulating. I don't expect that teaching will be a mission that gives significance to my life, but at least I'll be in contact with people, and my work will help others. I'm not doing it because the work is easy with lots of free time. I haven't got children at home. I live alone.

If this is the epilogue of work experience in a factory where the overwhelming majority of the workforce was male, the beginning, like all beginnings, had very different emotional connotations:

> I came here because I was looking for exactly this kind of opportunity. I wanted to work in industry and do what university had trained me for. I didn't want a makeshift job, nor a woman's job.

Alessandra remembered that she joined a friendly working environment, she was alarmed by neither the noise nor the immense spaces in the factory, nor the bland and grey expanse of the research laboratory. The reason was:

> I grew up in the countryside, with elderly parents, and in a small village where everyone talked to everyone else, eyeball to eyeball. I did the same here, with the same direct approach to the director as to the workers. I really enjoyed myself at the beginning. Everyone thought I was a bit strange to start with, but then they got used to me, everyone knew me and I knew everybody. I believe they liked me because I didn't shut myself up in the laboratory. As soon as I could I went round the factory driving a trolley. It seemed like a tractor to me, and I must say that was the best part of my job.

The laboratory was not competitive. There were substantially three work groups, and the manager let Alessandra decide which group to join. Alessandra described her relationship with her colleagues as friendly, and recounted how one of her male colleagues had confessed the anxiety of the men as they waited for a woman to arrive in the factory:

> When we got to know each other, they told me that they had accepted me, that I could feel myself one of them and no longer the newcomer. It was then that a colleague told me that they had all been terrified that a woman in a short skirt and stiletto heels would turn up. They had already decided that she wouldn't last a week in that environment. Instead I walked in, and I'm certainly not the paragon of femininity! I think that this was what, luckily, opened them up.

Alessandra's experience of entering a male occupational domain was not problematic, nor did she find it difficult to become an effective member of an occupational community consisting solely of men. What she found unsatisfactory was the work itself, and its lack of what she regarded as meaningful work experience:

> The only difference between myself and my colleagues is that they feel themselves part of one big family. They love the company, or at least they see nothing strange in continuing to work for it until they retire. But I feel exploited, just as much as the shop-floor workers. I'm grateful to the company for the experience I've gained. Yet slowly but surely I've come to realize that this work is meaningless. I need to know that I'm doing something useful, not that I'm working just to earn money to live. But I don't know if this has anything to do with being a man or a woman, or with being different kinds of persons. I can't talk to my colleagues about this. In their opinion I think like this because I haven't got a family. For them teaching is second-class work, woman's work.

According to the reputational scale applied by Alessandra's colleagues, a worker in industry is a productive worker, while the civil service and the state-owned industries are the domains of, respectively, bureaucrats and the welfare-dependent, i.e. second-sexed persons. The prestigious and sought-after jobs are, for them, in research or management. Alessandra's ideas were understandable and commanded respect, but they were 'real men'. Perhaps she had a more sensitive personality (for some) or perhaps she acted according to a political ideology (for others). Her criticism of the values system therefore fell upon deaf ears.

Alessandra was the first to have doubts about the parallel between work that gives a sense of being useful to others and being a woman. However, she realized that her colleagues attributed a 'male' meaning to their work, while giving up a career to teach was something that women did, not one of them. They quite understood that a woman might want to quit the game, because the game had been invented by men and for men. Alessandra might be different, but the game went on.

The diversity feared by the men seemed to concern the iconography of the woman as represented by fashion or on the glossy pages of the fashion magazines. Probably, the cultural imperatives of some organizational cultures which require men and women to dress in the same way, with one uniform for both sexes, constitute barriers against the anxiety provoked by women's femininity. By contrast, other forms of diversity which constitute an oblique criticism of the values system and seek to change it are ignored.

The criticism made by Alessandra or Fiammetta of the career system – and more in general a certain roundabout and understated accusation advanced by women managers that their (male) colleagues waste their working time on self-display and on signalling devotion, i.e. so-called 'face time' (Luciano, 1993) – seem to belong to this area of unexplored diversity. When the woman is positioned as the newcomer, a system of expectations is erected on her capacity to conform to local customs and usages, and she is judged according to how successfully she manages to integrate. The position of the newcomer is initially defined unilaterally. Subsequently the newcomer may negotiate other discourse positions.

I finally present a case in which positioning is imposed directly against the wishes of the person concerned.

A hostile culture and the position of the intruder

An intruder is someone who enters a situation without being invited and forces the others to respond to a more or less tacit request for acceptance. The refusal of this request is what characterizes the complementary position. It is, therefore, the right of participation that is being contested: the intruder assumes that s/he is equal to the others, and positions himself or herself as a member of the team. The group, in turn, actively resists any claim to membership, to the point that it gives priority to the affirmation of otherness over the values instilled in an occupation, like the solidarity among workers employed in dangerous occupations. And this was the case of Angelina.

Angelina was a young woman living in a small town which was swamped by tourists in the summer. There were consequently ample opportunities for work in the hotel and catering trade. This, however, is a sector with its own iron logic: work is seasonal, the hours are long, there is no trade union protection. Like other unskilled young women, and like their mothers with no further job prospects, Angelina had worked in this sector since she was 16 years old. She had long enjoyed fame in the town as a nonconformist: a political activist and a candidate for a small left-wing party, a feminist, and environmentalist, she led an 'alternative' lifestyle and was also a single parent. This latter was the reason why she had left seasonal hotel work for a permanent job, which nevertheless allowed her to stay at home for long periods. Recent legislation designed to eliminate sex discrimination in job placements had, in fact, led to her being hired as the first, and perhaps the last, female forestry worker.

At the time I collected this story, Angelina had left the forestry service and was a member of a cooperative for equal trade with countries in the Third World.

Angelina recounted an offbeat experience in which she enjoyed playing the part of the intruder. She was convinced that, in order to enter male occupations and to change their cultures, women have first to break down resistance and deal with male hostility by tackling it head-on. Afterwards mutual respect can be established and new spaces conquered. Although her early experience, in the town, was one of struggle, conquest and cultural change, her job as a forestry worker had undermined her previously unshakeable faith in the ultimate victory of women.

As was entirely predictable, Angelina refused to accept the sedentary, less dangerous work assigned to men nearing retirement or to those who had been disabled. She wanted no special treatment and insisted on going straight out into the forests. Hiring her had already created a scandal, but the forestry board had no legal alternative but to take her on. To the evident embarrassment of her superiors, and in the absence of reference cultural or managerial models, Angelina got her way:

> With sneers on our faces, we [the superior and Angelina] looked into each other's eyes, both certainly thinking: 'I'll show you!' My work squad's attitude was no different, they told me quite plainly that I was a pain in the arse, an intruder, and that this was no work for a woman.

As was equally predictable, Angelina refused to be intimidated either by verbal skirmishings or by being boycotted by her workmates:

> I tried to make everything ridiculous. Instead of taking offence or getting angry I used sarcasm. I was always cheerful and talked about my travels in Latin America and Africa to show that there aren't men's jobs and women's jobs. Not that it was easy. I had to battle for everything, even for the right to piss in privacy. When I walked off into the woods I let everyone know I was going for a pee. I turned it into a game. It was tougher when they tested me out with jobs that required physical strength or which could have been dangerous. I learnt to watch them out of the corner of my eye so that I knew what to do. But I often got into trouble and had to ask for help.

The hostility ebbed and flowed. Angelina was not the type to be put off even when on the verge of physical exhaustion. She sometimes felt that she had won when, during work-breaks, there was an atmosphere of conviviality. But she worried whether she could count on her workmates in difficult situations. Or, conversely, she worried that they would deliberately put her in danger to see if she could handle it. At any rate, when winter came, she was able to stay at home, be with her child and forget about her still resentful, but at least docile, workmates. This lasted until the next summer, when the event happened which had always been threatening: she was injured at work and suspected it had happened because of her workmates.

Although it was nothing serious, something, somewhere, changed irrevocably. Angelina did not rejoin her squad but was assigned an office job. The following summer she quit.

The dynamics of the accident are still unclear:

> I don't exactly remember what happened, and I can't say with certainty whether it was my fault, whether it was bad luck or whether someone set me up. Suspicion is a bad thing and I resist it, but I know my relations with my workmates were very different after the accident. They all came to see me, and

they were very sorry, but I felt as distant from them as they said they felt close to me. For me the incident was closed, even if I wished I knew more.

Angelina has not changed her mind over the possibilities of changing men's work into 'just work, that's all'. All she says is that today she bears yet another scar.

Whereas in the story of the guest and the host the two positions were symmetrical and had been constructed through a cooperative discourse strategy, in Angelina's story the position of the intruder resulted from the negation of self-positioning. This type of positioning simultaneously involves a positioning of the Other and an invitation which may be accepted, refused, misunderstood, or even, in the case of the intruder, imposed. One discourse practice contraposes the other. One cannot say that there is no dialogue, nor that such dialogue as exists does not establish an interpersonal relationship.

Liminarity and symbolic order

In the previous section we followed various narratives belonging to the single discourse of what I called 'travellers in a male world'. This discourse presupposes the existence of a territory marked out as male which is trespassed upon by females who are formally members of the community but who, in actual practice, must stake out their positions in the field. Various options are available, several subject positions can be taken up for oneself, and for the other, just as this discourse delineates a social structure which coerces discourse positions and sets up a series of expectations and social obligations. Inscribed in the complementary positions of guest and host is a social structure which everyone knows in its essential form, although it is a narrative which comes in innumerable versions. When we find ourselves in a setting of this kind, it is concrete people who bring their previous experiences, their anticipatory socialization to their roles; people who in actual discourse practices are the actors, directors and audience in these living narratives.

We followed six narratives (Table 4.1 on p. 109) which positioned certain features of the travellers, just as these were positioned by the 'others' as they took up complementary positions. In a dialogue-based process, positions are assumed, negotiated, changed, imposed: Giovanna was frozen into the position of guest, Rita initially failed to realize that she had been constructed into the position of visitor, Alessandra was an eager constructor of the newcomer who wanted to belong. Their discourse dynamic expresses the double reference (Mead, 1934) whereby the self and the other are reciprocally 'authored'.

In positioning the self, one also positions the other: a friendly culture offers a position, it extends an invitation which: (a) may be gratefully accepted – a cooperative position; (b) may not be understood – a mismatched position; (c) may be forced but open-ended. The frame that ties together the I–you–us interaction is collaborative and complementary in nature. By contrast, in a context of open hostility the pragmatics of the communication are symmetrical (Watzlawick *et al.*, 1967), so that Fiorella was marginalized, Fiammetta in the position of the enemy within, and Angelina was in the position of the intruder. The positioning of self and of the other follows a positioning-rejection dynamic which generates a dynamic of: (a) forced acceptance of a unilateral definition – a stigmatized position; (b) non-acceptance of one's position and pursuit of one's own definition – a contested position; (c) forced acceptance of definition by others as a declaration of non-agreement – a unilaterally imposed position.

The positioning of gender as a social relation among specific individuals in specific contexts is a 'liminary' activity, to use Victor Turner's (1969) term for it. That is, it is an activity which relates to the metaphor of the 'threshold' (*limen* in Latin): the invisible line that separates and unites the inner and the outer, a symbol of transition and transcendence.

The state or condition of liminarity enables communication between the structure – the institutional organization of positions and/or actors – and what Turner (1969) calls 'antistructure', that is, the social dynamic unit. The structure differentiates individuals, it renders them unequal within relatively rigid social positions. The antistructure is *communitas*, contact with the totality, an arena in which the individual or the group redefine the universal function of the structure in contact with age-old symbols.

In other words, one can talk of persistence and change, of structure and process, of institution and movement: all these are dualities which enable communication between static difference and processual difference. Just as the threshold between waking and sleeping represents what no longer is and what is not yet, so liminarity is the state of difference, of the 'original unifying unity of what tends apart' (Heidegger, 1969: 112).

The dialectical tension between structure and antistructure is the dynamic between the totality in the individual and the individual in the totality; it is structural ambivalence. Society is the dialectical tension between collective and institutional symbolic structures and semantic processes which define the structural and antistructural dynamic and guarantee the reverse movement from the particular to the total, from the individual to the collective. The structuring of the symbolic world is expressed in institutions, processes and dynamics which erect a symbolic order of gender based on static difference. Organizations express a symbolic order of gender which creates a subordinate difference, female and male domains, segregated occupations, differences in status, power and knowledge. But at the same time organizations stand in a position of liminarity between two structured social situations. The social relation of gender is problematized within wider society. The collective and global meaning of gender difference is historicized into radically different symbolic and social structures, where the threshold between male and female is crossed innumerable times. Female experiences in the male symbolic universe – and vice versa – give dynamic redefinition to the concrete meaning of the cultural and social system. The symbolic order of gender is redefined through the suspension of pre-existing structures, and it re-emerges with its contents changed to redefine successive structures.

The stories of women who are the first to enter a male work group describe a liminary space in which the normal expectations of behaviour are suspended and the participants are allowed to take up new roles. This is a space of transition – and the metaphor of the journey conveys the shock of the encounter – but it is also a transitional space because the journey has an end. Anthropologists use the expression 'going native' to indicate the fact that the more the researcher becomes an insider of an alien community, the more s/he shares its assumptions, and the less s/he is able to describe it with detachment. Not surprisingly, therefore, the stories which problematize the self/other relation share a marked sense of distance and extraneousness, where the beginning of the story is given by the narrator's status as the sole woman and is what is remembered of the story because integration never took place.

What is most interesting about these stories is their language of relational self-construction. They show that a gender identity is partly constructed by linguistic registers diffused in the social order and how social meaning is lived. The social order is an integral part of the development of self (Czarniawska-Joerges, 1994).

Let us now look at the narrative structures which sustain the construction of self as traveller, and the way in which the stories proffer a solution to the relationship with the Other. For brevity's sake, I shall refer to the types of narrative described by Murray (1989):

- Comedy involves the victory of youth and desire, and conflict in comedy is released in the course of an adventure or festivity, i.e. through sociality.
- Romance is the restoration of the honoured past through a crucial test, and conflict is resolved by battle.
- Tragedy involves the failure to conquer evil and exclusion from the social unit.
- Irony is the discovery that comedy, romance and tragedy are merely the schemes of mortals to control experience: individuals are not so pure, nor is the social order so healthy.

If we reread the stories with the help of Table 4.2, we find that the first two positions – of guest and of the marginal – are similar. The guest is unable to find a way to redress the situation. Having enjoyed the privileges of the guest, she does not know how to discharge her social obligation. Nor does the marginal know how to handle the situation and fantasizes that it will be changed by external forces. Both cases display the narrative structure of comedy; and not only is sociality the link between their positioning and that of the Other, it is the 'natural' solution: different obligations correspond to different positions.

Table 4.2 *Narrative structures and the moral of the tale*

Self-construction	Moral of the tale	Narrative structure
The guest	no way out of social obligation	comedy
The marginal	for collective redemption	comedy
The holidaymaker	equal discrimination programme	romance
The snake in the grass	use of personal power	romance
The newcomer	refusal to play the game	romance
The intruder	exclusion from the game	tragedy

Discord instead characterizes the narrative structure of the holiday-maker and the snake in the grass. Managing the conflict is therefore a test. In the former case, there is plainly a crisis and exit from it is framed in such contradictory terms as to constitute a play on words – equal discrimination (instead of opportunity) – which symbolizes the reversal in the subordination relationship. But also in the latter case there is determination to wield the power granted by organizational position, thereby shaking off a powerless (female) gendered presence. This is the narrative structure of the novel in which the protagonist passes a test by defeating the powers of evil.

Slightly different is the narrative position of the newcomer. She too in a certain sense is put to the test – crossing the threshold of acceptance or remaining an outsider – but she does not approach it as a battle and consequently does not grant significance to the test. This narrative structure may be called an anti-romantic romance.

The last story narrates the tragedy of the triumph of the forces of evil, defeat and exclusion from the social unit.

I reserve for myself the role of ironic narrator who insinuates doubt about the probity of the other narrative voices which actively construct, which collude, which benefit from a social order in which they find a place. As for the social order which expresses the place of gendered persons and of the relations which enable them to communicate, this can hardly be healthy if it prevents people from experiencing and inventing reciprocal relations which enrich their subjectivity.

The symbolic order of gender narrated in various work settings ranges from the place of honour to total exclusion. Gender relations can therefore be viewed as cultural performances learnt and enacted on appropriate occasions.

5

Doing Gender in the Workplace

Etiquette, good manners, civilized behaviour express the transformation of customs over time, and this change stretches a veil of oblivion over previous customs.

I give an example: the prescriptions that today almost all the scientific journals hand out to their contributors on the non-sexist use of language. When this custom, today generally accepted, appeared about twenty years ago, it provoked long argument with my (male) colleagues on the fact that it was only a formal adjustment which made no substantial change to gender relationships. It would be difficult today to take up this argument again with any degree of seriousness; on the contrary, the practice of writing and speaking while respecting gender diversity is well-nigh universal. Or take Norbert Elias's (1978: 288–92) masterly example of spitting. In a medieval treatise written in Latin – *Stans puer in mensam* – we are admonished as follows:

> Do not spit on or over the table
> Do not scratch your flesh with your finger
> If you are wise, spit outside the bowl while washing your hands

Erasmus of Rotterdam gave the following advice in his *De civiltate morum puerilium* of 1530:

> Turn away when spitting, lest your saliva fall on someone. If anything purulent falls to the ground, it should be trodden upon, lest it nauseate someone. If you are not at liberty to do this, catch the sputum in a small cloth. It is unmannerly to suck back saliva, as equally are those whom we see spitting at every third word not from necessity but from habit.

Giovanni Della Casa, archbishop of Benevento, advised in his *Galateo* (1558):

> It is also unseemly for someone sitting at table to scratch himself. At such a time and place you should also abstain as far as possible from spitting, and if it cannot be completely avoided it should be done politely and unnoticed. I have often heard that whole peoples have sometimes lived so moderately and conducted themselves so honourably that they have found spitting quite unnecessary. Why, therefore, should not we too be able to refrain from it just for a short time?

In 1729, La Salle wrote in *Les règles de la bienséance et de la civilté chrétienne*:

> You should take great care never to spit on your clothes, or those of others. . . . If you notice saliva on someone's coat, it is not polite to make it known; you

should instruct a servant to remove it. If no servant is present, you should remove it yourself without being noticed. For good breeding consists in not bringing to people's attention anything that might offend or confuse them.

In 1859, in *The Habits of Good Society*, we find:

Spitting is at all times a disgusting habit .... Besides being coarse and atrocious, it is very bad for the health.

We read the following observation in *Moeurs intimes du passé* by Agustin Cabanès (1910):

Have you noticed that today we relegate to some discreet corner what our fathers did not hesitate to display quite openly? Thus a certain intimate article of furniture had a place of honour . . . no one thought of concealing it from view.

The same is true of another piece of furniture no longer found in modern households, whose disappearance some will perhaps regret in this age of 'bacillophobia': I am referring to the spittoon.

We feel a 'natural' disgust on reading Elias's examples of the rules of good behaviour that govern the use of a handkerchief or spitting; and yet this reaction is not in fact natural, because it is the outcome of a social process of behaviour conditioning. Certain customs are prohibited, at least in the upper stratum of society, because they are unpleasant and reveal a lack of respect; or else they are prohibited *tout court*; or again they are prohibited for reasons of hygiene. Detailed prohibitions tend to disappear when the custom appears entirely obvious, when in the eyes of men they are laden with sentiments of disgust, distrust, shame or blame, even when they are alone (Elias, 1978).

The civilizing process, Elias argues, seeks to turn socially desirable behaviour into an automatism, a self-constriction, and to have it appear to the subjects' consciences as a behaviour bred of their free initiative, of their morality; to make them believe that it is in the interest of their human dignity.

The codes of courtesy which regulate the relationships between the sexes have undergone constant revision, expressing as they do social relationships between the sexes patterned on gender relationships that are not as unidirectional as we have been led to believe. In the type of matrimony practised in the absolutist courts, the woman was less oppressed by external constrictions than she was in chivalrous society, but the internal constraints imposed by courtly life increased. In bourgeois matrimony, the spouses were no longer subject to the constrictions of societal rank, but the regulation of the instincts increased *pari passu* with the self-construction of professional work.

Gender relationships today are rapidly changing, and however distasteful the analogy I have proposed with spitting may be, the movement of civilization seems to associate the two.

So far the parallel with the spittoon holds, and sexist language can be abandoned together with the spittoon with no concern for the self-restraint imposed on social behaviour.

I take another example from Elias, which this time refers to sport and bathing: activities in which men and women are in close proximity and are scantily clothed or naked. Only in a society in which close restraint has been wholly internalized, in which women and men are entirely similar, do strong self-control and a rigorous etiquette of behaviour constitute a curb on each, and can there be the bathing and sports costumes today so widely worn and – with respect to the past – such freedom. Civilized behaviour is founded on repression, the transformation of the instincts, self-control, the social regulation of the emotions and – paradoxically – freedom.

Is gender a kind of 'sphincter control'? By requiring the use of handkerchiefs or by prohibiting spitting, society elaborates rules which tame the physical urges in both children and adults. Gender, that which is permissible in the public interaction of sexed bodies, educates the sexes and represses the instincts. When a society (Italy being a current case in point) debates a law and argues whether sexual violence is an offence against morality or against the person, or whether sexual violence within the marriage can be prosecuted, that society is developing norms which regulate gender relationships and which set restrictions on male sexuality. It is a society which no longer considers assault on a woman to be an offence against morality, the expression of an ill-controlled urge.

The cultural elaboration of gender represses sexuality and creates greater freedom of behaviour for sexed persons.

Faced with this paradox, one may enquire as to the consequences of this regulation of the instincts on the type of society under construction. The question does not admit to a straightforward answer; but what one can discern is a redefining of the realms of the public and the private, and the constant and progressive confinement of the instinctive world to the private sphere. It has thus come about that sexuality and intimacy between men and women have been confined more and more narrowly to the ambit of socially legitimized matrimony. Can we therefore envisage a scenario constituted by some sort of twofold regime: genderless in public and gendered in private?

We cannot foresee what the contents of gender will be like in the years to come. But if we look at how the gender relation is negotiated in day-to-day relationships, we find that the change in the conception of gender is brought about in organizational life principally through face-to-face interactions. Let us assume, therefore, that gender is not (solely) a given, but that it is an activity. What do we do when we 'do' gender? Is it possible to do 'one' gender and avoid 'second-sexing' the other?

The dual presence at work

The previous chapters described gender principally as a category of thought which extends the meanings of sexual difference from sexed bodies to two symbolic universes: the male and the female. Gender is the prototype of social classification, and our social arrangements are the expression of that 'institutional reflexivity' (Goffman, 1977) which guarantees coherence, continuity and social reproduction between sexual difference and the attribution of gender. The term 'institutional reflexivity' refers to the social organization – that is, to practices in concrete social situations which ensure that society 'naturally' expresses the sexual division of rewards and labour. The gender we think is organized by a sexual segregation which takes account of 'natural' differences between the sexes and at the same time allows and directs the interactive production of this difference. Institutional reflexivity works through two complementary processes: one which reveals social arrangements along gender lines and in accordance with a separated symbolic universe; and one which conceals the contradictions between the social practices of sexed persons and symbolic universes. These are the contradictions of the dual presence described by Balbo (1979) and Zanuso (1987).

In other words, in everyday social situations we both produce a social presence coherent with the attribution of gender and handle the incoherences of the dual presence in such a way that they do not subvert the fundamental gender beliefs of our society. So adept are we at this that it is difficult to grasp the effort involved. For example, a physical feature presumed to derive directly from biological nature is that the male body is taller, stronger, more muscular and heavier: this may confirm or refute this contention, or alternatively it may measure the real variability of these sexual features; but the social mode of couple formation emphasizes pairings according to gender features, so that when we walk down the street we gain the impression that 'naturally' men are tall and strong and women are small and weak. Men do heavy, risky work in the open air, they carve out careers in the same way as medieval knights made conquests. Women devote themselves to lighter work, to tasks which require precision and patience, in physically and socially protected settings; work which is also a dead end because their aspirations lie elsewhere. It is pointless to repeat that the number of jobs in which the workers' physical features still count is negligible. At issue here are the beliefs that sustain social practices, and how social practices which openly contradict beliefs about gender are 'pardoned', minimized, remedied and concealed.

Beyond the sexual segregation which delineates parallel organizations between men and women, 'doing gender' means handling the dual presence. And this can be done both by re-establishing the social order of gender based on male dominance and on the systematic devaluation of the female as second sex, and by introducing the transgression and delegitimation of the principles on which that order is erected. At bottom, the so-called 'results' of feminism can be read both at the level of social consequences – that is, facts (how many women? where?) – and at the level of cultural presuppositions – that is, of the social legitimation of the beliefs that sustain the power relationships between the sexes. That which is labelled today as not 'politically correct' (i.e. socially subjected to restriction) yesterday either went entirely unnoticed or was the subject of heated political debate, and tomorrow, hopefully, will disappear because it has been incorporated into the ethics and aesthetics of society. Like the spittoon.

How we do gender is still a central question of the micro-politics between the sexes, in the social construction of the everyday reality of our society and culture. This assertion presupposes that gender is a routine, a methodical and recurrent accomplishment. In the definition provided by West and Zimmerman (1987: 126), gender 'is the activity of managing situated conduct, in the light of normative conceptions of attitudes and activities appropriate for one's sex category', and 'doing gender involves a complex of socially guided perceptual, interactional and micropolitical activities that cast particular pursuits as expressions of masculine and feminine "natures"' (ibid.: 125).

And organizations possess gender as well. For example, the research by Hirsch and Andrews (1983) and by Schneider and Dunbar (1992) on mergers and takeovers shows a social construction of these events based on the archetypes of the love affair, of marriage or of rape. When this discourse is applied metaphorically to the merger, the acquiring executive is the 'macho' and the target company is accorded the female gender.

By saying that also organizations do gender I mean that they contain specific social situations, and that doing gender in the workplace is different from doing it in other social situations like the street, a party, the family, and so on.

Doing gender in an organization therefore presupposes a set of already hierarchically normed interactions based on the sexual division of labour and on gender expectations. But it also makes it possible to regulate the interactions which produce more or less broad inequalities between men and women and more or less 'fair' conceptions of gender. In producing goods and services, organizations also produce social beliefs about gender relationships and about their equity, and they provide settings in which to experiment with and alter these relationships. Gender relationships in organizations not only reflect the symbolic order of gender in society; they actively help to create and alter it, albeit with processes and logics entirely their own.

For example, the Fordist factory expressed an organizational logic based on the hierarchy, on a marked sexual segregation of work, on an inflexible division between the planning and execution of work, between productive work and ancillary work which exalted the values of the masculine and of male domination. The productive logic which instead bases itself on quality, on service, on the involvement of the executors in planning and of the user in the delivery system, which requires lean and flat organizations and therefore reduces the significance and possibility of career-building, this logic speaks a less masculine language, lays less stress on competitiveness and more on competence, and increasingly assumes values that belong to the symbolic universe of the female but cannot be valorized as such as long as the female constitutes the second sex. And this is a contradiction that organizational discourses confront; it is not a so-called 'objective condition' that heralds the triumph of the female! The rhetoric of sexual difference and conditions of inequality are closely connected, but this is not a mechanical linkage. The limits of rationality, in thought as in the practices that used to be based upon it (planning, rationalization, the techniques of choice), also involve the entire symbolic universe in which rationality is inscribed – with the male as the paramount value – but they do not automatically entail the relaxing of the subordinate bond with the female as a chance to revalorize the contents of the other symbolic universe.

The dual presence can therefore provide a stimulus to cultural change and to the emergence of new articulations of the contents of the symbolic order of gender. It may in fact be seen as a breakdown in the symbolic order, and doing gender can be conceptualized as a process that produces order and repairs this order when it is breached, threatened or contradicted.

Maintaining the dual presence in the workplace requires interaction work, both in order to celebrate the recognition and attribution of gender and symbolically to remedy all those occasions that somehow transgress or contradict inner coherence. Doing gender and doing it in a way that destabilizes the social beliefs that legitimize gender inequality requires competences of perception, of interaction and of micro-politics. I shall now focus on these while analysing ceremonial work and the work required to repair the symbolic order of gender.

Dual presence and the deferral of the symbolic order

Doing gender involves symbols – using them, playing with them and transforming them; it entails managing the dual presence: shuttling between a symbolic universe coherent with one gender identity and the symbolic realm of the 'other' gender. We do gender through ceremonial work and through remedial work (Gherardi, 1994). In the former kind of behaviour we stress the difference between the symbolic universes of gender; in the latter we defer the meanings of gender to situated interactions. It is in the way that we weave these two forms of behaviour together that resides the possibility of doing gender without second-sexing the female.

Men and women are engaged in the ceremonial work of giving proper representation to the attributes and behaviour of their own gender, of acknowledging and anticipating that others will do the same, and of legitimizing this ceremonial in appropriate discourse strategies. It is impossible to avoid ceremonial work, because our first act of social categorization when encountering the other is to ascribe a gender identity.

Consider the relational difficulty that arises when we must telephone or write to somebody whose gender we do not know because she or he has an uncommon first name. Or, even more embarrassingly, when we have to engage in face-to-face interaction with an interlocutor who does not provide clear codes for the attribution of gender and does not emit appropriate gender display (Goffman 1976). For example, a front-office clerk in a youth centre had developed a whole range of 'tricks' (as she called them) to deal with her clients; that is, adolescents, in a life-phase where gender identity may still be ambiguous, problematic, and the body still immature. She possessed extremely sophisticated cultural tools with which to construe unisex clothing as female or male, and she used these tools to manage the social encounter with appropriate gender attribution. Similar problems have been reported to me when the interlocutor is of different sexual orientation. The heterosexual addresser tries to interact 'naturally' but does not know (a) whether it is more natural (that is, less discriminating) to ignore the diversity or openly to acknowledge it, and (b) how to relate to what is perceived as an incoherence between sex and gender and ignorance of proper etiquette.

Recognition of the gender position of another comes about both through precedence-granting and other courtesy gestures, and through the verbal appreciation of the 'gifts' of the other gender. A well-known example is the way in which thanks are expressed for help given even though it was not compulsory: a male colleague who fixes the lock on a desk is thanked by having his skills as a handyman praised – 'a real man about the house' (and office!) – while the female colleague who suggests an appropriate present for a child's birthday is thanked for her female intuition.

In the rituals demanded by etiquette, the sexes pay homage to the prerogatives of their gender (e.g. gentleness or strength), and in so doing they sanctify it and demonstrate competent gender behaviour. Offices differ from public places in that they are settings in which encounters are not just between a 'gentleman' and a 'lady' but also between the office boss and his secretary. Here, therefore, hierarchical rituals interweave with chivalric ones: if the former predominate, the position of subordination and that entailed by membership of the second sex are both reinforced (for example, when the office boss goes out of the door first and heads off for a meeting followed by his secretary a few steps behind).

The courtesy system, in fact, provides an interesting example of a 'double-bind situation' (Watzlawick *et al.*, 1967). In effect, there is a paradox in relations which is not to be found in analogous situations of social inequality: unlike other groups of disadvantaged adults, women are held in high consideration (Goffman, 1977), and this consideration is manifest in social situations as due acknowledgement of their gender identity and therefore as an expression of their inequality. Failure to respect the courtesy system marks an adult male as socially incompetent, but it establishes an asymmetric relation in which the man is in the one-up position.

An anecdote from my own work environment illustrates the various forms of escape from the impasse that the courtesy system constructs in different ways around the two sexes. An elderly and academically prestigious colleague of mine had returned from a visit to California where, I would think for the first time, he had been exposed to the rules of what is and what is not politically correct. After a meeting with a group of colleagues – all men and of lower rank/prestige – we started to leave the room. In opening the door for me, he asked, using the Italian courtesy form since our relationship was highly formal, 'Do you want me to open the door for you or will you react as if I'd grabbed your arse?' There seemed to be no way out for me because the question defined me either as a hysterical feminist (like those that he later described meeting on his American visit) or as a sweet and docile lady who knew her place in society and therefore also in academia. I decided on sarcasm and told him emphatically that I formally authorized him to open not only that door but also all the other doors and obstacles that might stand in my way in the future. I assured him that his ability to open doors (given his influence) was well known in academic circles. This made the rest of the group laugh, since they had benefited from his influence in their university careers, and saved my honour as a woman because I had acknowledged his masculinity (influence) and I had moved into the one-up position because I had stressed my power of authorization.

Age differences also help to define the meaning of the ritual. In the course of an interview (Gherardi, 1990), a technical worker in her forties explained how I should behave (as her double) when taking the lift. I should be the first to enter when I was in the company of the older male office-workers, because they had had traditional upbringings. With men of my own age, however, it did not matter because 'we don't worry about these things'. But if I found myself with two males who had recently started work in the office, I should still enter first. Although the reasons justifying the rule in the former two cases were offered spontaneously, in the latter one of younger men with fewer years of service (and therefore with a lower status?), the explanation centred on the resentment felt by the woman on the one occasion when the rule had been broken. In this case it was the man who belonged to the second sex by age, by hierarchical status, or both.

The courtesy system, in fact, is not as innocent as it may appear when considered solely as an occasion for the reciprocal recognition of gender identity or for the display of considerateness towards idealized femaleness. It is the prime arena for conveying relative rank: deciding who decides, who leads and who follows, who speaks and who listens, who has the power to position the Other, and so forth. Most organizational structures already contain a definition of the relative ranks of those who engage in interaction, and they often provide constructs organized along gender lines where men occupy a 'naturally' higher position, one which is the 'natural' expression of their natural abilities. We may take this as an extreme form of a social situation legitimized by social beliefs about gender: the position of the woman is clearly a female position which requires considerateness and care from a man occupying the one-up position in every respect and who positions himself as the provider and the honourer. The gender performance that thus takes place reconfirms beliefs about the differing human natures of the two sexes. We may deduce that it is relatively simpler for women to assume a one-down position; to be those who receive orders, listen, execute, follow, and so on, since this position is inscribed in social situations as institutional reflexivity. In other words, the one-down situation does not contradict gender identity; indeed it may bring advantages or specific resources in interaction, and it does not necessarily require all the relational work necessary to overcome the asymmetry of the relationship. The opposite is the case for men, who interpret subordination and the one-down position as a slight on their virility.

The political nature of gender rituals is highlighted by interactions among colleagues belonging to a peer group, or when the authority structure is at odds with gender lines. The fact that the bookshops are stocked with handbooks on 'What To Do When the Boss Is a Woman', or similar, signals that there is or could be a problem of authority/obedience, or at least an embarrassing contradiction. How can a man handle the courtesy system and activate the protector/protected frame when the relative ranks are in his disfavour, and when he risks resembling more a butler than a knight in shining armour?

The competence of each of them resides in the ability to minimize the gap and to create a climate of cooperation and trust, or to sectorialize the general situation into a number of sub-contexts in which she can appreciate his male skills (of being project oriented, of being able to fix things that have broken, etc.) and he recognizes the superiority of female gifts (of intuition, of tact, of relation). Genderism is competence in organizing social situations, and it may constitute a resource for a deliberately manipulative strategy.

The situation in peer groups is different, especially if the work context is competitively structured. Celebration of the attitudes and activities of each sex is normative-complementary in character. The strength of the man is complementary to the frailty of the woman, the mechanical ability of the man to the ineptness of the woman, his determination and assertiveness to her care and compliance, his belligerence to her diffidence, and so on.

If women assume the femaleness position (and the same applies to those men who do not adhere to maleness values), they automatically withdraw from the competition, and leave room for the 'tough who get going when the going gets tough'. Gender prerogatives can be used to mark out the boundaries of competition. The threat used to exercise social control is directed towards sexual identity. Or else it operates both as a threat and as a system of self-exclusion. It is in this situation that the organizational culture may make a major difference in the structuring of these social situations: the more the description of the work, of the talents required to perform it well, of the characteristics necessary to get ahead, of the dedication required by the work and/or to the organization are defined within a symbolic universe of the masculine, the more female competition is discouraged, is self-selected, is defined as unfair competition, and the less the men who do not support this values system are real men. The corollary to this organizational culture is that when a woman competes or when she achieves high status, it becomes legitimate to suspect or to insinuate that she has lost out on femininity. She's married, she has children, she has a happy and female domestic life; what has she had to give up in order to become an organizational woman?

An episode taken from the Italian press well illustrates the diffusion of these ingrained assumptions. In summer 1992 a woman was appointed to one of the top jobs in the Italian judiciary (directress of criminal affairs for the Ministry of Justice). The press gave great prominence to the exceptional nature of the promotion in tones of complacent emancipationism. All the newspapers dwelt at length on her curriculum vitae. This, of course, was perfectly natural. But the guild of women television journalists complained at the way that the news had appeared in the press. All the newspapers, in fact, had reported that the woman was divorced, childless, lived alone, had no hobbies, but she made her own tomato sauce and she enjoyed cooking! The readers could rest assured that as well as professional competence, gender competence was secure. The situation had been ratified!

There is a certain class of celebration work which comprises ratification rituals (Goffman, 1971). These are performed for or towards someone who has changed his or her status in some way, and they function as reassurance displays. The examples range from congratulations, through expressions of welcome to a new situation, to friendly (or apparently friendly) teasing.

These ratification rituals may disguise an ambiguous position if they are repetitive and if they involve people who meet frequently. A recurrent case is one in which a work group is predominantly single sex: here the lone woman or the lone man usually receives expressions of welcome, insistence on the exceptional nature of the situation, reassurances of non-aggression, and protective displays – as long as s/he is not in a position of authority. If the person is a woman and if the ratification ritual is repeated, elaborate and lengthy, the exceptional nature of her presence, and the benevolence of the group which accepts her as an equal and pays homage to her femininity, is insinuated even more strongly. In this case, what is ratified is a condition of symbolic subordination and the object of the reassurance is the group, which feels threatened by diversity.

When the person is a man who wields the same power as his female colleagues (which implies that the group is led by a woman), he is not usually subjected to over-ratification. More commonly he is teased by his other male colleagues with expressions such as 'blessed among women'.

Similar expressions are rarely addressed to women. This example shows that in rituals for the celebration and symbolic construction of gender the position of subject is in turn occupied by people of different sex, but that the same rituals have differing impacts according to the sex of the recipient. The celebration of male-dependent femininity disguises a ritual designed to preserve such dependence, as if the strength of the bond with the second sex would slacken if nothing was done to pay homage to it.

In celebrating our masculinity or femininity, when encountering people of our own or the other sex, we feel pleasure at momentarily becoming part of the sacred. In these brief rituals, 'individuals perform for and to another, attesting civility and goodwill on the performer's part and to the recipient's possession of a small patrimony of sacredness' (Goffman, 1971: 89). For an instant we are no longer just a sexed body but part of the 'mystic body' of Male or Female.

The pleasure that derives from ceremonial work is a possible explanation for why men and women prefer to work in mixed rather than single-gendered environments, and why so many women have told me that they are annoyed by 'colleagues who don't even notice that you're a woman, or they don't realize that you've made yourself look nice for them as well . . . to brighten the place up'. Statements such as these implicitly express what Goffman (1967: 5) calls face-work: that is, the work involved in maintaining 'an image of self delineated in terms of approved social attributes' – including the attributes of gender, which must be respected and which it is ill-mannered to ignore. There are, therefore, rules of self-respect which require us to acknowledge and to celebrate our gender membership, and rules of considerateness which express the reciprocity of interaction. There is also the pleasure we gain from the ceremonial work and our emotional involvement in maintaining the identity of our own and the other's gender. And finally there are the appropriateness rules and situational constraints that apply in the environment 'work'; that is, in a public place like the organization.

One of the commonest rituals in organizational life which celebrates both gender membership and the particular regard due to the female sex is courtship. This too assumes organizational features. The aim of the ritual, however, is distorted because it is not the formation of a couple and the granting of sexual access that is at stake, but ritual acknowledgement of gender identity and reinforcement of the attract/be attracted frame. In organizations especially, the courtship system intersects with the courtesy system, since its aim is only superficially sexual. It is more directly concerned with the display and recognition of gender identity. The man who uses the courtship ritual employs conventional language to show his interest and implicitly sends a message of reassurance to his interlocutor – worthy of receiving the attention due to her sex – even when he is not asking her to grant sexual favours but to search in the files for an unpaid invoice! The woman who assumes a complementary position in the ritual game confirms her benevolence towards the man and affirms herself as young and beautiful – that is, able to attract and to arouse interest. When the attraction shifts from the physical to the intellectual, the formal recognition of leadership is a ritualized courtship of the ability to attract/ be attracted.

Organizational courtship also intersects with the courtesy system because, depending on the organizational culture, indulgence or abstinence may be taken to be an act of discourtesy or a lack of tact. At the risk of cliché I quote the example of Latin cultures compared with Anglo-Saxon ones. In my experience, language, fantasies and games-playing centred on courtship as an end in itself are much more common in Italian, French and Spanish organizations. Those who systematically abstain – whether men or women – are dismissed as cantankerous, ill-mannered, lacking in relational competence. More recently, the debate on gender relationships has created ambiguity and uncertainty. Are those who abstain showing a new relational competence, or are they people who wish to keep their distance and therefore deny symbolic access to that aura of diffused, suffused and apparently innocent sexuality? Discussion of this ritual with Anglo-Saxon colleagues has made me aware of what may be a cultural difference in sexuality and the social legitimacy of its public expression.

Finally, one notes that although the regulation of courtship among colleagues is left to habit and to power relations between the sexes, this is not so when it is the organization itself that imposes such behaviour as part of role prescriptions/ expectations. In general, in those situations in which the organization 'meets the public' both men and women employees are required to assume the attract/be attracted frame, to use courtship rituals, and sexual innuendo (as product advertising well illustrates).

In our working lives we create both material products and the symbolic product of a role assumed by a sexed body and performed by a gendered actor for an audience which not only judges the appropriateness and coherence of the performance with the symbolic universes of gender, but actively participates in the production of competence rules.

We might say that the first competence rule imposes the celebration of the symbolic order of gender as the archetype of separateness and univocality between what is male and what is female and the 'symbolic' subordination of the latter to the former. The second competence rule prescribes the behaviour required to overcome the ambiguity of the experience that reveals the dual presence and which historicizes the forms of subordination according to the place, according to the circumstances, and according to the local culture which expresses what is 'fair' in the relationship between the sexes and in the discourses that constitute the social representation of gender.

For example, the realm of work (and also the word itself in many languages) is clearly masculine: men assume the burden of labour as work, women the burden of labour as childbirth. This is a symbolic construct common to almost all Western cultures; and the celebration of the symbolic order of gender consequently places organizations in reliable male hands. But if men are excluded from female labour, women are not excluded from work. How can women cope with this? Through remedial work which makes their presence 'discreet': women enter organizations, but 'take their place' in segregated jobs; in their work roles they express their femininity and the continuity of maternalism; in public places (that is, in the presence of men) they adapt to forms of male sociality, the homosociability described by Kanter (1977), and they use language differently (Lakoff, 1975). Although the literature has often pointed out that women must work harder than men to make themselves 'visible' (the prerequisite for a successful career!), it has neglected the fact that men and women collaborate actively, if not consciously, to render the female presence feminine, discreet and almost invisible.

This collusive manoeuvre is a celebration of the symbolic order of gender, but the kinds of interaction in which this manoeuvring takes place differ, because 'doing gender' stands at the intersection between the difference/deferral of the meanings of male and female and the material and symbolic structures which create inequalities on the basis of difference (second-sexing).

The ceremonial work which sustains the symbolic order of gender (where male is male, and the female is second-sexed) is one of Durkheim's (1912) 'positive rituals'; namely, those rituals which involve doing, paying homage, recognizing or celebrating. Negative rituals, by contrast, involve avoiding, maintaining distance, forbidding; and when in interaction the symbolic order is broken, then remedial work is required (Goffman, 1971; Owen, 1983). The dual presence, that is, the transverse experience of gender, is a breach of the order, and as such requires a ceremonial which is simultaneously 'supportive of the symbolic order of gender' and 'remedial' of the offence.

What makes the work of repairing the symbolic order of gender so frequently laborious is the difficulty of preserving difference without reproducing inequality. Those involved often find themselves caught in 'double-bind' situations, given that not all the situations in which a rule is broken are as simple as those where: (a) a man makes a risqué comment (tells a story, makes a joke) in the company of one or more women; (b) he apologizes, or has asked for permission beforehand; and (c) the women present pardon him or minimize the gravity of what he has done.

Whatever difference in magnitude there may be between a coarse remark and the segregation of female work, they are both rituals of recognition of the separateness of two symbolic universes.

Different, though, is the situation which involves a serious double-bind. For example, when a woman is finally accepted as an equal in a male environment, she is frequently made the object of those displays of appreciation and intimacy that typify the community of men. A remark made to me on several occasions in my investigation of occupational community cultures (Gherardi, 1990) concerned the emblematic 'slap on the back'. This situation is well illustrated by the story of a young woman engineer who joined an entirely male research team. For a whole year she was marginalized and teased as an 'angry feminist' because she repulsed the advances made by her colleagues. The situation changed dramatically one day when the boss, in the presence of everyone, praised her work and as a sign of appreciation gave her a hearty slap on the back – something famously not done to a woman but to 'one of the boys'. Very often, when a woman gains acceptance by men, and when her work is valued, forms of communication normally exclusive to males are extended to include her as well. This implicit devaluation of femaleness either seems to pass unobserved or it is taken for granted, but such interactive behaviour also signals that the forms of female sociability are restricted to women-only groups and to situations of female intimacy, while homosociability tends to be the model of behaviour in mixed social settings.

How do women react to the symbolic 'slap on the back'? That is, how do they react to situations where they are accepted as people but devalued as women? If they respond to only one of the terms of the message, they ignore and disqualify the other. They resort to a collusive manoeuvre to become honorary men, thus disqualifying their gender, or else they save the honour of their gender but show poor communicative skill by ignoring the main content of the message (acceptance). Responding to both terms of the message requires a ritual which signals that an infringement has been committed, together with a readiness for repair so that the symbolic order of gender can be re-established in terms of difference. Sarcasm, for example, is a way out of the impasse because it is a metacommunicative device which changes the content of the message but leaves its form intact – and sarcasm has also acquired the meaning of a postmodern tool of resistance. Our woman engineer, for instance, had the presence of mind, once she had thanked her boss and her colleagues, to ask them in future not to slap her on the back but to kiss her hand. This is a paradoxical form of communication, but it is quite normal in handling interactive situations comprising a double-bind and requiring, simultaneously, a ritualistic form of communication which is 'supportive' of the symbolic order of gender, one that is 'restitutive' of the violation of that order and one that is 'resistant' to the domination that it expresses.

When we speak of 'doing gender' as an interactive activity, situationally and historically constructed, we are defining the rules and norms which regulate equal gender citizenship in a particular culture and therefore determine the amount of remedial work required – along a continuum ranging from gender 'play' (and playfulness) to the open conflict of the war between the sexes.

An organizational culture expresses the ceremonial work and the restitutive work implicit in doing gender and revealed by the most overt forms of remedial interchange: accounts, apologies and requests (Goffman, 1971).

In organizational life men and women are equally engaged, as Heritage writes (1984: 136), in 'descriptive accountings of states of affairs to one another'. Gender is an implicit variable here because an evaluation of a matter changes according to whether the subject and the other protagonists are men or women. Accounts fix the rules of gender fairness, they approve or censure the behaviour of differently gendered people, they socially construct the male and the female of the organization, and they remove the ambiguity from ambiguous situations. The gossip or light conversation or humour, which often address the theme of sexuality, offer excellent access routes to the gender codes of an office culture because they contain both suggestions on how to make correct representation of one's gender membership and instructions on how to save face when this membership is offended.

Within the various forms of sociability in an organization, when both men and women are present, it is very often the task of the women to develop communicative competence in male discourse, to take responsibility for repairing the embarrassment caused by their 'diversity', and to make amends for the intrusiveness of their presence.

In managing interpersonal relations, women are generally more responsive than men to non-verbal cues (Henley and Freeman, 1979; Spender, 1980). They are expected to be more personable, to display more emotion and to contribute, constantly, to the power and status of others. Conventional femininity is a requirement of subordination and it is a strategy for what Goffman (1967) labelled 'impression management'.

Conversational analysts have pointed out that women use the interrogative form more frequently, and that this expressive genre can be linked to a remedial ritual taking the form of a request; that is, 'requesting permission to intrude' (Goffman, 1971: 115). There are many ways to request permission to intrude: 'Can I ask you something personal?' 'I'd just like to add something.'

Requests as remedial rituals indicate that 'the actor gives up his (her) autonomy in regard to deciding the matter; the recipient of the request retains his (or her) authority, it being assumed (s)he alone was the one to decide the matter' (Goffman, 1971: 114-15).

Female experiences of the woman as intruder, foreigner or fraud (McIntosh, 1984) may be read as breakdowns in the symbolic order of gender and as repair strategies and practices. Peggy McIntosh writes of 'feeling like a fraud' to describe the sensation when, in order to take part in public life, a person has assumed a disguise and is about to be unmasked. A gross error has been committed in the selection and accreditation of this person, and soon all will be revealed. These are feelings of non-belonging and of extraneousness; they are not exclusively female experiences, but they are made manifest when a woman takes the conversational initiative and apologizes for doing so, when she expresses her doubts as to the importance of what she is about to say, when she minimizes her competence to speak on the subject – that is, when she requests authorization, protection and benevolence.

I suggest that women's lack of an assertive style can be interpreted as a ritual which repairs the offence caused by the infringement of the symbolic order of gender when they speak. If we employ the metaphor of territory to analyse gender relationships, we note that the dual presence is handled by asking permission to trespass on someone else's territory, by giving justifications for doing so, and by apologizing for having done so, whenever women enter male domains: the public, production, conversation, and so on.

People entering work strike a bargain with the employer: they act *as if* they are exchanging their labour or services for remuneration, but they are making their bodies available for use in ways and for the period envisaged by the contract (Pateman, 1988). And jurisdiction over femininity and the female body differs in just the same way as forms of subordination differ according to the sex of the worker.

Also unequal between the sexes are the ethics and moral codes of professionalism. For example, the same behaviour may be socially condoned if the perpetrator is a man and socially condemned if it is a woman. One is reminded of the dual morality that used to regulate adultery. An example from my personal experience is the instrumental use of a network of persons made by a male colleague to enhance his visibility and to advance his career. This colleague joined the network and offered to organize a conference but then subsequently withdrew. The instrumentality of his action was clear to everyone, but since there was an even balance between what he had given to the collectivity and what he had taken, the affair was soon forgotten. When the same thing was done by a woman, it left behind a trail of resentment and mutual recriminations of exploitation and abandonment. The same double morality is manifest when a woman loses her temper in a meeting, is verbally aggressive, uses foul language, does not answer a call for help, and therefore does not display the gendered behaviour expected of her in the workplace. In other words, to do these things without having to pay the consequences, she must invent some negotiation strategy to remedy the offence given. The prescriptions of gender behaviour and virtue constrain both the sexes: those men who by character or conviction are less competitive, or who believe that the only true winner of the organizational game is the organization itself, often complain that they must defend themselves against colleagues who mistake their helpfulness for weakness.

In Figure 5.1 I have tried to sum up the dynamics that sustain the practice of doing gender. I have started from the assumption that the presence of women in the workplace breaks with the symbolic order of gender based on the separation between male and female, public and private, production and reproduction. The co-presence of the sexes in the spheres of the social gives greater ambiguity to gender-based social differentiation, and the way in which people handle the dual presence – and the dilemma between diversity and inequality – creates the space for a historic transformation of gender. In the first stage, gender is celebrated as

1st stage   Symbolic order of gender based on the separation of male and female

Action   Ceremonial work

Competence rule   Acknowledgement of gender as separatedness and univocality

2nd stage   Symbolic order of gender based on the dual presence

Action   Remedial work

Competence rule   Acknowledgement of gender as ambiguity and the discursive
                         construction of a situated meaning of gender

Figure 5.1   *The deferral of the symbolic order of gender*

a ritualization of separateness; in the second, the ambiguity of the dual presence is remedied – each ritual requires a specific competence rule.

Ceremonial work and remedial work are much more closely intermeshed than may have appeared from this necessarily brief discussion. And they are both finely balanced on a razor's edge, because men and women equally exploit their competence in managing the micro-politics of gender; both are concerned to ensure that the game continues, to save face, to experience reciprocal attraction and repulsion but also to gain the advantage. They are both caught in the gender trap, and in describing the competences required to manage the dual presence I have also implicitly illustrated some of the relational resources that are deployed in negotiating the contents of gender.

In the next section I intend to examine some of these resources more closely: hypocrisy as superficial adherence to equity values, irony as the destabilization of gender values, trust as the ability to change the frame from asymmetrical to reciprocal, embarrassment as a signal of a change in customs.

Hypocrisy, irony, trust, embarrassment

Our everyday morality is certainly not benevolent towards hypocrisy; even less does it consider hypocrisy a resource for change. And yet in recent years a number of organization scholars have lifted the prescriptive veil of ethics to show that organizations have good reasons not to condemn hypocrisy, and that an incoherence between values and actions may prove advantageous to them in the long run (Feldman and March, 1981; Brunsson, 1989).

One talks of hypocrisy in organizations to indicate a lack of coherence between what they say, the decisions they take and the actions they perform. Hypocrites are said not to practise what they preach: an expression which effectively conveys how discourse is used to conceal action, but which also presumes that discourse and action are not reciprocally influential. If instead we presume that, in the long term, declared values and actions will converge, then hypocrisy is a transitional stage towards coherence, a tactic of gradual approximation. Hypocrisy signals a contradiction between conscience and self-interest, and it is the 'assertion of a value as a symbolic substitute for action' (Feldman and March, 1981: 176).

When hypocrisy is framed as a symbolic substitute, it is perhaps possible to dispel the moral repugnance aroused by talk of hypocrisy, and look instead with amusement at how hypocrisy is a resource for changing gender relations.

Today, at least in Europe, organizations are forced to construct a façade which asserts their commitment to equal opportunities between men and women. European legislation prohibits discrimination on the one hand, and rewards those who apply policies promoting female 'human resources' on the other. The social and political climate obliges organizations to assume a public image of social responsibility. Part of this responsible and progressive aura is commitment to equal presence, to non-sexist language and to the hiring of women to fill non-traditional jobs. In Italy, for example, all municipal administrations have recently revised their statutes to introduce rules ensuring that the sex of job applicants is not specified, and that the female form is used to designate women's occupations or political appointments. Industrial relations in organizations have introduced forms of bargaining explicitly designed to affirm gender difference: equal opportunities commissions, opportunities counsellors, and contractual clauses explicitly in the interests of women. A recent example is an agreement reached at Zanussi (a large company producing domestic appliances, 85 per cent of whose workforce is female) which introduces a sexual harassment hotline in the company, as well as the self-organization of working time by three-member teams who together manage eighteen hours of work. An ingenuous observer might be led to believe that, given this legislative effort – local, national and communitarian – and the commitment of the mass media, major changes in gender relationships are now under way. A cynic would instead read the signals to predict a large-scale counter-reaction, what the Americans call a 'backlash'.

True hypocrites profess values which in part have been imposed on them, which in part they share, and which in part leave them indifferent. They take decisions in the name of those values and leave it to the inertia of routine action to dilute their consequences on courses of action. But it is not just attrition and depreciation in transition that brings values and actions into coherence; there is also an unexpected effect: the discovery of new opportunities or, if preferred, a self-fulfilling prophecy effect. The symbolic world is not static; it follows its own dynamics. The affirmation of certain values has opened the way for the few symbolic actions that those values represent (the various tokenisms). Thus alternative values and actions have been sustained which may have produced different insights and yielded new opportunities which, in their turn, have brought about greater commitment to pursuit of the initial course of action.

This is not an isolated and utopian case of innovation, since it is to be found in other instances of organizational change. For example, I came across similar dynamics when studying (Gherardi, 1985) one of the first Italian companies to introduce computer aided design. This technology had been purchased because the engineering company concerned had received major public financing for the purpose, and because it had a cultural tradition which always attributed great value to being the first Italian company to introduce technological innovations. Although the choice of the system was imitative and constrained by the amount of financing received, once it came on stream its advantages were realized, and the desire to believe in the advantages thus intuited laid bare the limitations of a foolhardy purchase. It is not new for those who study decisions to find that opportunities for action are discovered during the course of action, or are produced themselves by the process.

Hypocrisy may therefore ideologically cover experimentation with a course of action which few believe in, which is undertaken with little enthusiasm if not outright resistance, which begins already with the intention of shelving it as soon as possible. But we also know that intentions and results are often loosely coupled, and that the process itself of putting intentions into practice may lead to the discovery of new intentions or alter initial ones.

Faced with a strong ethical imperative for coherence between values and actions, the ambiguity of courses of action creates room for experimentation. There is no doubt that equal opportunity initiatives attempt to instrumentalize the female presence for the purposes of legitimation. But it also true that they have enabled many women to instrumentalize organizations in order to create spaces for other women and to combat the devaluation of the female. Hypocrisy is an ambiguous relation between values and behaviour, between vice and virtue. For example, a recurrent theme in the rhetoric of the female is the duplicity of women, their use of oblique methods to achieve their ends, their manipulative use of power, their indirectness in relationships, and so on. Indirect actions, which offend moral common sense, are inscribed in the code of dominance and subordination relationships. They are a form of resistance to the social control which expresses itself in the professing of façade values in order to maintain a certain freedom of action and of personal creativity. One may therefore ask how many women and men only superficially profess the traditional values of femaleness and maleness, and how many forms of resistance are raised in covert and private form. Doing gender has a prescriptive side to it, and expectations of coherent behaviour among the characteristics attributed to a sex are empirical evidence of it.

Behaving in a female manner and professing the values of femaleness makes it easier to manage the dual presence, leaving room to choose where, how and when to resort to open opposition rather than to covert resistance. War, guerrilla action and skirmishing require different settings and instruments and are not mutually exclusive.

Not least is the pleasure of the ambiguous relationship between individual discourses, decisions and actions, the allure of transgression. We transgress by ignoring the prescriptions of gender: by doing a typically male job, by not having children, by rejecting the trappings of femaleness in self-presentation. But we can also transgress by flouting transgressive models: by emphasizing our female appearance, by exploiting gender privileges, exploring gender as a game. Hypocrisy protects the explorer and the innovator by providing symbolic substitutes. Can hypocritical endorsement of gender relations create room for experimentation by people of different sexes jointly in search of solutions? Can it help them feel more at ease in their sexed bodies? If so, complicity may be a bond which reveals the contradictions between gender as we think and want it, and gender as we do it. Exposing contradictions without claiming to resolve them is the prerequisite for a Socratic attitude towards self-knowledge based on irony as its resource.

Irony as a metacommunicative resource, as an instrument of resistance, as a postmodern attitude, has undergone a renaissance in recent years (Derrida, 1971; Rorty, 1989; Ferguson, 1991) which I shall not elaborate on here but merely mention. My concern instead is to illustrate the pragmatics of irony; that is, the destabilization in gender arrangements that ironic discourse can produce. Irony, in fact, insinuates doubt. It suggests that the world can be described in different terms, but it does not propose these other terms as alternative, 'better', 'more correct', or 'truer'. Irony is a processual invitation; an invitation to consider how things (gender relationships, for example) can be redefined; how common sense can be problematized. Irony does not offer solutions; instead, it calls the linguistic games which produce a certain vision of the world into question.

Irony thus becomes a valuable resource when gender must be positioned within the relations between women and men; but it is less so when a description of a male-centred world is to be contrasted with a female-centred one (Flax, 1992). To give better specification of the attitude of the ironist, I draw on Rorty (1989) and begin with his concept of 'final vocabulary'; that is, the set of words that someone uses to justify her/his actions and beliefs, and to tell her/his life story. It is a 'final' vocabulary in the sense that 'if doubt is cast on the worth of these words, their user has no non-circular argumentative recourse' (Rorty, 1989: 73). And 'to be commonsensical is to take for granted that statements formulated in that final vocabulary suffice to describe the beliefs, actions and lives of those who employ alternative final vocabularies' (ibid.: 74).

Awareness of a choice between several vocabularies, of the contingency and fragility of each of them, of the historicity of affirmation of one rather than the other, of the non-neutrality of linguistic games, produces an ironist.

For Rorty (1989: 73), an ironist is someone who fulfils three conditions:

1. She has radical and continuing doubts about the final vocabulary she currently uses, because she has been impressed by other vocabularies; vocabularies taken as final by people or books she has encountered.
2. She realizes that argument phrased in her present vocabulary can neither underwrite nor dissolve these doubts.
3. Insofar as she philosophises about her situation, she does not think that her vocabulary is closer to reality than others, that it is in touch with a power not herself.

The ironist is therefore someone who has lost her innocence and is no longer able to believe in Truth and in the Real, because these are outcomes of discourse, and every discourse has its distinctive rules and procedures which govern the production of what counts as meaningful. Every discourse at the same time allows some possibilities and disallows others: the ironic touch stresses the possibility of switching from one discourse to another, of casting doubt on the rules and procedures which govern a discourse and the relations between language and people.

We are the products of a discourse while at the same time we produce discourses: our subjectivity is produced by the categories of female and male that operate beyond the individual's control. But we can introduce the instability of these categories into our discourses. We can play with them, try to see the world differently by changing positions, lay bare the power relations which tie us to a gender identity.

Of course, to convey an ironic message we must be self-ironic, we must also cast doubt on our own final vocabulary. That is to say, we must not take ourselves too seriously, and we must stop believing that we have direct access to the truth. This conflicts, for example, with that brand of feminism that asserts a truth principle – male domination – from which it derives a political consequence. Perhaps the political nature of irony is not as evident as a political programme, but it undermines the foundations of all power based on the monopoly of absolute truth. As all totalitarian regimes (discourses) well know, it is impossible to respect a power structure which makes you laugh.

Irony as a philosophical position consists of a Socratic discourse strategy in which the questioner interrogates her/his interlocutor while feigning inability to grasp the argument and in the pretence of being ignorant. The device consists of admitting a concealed contradiction as true and then subsequently revealing its falsity, so that the adversary falls victim of her/his presumed superior knowledge. Irony as a communicative frame raises doubts over the truth and seriousness of what is asserted. Irony may therefore be employed as an offensive or a defensive manoeuvre in interaction. Alternatively, there may be complementary irony in which contradictions are mocked and communication takes place between two ironic interlocutors. What makes the difference is the power relationship: in asymmetric relations, irony acts as a destabilizer; in symmetric relations, it may generate new relations based on the reciprocity and instability of the interlocutors' positioning of each other in the discourse. But this presupposes trust and that both men and women are interested in changing gender relationships; if not in all social relations at least those in the workplace.

Relationships between people of different sexes who work together have an interaction structure that is often absent from other types of inter-action. For example, most communications among co-workers are shaped by occupational roles, and they are binding. Reciprocal status is largely inscribed in a system of legitimized authority. Reciprocal knowledge is expected to be long-lasting, so that acknowledgement/display of gender identity need not be repeated at every encounter. As public settings, moreover, organizations provide women with a relatively safe physical arena: their presence has an explicit purpose which is not to be misunder-stood; their vulnerability and exposure should not be exploited; their accessibility should be unequivocal. Theoretically, there should be more room in organizations for the negotiation of the contents of gender relationships than in the private sphere. Yet in organizations too, institutional reflexivity imposes the classic asymmetric alignment of gender (Goffman, 1977). In the reciprocal positioning that occurs within discourse, those who assume a dominant alignment position themselves as superior and the other/others as inferior. For example, someone who speaks to others as if s/he was the teacher and they were the pupils, not only gives him/herself a one-up position and the others a one-down position, but the latter may also perceive this manner of address as condescending and pedantic. In conversation, we often find ourselves in asymmetric discourse positions, both because of structural conditions (for example, when hierarchical relations impose the frame give instructions/ receive instructions) and because of contingent ones (complementarity in conversational turn-taking, in giving/receiving information, in speaking/ listening). What creates problems is not the asymmetry but the fact that the asymmetry is based on male dominance and reflects the institutional arrangement of the sexes.

Certain of the frames that structure conversation also and automatically comprise a gender positioning. Of these, the protector/protected frame is paradigmatic. The colleague who tells me about a meeting I have missed positions himself as expert, as better informed, as in control of the situation. He portrays himself as privy to 'what is behind' official discourse, and by giving me his interpretation and his advice on how to behave, he is assigning me a female position. When I do the same to him, I am perceived as maternal, as assigning a filial position to the other.

The asymmetry of this situation seems to be sustained and perpetuated by the fact that women and men are socialized to different discourse strategies. This, according to Tannen (1991) inevitably gives rise to a symmetrical misunderstanding between the sexes. In communication, women seek intimacy with the other, connection and a sense of com-munity; their speech stabilizes and maintains the relation. Theirs is an orientation towards a symmetry of connection. Men instead seek status, they strive to assert their independence (because otherwise they reveal themselves as insecure and incompetent). Their speech presupposes and reaffirms an asymmetry. Under the hypothesis that communication between the sexes is cross-cultural communication, misunderstandings arise when the values of connection conflict with those of status.

Is the situation therefore irremediable? It might appear so if we assume the inevitable correspondence between women and the female discourse position on the one hand, and men and the male discourse position on the other. However, for all the sex-based differences discovered by linguists and conversational analysts in the use of language and in conversation, presupposing their asymmetry does not preclude the possibility that a discourse frame can be altered from asymmetrical to symmetrical.

In a symmetrical frame, positions are interchangeable. The reciprocity may be real or only potential, but the interlocutors have made a binding agreement on their parity of status. Reciprocity presupposes trust because the reciprocation may be deferred in time, and it simultaneously sets up an obligation. An asymmetrical discourse relation can be changed through a process of metacommunication; that is, cooperation is required to reframe the situation. For example, the protector/protected frame can be renegotiated in the same way as the give help/receive help frame which enables reciprocation by redefining the situation in terms less connoted by gender archetypes.

A relationship which has negotiated the symmetry of positions may comprise the trust required to detach the interlocutor's sexual identity from its discourse positioning, so that it may varyingly assume female or male positions without jeopardizing their credibility and gender competence. The reciprocity relationship entails a change of frame in the interactive relation, because the positions of the One and the Other are no longer defined as independence/dependence but as interdependence. Growing social differentiation has considerably increased social situations of interdependence between the sexes, compared with a simpler society in which the rigid sexual division of labour was matched by separate symbolic universes of gender. The dual presence instead envisages a new form of interdependence between the sexes engendered by a structural change in society to which corresponds a change in the psychic habitus.

I want at this point to return to Elias and the demise of the spittoon in order to discuss the role played by embarrassment in the management of those interactions that are not yet fully or univocally regulated by a new code of good manners in the relationships between the genders.

Elias maintains that changes in the psychic structure of the individual are produced by structural changes in society, and that it is the psychological functions that control actions which change over time. More specifically, civilization is driven by the specific dynamics of the relations among individuals in society and between the agencies constructed expressly to exercise external control over human behaviour and the forms of self-control exercised by individuals themselves. It is not necessary to go too far back in time to realize that a set of external restraints on the behaviour of individuals and organizations has been institutionalized in the form of prohibitions on sex-based discrimination, of equal opportunity legislation, of the cultural control of sexism in language and in socialization processes at school, in the family and in the workplace. Symptomatic of the change in the psychic habitus is the embarrassment that surrounds the management of those men/women interactions that are characterized by a double-bind.

Embarrassment is a social invention contingent upon the standards of civility and education historically in force (as the evolution of etiquette teaches us), and it is also an emotional state which functions as self-censorship. For a person to feel embarrassment, s/he must have developed the capacity to reflect on her/his behaviour. It is therefore a metacognitive emotional state which presupposes a language which allows identification and description of how that person behaves in public. Here too one notes that the concept of gender is a recent social acquisition, and that studies of gender have triggered a metacognitive dynamic by revealing and scrutinizing a set of behaviours which used to be taken for granted but which today are laden with negative emotive force. We have not yet reached the point of the disgust aroused by the spittoon, but the emotional dynamic that has been set in motion is moving in the same direction: from embarrassment, to shame, to a sense of guilt.

These forms of emotional cognition render people sensitive to distinctions of which they were previously largely unaware, and they induce them to develop forms of self-censorship of behaviour and of self-control of impulses.

Organizations, too, are susceptible to a feeling of shame, defined as the fear that one has failed to present a positive image of self and/or to obtain social esteem. Consider how affirmative actions have been portrayed and the rhetoric of persuasion that sustains them: the organization found it in its interest to construct an image of itself which included values of egalitarianism, emancipationism, the enhancement of human resources, and so on. In doing so, it seems to have been motivated more by an image strategy than by fear of legal sanctions.

I have emphasized the process of civilization as progressive social differentiation. Under the hypothesis that this corresponds to an analogous differentiation in the individual's psychic apparatus, we must enquire as to the place occupied by psychic identity in that individual's psychic economy. It is now increasingly common to speak of identity in the plural – that the idea of the unitariness of the ego has been superseded by that of the 'multiple self' (Elster, 1986; Fabbri and Formenti, 1991). The single and immutable ego is therefore an illusion, just as the belief that the ego was the seat of decision-making was an illusion. The ego appears instead to be a momentary aggregate, a social construct employed to describe the various states in which subjectivity manifests itself. Elster distinguishes among a number of such states: the weakly integrated ego, the self-deceptions of the ego, hierarchical egos, successive egos, parallel egos.

The image sustaining this multiplicity is that of a turbulent inner community formed by a set of personages pitted against one another in interminable conflict. Identification, therefore, is the process whereby we find our object-investment in various situations and guises under constant threat of disaggregation (Demetrio, 1994). The egos are always more than the weakened egos, as marked by multiple social memberships, by the social negotiation required to cope with the lack of integration of the various memberships – the ultimate expression of social complexity. The rethinking of the ego in psychoanalysis also displays the same pattern of transformation: 'the psychic structure is polycentric. It is a field of many lights, dazzling flashes, eyes, its energy is distributed' (Hillman, 1985: 30).

Thus the metaphor of dramaturgy so dear to Goffman's sociology moves back to centre stage and with it, emphatically, the idea of the presentation of self not as an end in itself but as constitutive and formative of interaction. If, in fact, in the egoic theatre the various egos arise at the moment in which impulsive needs emerge, the ego is the expression of a relation or a connection, not of a substantive entity. All that remains of the idea of a subjective entity is the purely corporeal and physical datum. And it is a datum of no little consequence. We may in fact hypothesize that this differently sexed body continues to perform an important organizational role in the multiple egos and in social memberships; but it will not always stand in the foreground, not always will it colour the climate of social situations.

Emotional rationality

My foregoing examination of how gender is produced in social situations has highlighted its ideological character and the manner in which it reproduces and legitimizes the choices and restraints that derive from attribution to a sexual category. Social control over the structures and institutions that reproduce gender relationships is based essentially on the devalorization of the female. If the female and the male did not stand in a hierarchical relationship, if men and women were wholly interchangeable, what need would there be for two different social statuses? At the level of interaction, gender presupposes sexed bodies; and we have seen that through metacommunication it is possible simultaneously to negotiate the unfolding of gender identity and the inequality relationship that rigid gender constraints construct around it.

Could or does the calling into question of rationality in all spheres of knowledge create the conditions for the emergence of an organizing principle based on emotionality? Could a valorization of emotionality come about in our society, given the female connotations that attach to it?

If organizations were less rational and more emotional, would the relationship between the genders be different? These are questions which require us to look more closely at the place of emotionality in organizations – meaning by this term both the emotions in the strict sense, feelings, and more in general the knowledge produced by the normative-affective dimension of action.

Let us start with a feminist critique that deconstructs the concept of bounded rationality by contrasting it with that of bounded emotionality. With this concept, Mumby and Putnam delineate 'an alternative mode of organizing in which nurturance, caring, community, supportiveness and interrelatedness are fused with individual responsibility to shape organizational experiences' (Mumby and Putnam, 1992: 474).

What I like most about the contrast between the two concepts – as they are used here – is the different meanings assumed by the term 'bounded'. Bounded rationality places the stress on limitation, on a connection which imposes closure, whereas bounded emotionality involves the creation of a link, of establishing a connection. Mumby and Putnam say that 'individualizing is joined with relatedness' whereas, classically, the process of individualization was based more on separation than on the creation of new/different links.

Comparison between the two concepts (Figure 5.2) shows that limitations derive, for example, from commitment or responsiveness to others and not from abstract organizational rules, just as tolerance may be shown towards ambiguity instead of resistance by giving greater rigidity to the system. Thus, instead of a hierarchical chain of means and ends, a plurality of values not necessarily hierarchized according to a single criterion can be considered, thereby overcoming the fragmentation of both work and of the individual.

Finally, in the bottom row of the table, Mumby and Putnam contrast feeling rules based on the organizational control of the emotions with feeling rules that emerge spontaneously in social and workplace interactions.

This, in my view, is the weak point in their analysis. In contrasting what they call, following Hochschild (1979, 1983), emotional labour – that is, the organizational control of the feelings placed entirely at the disposal of the work task (the smile fixed on the face of the air hostess together with her make-up, as in Ferguson's (1984) example) – with the feelings that arise from spontaneous relations, Mumby and Putnam indirectly confirm the rationalist assumption that there is no place for feelings in the organization, precisely because feelings cannot be prescribed. Prescribed feelings of human warmth remind one of the paradoxical injunction of Watzlawick *et al.* (1967): be spontaneous! The commodification of feelings is somewhat alien to the fact that the feelings, or better the emotional structures, have an independent life of their own and cannot be engineered, even if they do not enter the discourse of either the organization or organization scholars.

Bounded rationality	Bounded emotionality
Organizational limitations	Intersubjective limitations
Reduction of ambiguity	Tolerance of ambiguity through satisfying
Hierarchy means–end chain	Heterarchy of goals and values
Mind–body dualism	Integrated self-identity
Fragmented labour	Community
Gendered and occupational feeling rules	Relational feeling rules

Figure 5.2 *A comparison between bounded rationality and bounded emotionality*

Source: Mumby and Putnam, 1992: 474

The official rhetoric of the organization attempts to persuade its members to control their feelings: it exhorts them to decide without being influenced by the passions, it prescribes bureaucratic impartiality, and it demands smiles and flattery when they interact with customers. But the effects of this rhetoric on actual behaviour may be very surprising and they may distort the intentions of whoever enunciated such principles.

When I was researching blue-collar communities, I was taught a simple rule for interpreting managerial discourse which I confess I still semi-consciously adopt. This is the 'rule of systematic distrust' and it runs as follows: they (managers) never do anything or say anything for free; if they say something then they have good reasons for doing so. This pragmatic rule of mine brought out the hidden subtext in official pronouncements and revealed their underlying power relations. The workers equally resisted attempts both to rationalize and to commodify feelings. Organizational discourses laid bare the difficulty of dominating the desire for rationality as much as the desire for expressiveness.

I give a brief example of what I mean by the impossibility of prescribing feelings by recounting an episode which involved me personally. I should point out first that I have for some time been concerned about the fashion for what I call, for brevity's sake, 'the quality of service' – a slogan which translates into the training of contact personnel in the 'personalization' of their relationships with customers: using their first names, sending them birthday greetings, enquiring after their health, and so on. The ethical implications of this invasion of privacy and commodification of the warmth of human relationships leave me almost nostalgic for the Weberian bureaucrat. Dogged by this suspicion that the client is being manipulated, I verbally assaulted a person, a hotel receptionist, who was instead being spontaneously polite. I had arrived in the hotel to teach a course to trade unionists and I was irritated because the car park was full and I was late. When I had registered, the young receptionist gave me my key and wished me 'Happy name-day'. She was surprised by the abrupt tone with which I asked 'And how would you know?' instead of returning her smile. I had imagined a Big Brother computer program which signalled all the customers' private information to the front desk. In actual fact, the girl had the same name as mine and told me that at home everyone forgot her name-day because it did not correspond to a saint as popular as those of her brothers and sisters. I felt extremely embarrassed, but I believe that this episode is symptomatic of what will happen to all those organizations which are now investing in plastic sentiments that could, instead, rebound on them with a sort of boomerang effect.

One may therefore legitimately suspect that emotionality is now undergoing a process of defeminization with the intention of ascribing it greater legitimacy. Symptomatic is the recent interest shown by organization studies in this topic (Lutz and White, 1986; Sutton and Rafaeli, 1988; Franks and McCarty, 1989; Rafaeli and Sutton, 1987, 1989; Van Maanen and Kunda, 1989; Sandelands and Buckner, 1989; Sutton, 1991; Fineman, 1993); an interest which also stems from the cultural approach to organizations. Although this literature is still rather meagre, it reveals a common preoccupation with the control of the emotions and the organizational regulation of feelings. Feelings seem to arouse fear even among those who study them, and when the organization is studied it is often from the point of view of control, without examining the hypothesis that the emotions can be controlled and it is they that give form to the control itself.

The preoccupation of scholars with control over emotions originates from the manner in which the emotions symbolize an inner state of the subject which is closer to physiology than cognition. This has had profound repercussions on how to study the emotions and on which scientific discipline should study them. The opposition between reason and emotion is based on the hypothesis that affect and cognition are independent processes. The image currently associated with emotion is that of a disorganized response which interferes with the efficient functioning of reason and action. Early psychologists distinguished between intellect, will and emotion. For the latter they employed the vocabulary of the things that happen, as if the person who felt emotions was the passive victim, a prey to alien forces like hate, love, rage or fear.

A different conceptualization of the emotions arises if one changes the ontological referent and passes from the question 'What are the emotions?' to 'In what situations and in what ways can the emotions be considered acquired responses, determined by socio-cultural prescriptions and behaviour?' This is the perspective adopted by social constructionism (Averill, 1980; Harré, 1986; Sarbin, 1986), which profoundly innovates the field of research because it shifts attention from the subject's inner states to the social and situational context, to the learning of the language of emotions, to the cultural variability of the emotions and of their expression, to the social functions of emotions.

This is also a promising perspective for organization studies should they wish to study, not a purported cold and abstract rationality which identifies the emotions with the devil, but an emotional rationality where reason is coloured by sentiment and is part of everyday reasonableness.

In order to heighten the awareness of reason, theoreticians of the social construction of the emotions offer a number of key concepts:

- First, a methodological pointer: the meaning of an emotion lies primarily within the socio-cultural system (Averill, 1980). The emotions are constituted and prescribed in order to buttress cultural systems of beliefs and values.
- The emotions have socio-cultural content in the sense that they adapt to social contexts and regulate cognition and behaviour. There are justified and unjustified, appropriate and inappropriate emotions. An emotion is an integrated response which commits agents to moral values and rules (Armon-Jones, 1986).
- Emotions are transitory social roles, institutionalized ways of interpreting and responding to particular kinds of situations (Sarbin, 1986). Just as Othello is the jealous husband, other roles of pain, of deserved success, of envy or of defeat have emotive prescriptions of a duration, intensity and complexity in relation to the social position, gender and age of the agent.

I provide an example of the relationship between occupational culture and the structuring of work feelings, my thesis being that it is the emotions which create the meaning of work. I shall compare two offices belonging to the same organization – a university – which perform routine administrative and secretarial work. These two offices are both headed by a woman, and they are staffed by a small number of workers (four women, and eight men and women) with different job classifications. I shall call the first Pinkland and the second Greyland.

At Pinkland, the head was an Artemis who had her office at the end of a large room containing four desks arranged symmetrically, and separated from the public by a high counter surmounted by a glass screen stretching right across the room. Although the office was only open to the public (the university teaching staff) at specific times, the fact that these times were not respected did not particularly bother the work group. The office head and the secretarial staff had established close personal ties and a bureaucratic counter-culture. The values of the group can be summed up in the following two rules: we must be irreproachable towards the outside (do a good job, do not give anyone reason to complain, show ourselves to be firm and competent); towards the inside make sure that you are comfortable. 'Doing a good job and doing it the way we want' could stand as the motto for their culture. They ignored official job classifications and had divided work tasks among themselves according to individual preferences. A particularly vivacious secretary preferred to handle a certain type of paperwork because otherwise she would have been bored and time would have hung heavy. Another preferred typing and more routine work, even though she had a higher job classification, because they gave her time to think. The sense of well-being in the group was a collective achievement which symbolically mediated between thought and action. The moment of symbolic mediation came twice a day when the workers arrived in the morning and when they resumed work after lunch. At these times the head paused to chat with her staff, and it was clear to everyone that this was a sort of 'time out' of idle gossip, relaxation, and enjoyment of the sense of well-being. It was the production and consumption of well-being that took place at these moments, and complaints about work were implicitly banned. Indeed, work was never mentioned, because the understanding was that 'work' was the time spent in the office and which everyone tried to pass as enjoyably as possible.

The climate in Greyland was different. The office head was an Athena who was responsible for the office although her job classification was lower than that of some members of her staff. She was a young unmarried woman with a strong sense of loyalty towards the administration and she regarded bureaucracy as a set of rules which must be respected without question. She ran a service which was hampered by the pressure applied by the users (students) during the three hours a day when the front desk was open to the public. She often had to cope with the problem of asking staff to do overtime, and she openly complained about the fact that the work group consisted solely of women who had family responsibilities and were therefore uninterested in their work and resisted overtime. The office-workers defined their work as bureaucratic and catering to an irksome clientele. All of them took turns at the front desk, and they were highly professional in their work performance because politeness raised an aura of defence against the user and of respect for the sanctity of rules and procedures. However, the hours spent at the front desk built up negative feelings, and in the afternoon conversation was often devoted to descriptions of emotional burn-out. They also felt themselves to be judged negatively by a boss who did not trust them, and they felt they were being watched.

The moment of symbolic mediation came when the manageress tried to find someone to do overtime or to help her remedy an error committed by the office and pointed out by someone else in the university administration. It was especially the overtime problem that provoked collective complaints over the work, its lack of organization and bureaucracy. When the front desk was closed, the office became a place where the workers could unload their grievances, but the socialization of negative feelings led to enduring discontent, not to emotional recharging. Many had left or would have liked to leave the office and, as a sort of self-fulfilling prophecy, the personnel office sent the 'more bureaucratic' persons available to it because of a generic feeling that its work was highly bureaucratic.

Pinkland and Greyland had very different emotional climates, and it was these that gave different meanings to work tasks that, from an objective point of view, were equally routine, boring and repetitive. The emotions make the work, and occupational groups elaborate their feeling rules in the presence or absence of rules of emotional control imposed by the organization, they establish collective programmes which represent their 'know-how' on how to cope with strongly emotional situations (by excess or by default), and they identify a class of emotion elicitors which they classify using a specific vocabulary. Study of emotions in stable groups of people working together sheds light on the language of the emotions because it enables analysis of local vocabularies and the dynamics of their creation.

The vocabularies used in Pinkland and Greyland to express work feelings differed because they were specialized in the description of different feelings. To give an idea of the fundamental modalities of the emotions, in Pinkland the vocabulary of happiness comprised expressions centred on the experience of relaxation (to gratify, to satisfy, to amuse), that of sadness had connotations of depression and affliction, fear those of agitation (to preoccupy, to worry, to alarm), anger those of irritation (to annoy, to rile, to enrage, to hassle), and disgust those of unpleasantness (being bothersome, repellent, offensive, irksome). At Greyland the vocabulary of happiness was more exalted and had connotations of seduction (to interest, to entice, to attract, to enrapture), sadness those of demoralization (to depress, to sadden, to offend, to hurt), fear those of intimidation (to appal, to frighten, to terrify), anger those of exasperation (to infuriate, to annoy, to exasperate, to jolt), and disgust those of being odious (distasteful, ignoble, shocking).

These two vocabularies display diverse contents deriving from emotional states associated with conventionally regulated patterns of emotional behaviour. Let us analyse them from the point of view of the emotional state described and expressed in situational scripts. Both Pinkland and Greyland speak of 'happiness'. In the former case this emotion is manifest in a context in which people are the active agents of relaxation, gratification, satisfaction, amusement. Pinkland follows a behavioural script to produce this state of mind. The vocabulary of happiness at Greyland has more marked overtones because it denotes a desired state. It expresses an expectation which is rarely fulfilled. People passively wait to be seduced, intrigued, interested or attracted, while the situational script for emotional states is anger and its socialization through the stable definition of the situation as distasteful. The logical consequence of this model of emotional behaviour is that people extol life outside work as endowed with sense, while every request for increased overtime serves to prolong the torture. This strategy was adopted both by the women, who in fact did not complain of particularly onerous family responsibilities, and by the men. The difference was that the women were offended by their boss's lack of sympathy towards them and consequently stiffened their resistance.

The gravity of these negative states of mind emerges clearly from comparison between the vocabularies used in Pinkland and Greyland to describe situations of fear or sadness. The inhabitants of Pinkland talked about 'worry' or 'alarm'; those of Greyland were 'appalled', 'frightened', 'terrified'. In the former case depression was an affliction, in the latter it was demoralization.

And yet the two work contexts were not dissimilar to the extent that work in the one can be described as 'gratifying' and in the other as 'alienating'. The people concerned instead expressed these sentiments because the circumstances authorized them to do so. In Pinkland and Greyland a 'positive' or 'negative' attitude to work was adequate emotional behaviour because a set of emotions had been codified and sustained by explicit social practices which had been assigned prescriptive value in order to maintain the occupational community that had generated them and which, through them, expressed its moral order. In other words, the emotions appropriate to Pinkland and Greyland were transmitted and maintained through a process of social learning. The 'spontaneous' emotional response of a member of Greyland or Pinkland in the appropriate situation signalled that the values associated with that emotion had become the constitutive patrimony of its social identity. A clearer idea of the process can be gained by imagining the reactions and expectations of a worker transferred from Pinkland to Greyland, and vice versa. Probably the transferee from Pinkland, on finishing her spell at the counter, would expect to release her tension by 'chatting' with her colleagues and relaxing after the toughest hours of the working day. The transferee from Greyland would instead wait until there were no indiscreet ears in the office before she complained about the public, about its idiotic demands, and about moronic bureaucracy. In their socialized form, emotions have a non-natural content and function because they reflect and sustain the (religious, moral or political) beliefs, interests and values of a community. They confer an affective meaning on abstract rules, and the sentiment with which a moral is transmitted demonstrates the sincerity of the subject and not just the significance and importance of the rule (Armon-Jones, 1986).

Occupational communities exercise control over the appropriateness of the emotional responses of their members, over the evaluation of emotional objects, and over emotional behaviour. The four classes of rules described by Averill (1982) in relation to rage and subsequently generalized can be transferred to the organizational setting as the rules elaborated by communities to regulate emotionality:

1. *Evaluation rules* concern the way a situation is perceived and assessed. Evaluations determine the intentional object of the emotion – for example the object of anger is the vendetta waged to right a wrong – which is part of an emotional syndrome, a meaning imposed by events.

2. *Behaviour rules* regulate the way an emotion is organized and expressed. These are implicit rules which separate the appropriate expression of feelings from sentimentality and emotional coldness.

3. *Prognosis rules* regard the time-course and progression of an emotional episode. Whereas some emotions are short-lived (e.g. shock), others develop through various stages (e.g. distress). In an organizational setting, conflict between an underling and a supervisor, for example, may assume the harsh tones of rage, but there are social expectations of its 'natural' sequence which vary according to situational factors. If the appropriate sequence is not followed, the authenticity of the emotion is doubted and hidden motives are looked for.
4. *Attribution rules* relate to the way in which an emotion is explained and legitimized. These rules arrange the estimated object, behaviour and prognosis into a meaningful whole.

Routine work in bureaucratic organizations may arouse very diverse emotions and feelings in different occupational communities, as in the case just described. These emotions are socially constructed and they follow their own logic. They establish subjectively rational patterns of behaviour in situations where objective rationality – with its assumption that all rational subjects will behave in the same way – is a pure and irrelevant abstraction.

My argument is that feelings are at home in organizations. Indeed, the true glue of organizations is the emotional structures that map out invisible walls and corridors according to the positive and negative feelings that tie people together. I feel uneasy when I read articles by colleagues who seek to show 'the ugly face of organizations', because although in many respects the destructiveness of the organization is its dominant characteristic, in several others organizations are places in which people undergo significant life-experiences: they feel joy, exaltation, enjoyment, play, friendship, and so on. I personally prefer to stress that the members of organizations use their creativity to develop resistance strategies and to assert their primary human nature even though they are at work; that is, even though they operate within a context of constraints which does not address attention to those constraints and to the intuitions that underlie them.

From my point of view, emotionality as an organizing principle is a dynamic that enjoys full citizenship in the life of organizations but not legitimacy in the organizational discourses either of organizations or of those that study them, because emotionality belongs to the symbolic universe of the female and is therefore devalued. Doing gender consequently also entails revealing the hierarchy of values according to the gender criterion. Emotionality is omnipresent in organizational life; we should not ask wherein it lies, but rather how and why it has been hidden and systematically made invisible.

It was when I joined various occupational communities in a particular organization (Gherardi, 1990) that I discovered that work requires emotions and feelings for its execution, and that emotions and feelings require work for their maintenance. Being at work, getting things done, presupposes a whole range of activities which are only partially and imperfectly set out in job descriptions, in procedures, in work schedules; but what is described and contained therein is 'work' and is therefore prescribed and remunerated, while all that is intangibly 'done' to perform such work, all the self-organization required to circumvent organizational norms and to make them 'intelligent' is not seen and is often obstructed.

Work therefore involves two logics, one governing procedures and one governing relations; or better, all work is constituted by performative work (activities) and relational work (establishing and keeping open the channels of communication and relation through which activities are carried out). Even the work most closely tied to execution – such as that performed by a pair of assembly-line workers observed in my research (Gherardi, 1995) – presupposes relational work: in order to 'synchronize' oneself with one's workmate and to negotiate the work rate, in order to know when and how to call in the foreman, and which foremen to call and which to avoid, in order to give information and feedback to the team working upstream and to coordinate with those working downstream, and so on. Observation of secretaries at work reveals even more clearly the amount of time strictly devoted to office duties and the amount spent on maintaining good channels of communication with other offices. The difference in status and power, however, is evident, in that the relational work of the manager is called 'productive' while that of workers and secretaries is denied and negatively sanctioned.

Producing a social system requires undertaking activities and employing resources; resources which are mostly emotional.

Emotions are forms of communication both internal and external. The reception of these signals usually engenders behaviour (one's own or that of others) adjusted to the situation that has elicited them. To borrow a metaphor from ethology in order to locate the sources of emotion in organizations, we may say that the emotional life of these social 'mammals' hinges on four classes of important inanimate entity: the territory, nutritional and toxic elements (i.e. resources and losses), and threats. Within the species itself there are five main classes of individual: parental figures (caregivers), their offspring, workmates, competitors and cooperators, while there are two important classes of other species: predators and prey (Johnson-Laird and Oatley, 1988).

Aggressiveness and submission, sexual rivalry, social dominance and the protection of the territory, cooperation for sustenance, anger and fear in coping with hazards, sadness over loss, happiness at success, disgust – these are all emotional states which I have ironically ascribed to a non-human society but which are also present in organizational life and may provide both the key to interpretation of the dynamics of survival and 'territorial' defence, and a guide to action and choices oriented more by affect than by rationality.

It would be superfluous to insist again that organizational life is coloured by the emotions. What I wish instead to stress is that emotional life gives rise (or does not) to organizational activities. One single example will suffice: many forms of cooperation, from mutual help among colleagues, to scientific collaboration, to voluntary associations, to company mergers are often born from (or are impeded by) affective affinities and bonds among people. But organizational cultures also possess dynamics and mental schemata with which emotional experience is ordered and conveyed to the outside world in the form of artefacts. Study of this dimension of organizational culture has been conducted principally by Gagliardi (1990), who proposes a reading of organization culture framed not only by Logos and Ethos but also by the 'sensory and aesthetic element – the Pathos'. An organizational culture, in fact contains those

> sensory maps which become active in the interaction between our senses and the artifacts of the organization in which we live, belong to what has been termed the 'knowledge by clue' which rises out of concrete and sensory experience and relies on subtleties not formalizable and often ineffable. (Gagliardi, 1990: 20)

An organization's culture therefore expresses how its members feel, and it also socializes them into feeling and perceiving in a given way: not only reason but sentiment are the links between thought, choice and action. Aesthetic understanding of an organization, therefore, concerns the way in which an organizational culture codifies its taste-judgement of sensory experience, and it also provides researchers with understanding/knowledge about their object of study (Strati, 1992b).

The pathos of an organizational culture therefore expresses the link between the sensual dimension of experience and its cognitive dimension, and between these and action. Let us examine this latter link.

We have seen that the execution of any form of work also requires relational work based principally on the intelligence of the sentiments (Witkin, 1974) and the capacity to relate. But not all jobs have the same emotional charge, and not all occupational/organizational cultures develop elaborate codes for handling emotional life. I cite two examples in support of the thesis that emotionality is an organizing principle.

The first concerns the elaboration of deontological codes by occupational communities exposed to the distress, the pain, the aggressive behaviour of their users and over whom they often exert a form of social control while providing help. I am referring here to social workers, health workers, the police, and similar occupational categories. Their organizations may indeed prescribe empathy towards the user and commodify human warmth, but in contrast to the airline companies which require their hostesses to smile, they are much more concerned with emotional burn-out among their employees: their emotional stamina is an organizational problem and it is sustained by special structures and procedures. It is the work group itself, however, which devises the rules that establish the 'correct distance' *vis-à-vis* users, which socializes its members into methods and stratagems to keep them at arm's length, which uses humour, anecdotes and ritualization to help its members cope with painful experiences (Strati, 1986; Gabriel, 1991).

Occupational communities of this kind frequently possess principles of internal organization which tend either to annul or to minimize hierarchical distances. They use, that is, a principle of competence rather than of authority; they adopt a system of diffused leadership in which their members not only alternate as leaders but act both operationally and emotionally as such. The members' professional and private lives tend to merge, in the sense that they are often friends outside work and that the individual's private life is nurtured by the others. Cooperation and solidarity are recognized as positive values which must be respected when action is urged in their name.

When I teach training courses to social workers I often see reproduced in the classroom attributes which have by now become professional skills: the ability to listen, help for the individual in difficulty, all-channel communication. I ask myself whether the habituation and socialization to work within care structures can help those abilities that common sense attributes to the female to spread. Moreover, although there is a balanced distribution of care workers by sex, this type of work and organization is considered female and is, in fact, organized more by emotional rationality.

The second example concerns organizations which are voluntary in nature and whose members have joined mainly for emotional and ideological reasons; organizations which may be interest associations, non-profit associations with a large number of volunteer members, clubs, or similar.

The value premises of these kinds of organizations are the criteria governing the formulation and selection of strategies: the emotional propensity to internal democracy gives rise to forms of work organization predicated on egalitarianism, community, mutual support. In trade unions, for example, tensions among the various categories and their attempts to break away are resolved by appeals to solidarity, by the all-encompassing idea of a union which represents workers, or even workers and non-workers; a 'trade union of rights', as the CGIL in Italy defines itself.

Several studies have been made of feminist organizations and of the features of female organizing. Their principal findings chime with those advanced here, which for brevity's sake I have called 'bounded emotionality'. On the basis of my own experience I would not attribute these features solely to the presence of women, since I have found the same pattern in many other democratic organizations. In my view, it is these organizations' need for integration that, by using emotional commitment to the organization's ideals as leverage, enables them to rely solely on instruments of control based on emotionality and culture. The prevention and punishment of opportunistic behaviour, for example, is only possible by means of third-degree control (Perrow, 1972); that is, by means of control exerted by operating on the ideological premises of action.

Put in other words: if care, nurturance, community, supportiveness and interrelatedness are part of the value premises of an organization, do we have organizing principles and criteria for action choice based on emotionality? And again, if it is true that the dominant principles of the most recent organizational philosophy are the simplification of structures, flattening of the hierarchy, a culture of quality (i.e. the unifying of the planning and execution of work), strategies of cooperation among organizations rather than of competition, networking skills within and across organizational boundaries, integration through culture, then has emotionality been recognized as a productive force and has it now been incorporated into the official vocabulary?

If the answer to these questions is 'yes', then, say Calás and Smircich (1993: 73), we will not have long to wait before this kind of advertisement starts to appear in the press:

HELP WANTED

Seeking transforming manager. Impatient with rituals and symbols of hierarchy. Favors strengthening networks and interrelationships, connecting with co-workers, customers, suppliers. Not afraid to draw on personal, private experience when dealing in the public realm. Not hung up by a 'What's in it for me?' attitude. Focuses on the whole not only the bottom line; shows concern for the wider needs of the community. If 'managing by caring and nurturing' is your credo, you may be exactly what we need. Excellent salary and benefits, including child care and parental lives.

Contact: CORPORATE AMERICA
FAX: 1–800–INTRUBL
An Equal Opportunity Employer
We do not discriminate on the basis of sex,
race, disabilities, or sexual orientation.

Should we be pleased? The so-called 'feminine-in-management' literature says we should, and so do the great gurus (men) of business. But Calás and Smircich go on to reveal the process well known in certain sectors of activity: when occupations are 'feminized', their status and market value decline. This process is accompanied by the globalization of the economy, so that as men move on to the supra-national stage 'to serve with pride and distinction', women will 'extend the household up to the national border' and provide 'carefully done, high-quality, cheap work, performed by docile workers' (Calás and Smircich, 1993: 77, 78).

The rhetoric of the female conducted within patriarchal discourse does not change the definition of women as the second sex. It simply per-petuates the power structure based on sex. However, the same discourse repeated is never the same discourse. In my view, the ambiguity inherent in the tension between apparent valorization and subsequent devalorization generates a dynamic of cultural change. Hypocrisy creates room for the negotiation of the power relationships between the sexes and of the meanings of gender precisely in those areas where values become loosely coupled with actions. Changes in social relationships between the sexes, the constant redefining of the realms of private and public, lead to a redrafting of codes of behaviour and to a remodelling of the individual and societal psychic structure. Like the disappearance of the spittoon, that of the process of second-sexing the female will be lengthy and contorted, but the tension between symbolic universes that express diversity and the social relations that on this diversity build inequality is dynamically productive of civilization.

6
Gender Citizenship in Organizations

'So I observed,' said Hewet. 'There is a thing that never ceased to amaze me. . . . The respect that women, even well-educated women, have for men,' he went on. 'I believe we must have the sort of power over you that we are said to have over horses. They see us three times as big as we are or they'd never obey us. For that very reason, I'm inclined to doubt that you'll ever do anything even when you have the vote.' (Woolf, 1978: 212)

This conversation, obviously, takes place between a man, Hewet, and a woman, Rachel, at the beginning of this century when the vote for women was a social issue and a symbol of citizenship. Virginia Woolf belonged to the Bloomsbury Group, which, in the Victorian age, attacked the ruling order for its militarism, its repressive colonialism, its uncontrolled capitalism, its sexual inequalities, the rigidity of its customs, its hypocrisies, and its philistinism (Williams, 1981). The Bloomsbury Group envisioned a more civilized order brought about by the removal of absurd restrictions for people to live in freedom. However, although the group identified a source of social inequality in gender, they ignored the paradox that the removal of restrictions (for example reform of the educational system) would have been to the sole benefit of men, since the large majority of women fell outside the system. The Bloomsbury Group personifies a utopian dream of universalist social democracy which believes in reform as the instrument of social change but is still unaware of the paradoxes that this may generate.

The law both assimilates social change and is an instrument of social change – this we know from history – but how can the horses' point of view be changed? Are horses able to grasp sexual difference? Will they cut men down to size? The parallelism between women and horses proposes the symbolic relation of domination: the horse (and every other mount of mythology) represents the dominated inferior being; it symbolizes the instinctive forces dominated by the spirit (the horseman). The horse as a vehicle is a symbol of the body, and those who maintain and dominate their mounts belong to the spiritual cavalry and also to chivalry understood as a historic social order. In what capacity do the dominated, horses or women, participate in the same social order?

Only twenty years ago, while a respectable cavalry major was teaching me to ride he repeated the same old cliché: 'Horses and women should be treated with an iron fist in a velvet glove.' I suspect that the velvet glove is represented by the granting of formal rights; but are we sure that the iron fist has not been changed in the process, that it is has not grown rusty?

The extension in recent decades of the sphere of rights connected, directly or indirectly, with the condition of women in society is undoubtedly of great social and cultural importance. And the changes which, at least in Europe, have been made to labour law have had a major impact on the organization and on the organizational culture of so-called everyday rights. But it is not at the level of the law and the *de facto* change induced by it that I wish to proceed; I shall concentrate instead on cultural and symbolic change in the social construction of gender within organizations that has progressed in parallel. To do so, I shall explore a metaphor – gender citizenship – in order to show how gender can assume different connotations internally to an organizational culture, and generate a multiplicity of courses of action. My aim is to have 'gender' recognized as a social relation, instead of being denied by supposed gender neutrality.

I have chosen the concept of citizenship principally because of its strong symbolic value as a complex of meanings handed down to us by previous generations. These meanings have undergone a process of transformation, and this transformation has been institutionalized. The analogy with gender should be clear.

My second reason for choosing citizenship is that it provides common terrain for broader debate encompassing the condition of postmodernity and the demands for affirmation by various diversities. This sets up the interesting paradox where the concept of citizenship suggests a common identity even though many citizens are excluded from it or wish to differentiate themselves from it. Citizenship is the sign of membership, of 'sameness' rather than of diversity, and it generates further paradoxes and ambiguities when we interrogate ourselves on the presence/absence of women as title-holders of citizenship.

Feminist political scientists (Sapiro, 1981; Diamond and Hartsock, 1981; Zincone, 1984, 1992; Jones, 1990) have conducted rich debate on the ambiguity of the concept, and certain contributions to this debate will be drawn upon here, although my principal concern is to explore the metaphorical force of the concept when it is transported to a more restricted setting, from the state to the organization. As a further case of institutional reflexivity, current debate on citizenship can also be transferred into organizations. In both cases the leitmotif is the same: difference and how to accommodate the models of universality and particularity in thought and action. 'Equal and different' has been a feminist slogan which one can use to indicate many other diversities, but the same problem. The practices of citizenship have helped to change the concept of citizenship into tolerance for diversity and ambiguity; and the jurisdiction is both accepting these deferrals of meaning and actively diffusing them through its normative action. Thus, today, one may justifiably talk of gender citizenship as women's right to be equal and different, and as a universal right (of women and men as well) to be released from the prison of gender.

In the literature of organizational studies since Barnard (1938), examination has been conducted of the participation of the members of an organization in producing that common good known variously as organizational life, the culture of the workplace, the organizational climate, well-being (or the lack of it) and the material conditions of its production, the civilization of the workplace. Common to all these reflections is the notion that there is something more than economic exchange involved in the regulation of the individual/organization relation, and that it is constituted by a 'willingness to cooperate', by a pro-social form of behaviour, by an organizational commitment.

The concept of organizational citizenship behaviour (OCB) has been proposed by Bateman and Organ (1983) 'to denote those organizationally beneficial behaviours and gestures that can neither be enforced on the basis of formal role obligations nor elicited by contractual guarantee of recompense. OCB consists of informal contributions that participants can choose to proffer or withhold without regard to considerations of sanction or formal incentives.'

The literature has explored ways to develop OCB and has sought to identify its motivational base (Organ, 1990). My concern here is to suggest that there are several components of OCB which express the quality of gender citizenship within an organization.

Assessment of this proposal requires us to ask if and how gender citizenship can become part of a conception of 'civic virtue' and in what sense fairness in the gender relationships may be considered as 'organizationally beneficial behaviour'. One can straightforwardly answer the first question by saying that for civil society today the justification of social inequalities as 'natural' is repugnant, and that, since civil society condemns discrimination, the behaviour which endeavours to achieve substantive equality is therefore a civic virtue. Graham (1986) has argued that OCB logically comprises those behaviours which define civic virtue, and that the concept of citizenship entails an obligation to participate appropriately in the government of the common good, if I may anticipate the second point.

If the organization is the beneficiary of OCB, then it is necessary to specify what the organization is and what it is that organizational citizens cooperate over when they express a civil commitment. Obviously, if the term 'organizationally beneficial' is synonymous with 'managerial', the suspicion of manipulation and of an attempt to extort more effort for unilateral gain is legitimate. There is no doubt that organizations – as corporate bodies – have understood the benefits that derive from non-discriminatory behaviour and from commitment to equal opportunities. Indeed, the development of affirmative action programmes has pivoted on the image of the firm and on indirect benefits. What one fails to understand is why simple members of the organization, workmates, should commit themselves to behaviour designed to achieve gender citizenship when they do not stand to gain any benefit from it for themselves.

My proposal is to consider the expression 'organizationally beneficial' in terms of the social dimension of organizational life, of the organization as the social construction of a delimited sphere of civil society. Life-quality in this sphere of our social existence is a common good produced by all those involved in the process, and it is enjoyed or consumed by these same producers. The willingness to cooperate, therefore, takes as its goal the social construction of an environment which respects human dignity, favours the development of human characteristics, and enhances human well-being. The equity of exchange in asymmetric power relationships thus becomes of crucial importance; and so too does individual moral responsibility for the production of that common good which we call organizational life. Consequently, participating – as producer and beneficiary – in organizational cultures more or less respectful of differences (not only of gender differences but all of them), and more or less concerned to redress inequalities, makes a difference both for the individual and for a society which contains more or less fair organizations. Accordingly, the way in which one 'thinks' gender and 'does' gender within an organization is part of a civic discourse and is integral to the process of civilization. That which is socially fair in the social arrangements between the genders is historically produced by the social institutions, and one such social institution is the organization.

The concept of 'fairness' is crucial for understanding OCB. One of the principal conclusions of this line of thought is that willingness to engage in OCB depends on a perception of fair treatment by the organization. This entails an exchange which is both economic and social, and based on different ideas of fairness. Organ (1990) maintains that whereas fairness in economic exchange requires a specific quid for a particular quo, fairness in social exchange requires diffuse obligations which are vaguely defined in their nature, value, and temporal definition of benefits given and received. Social exchange 'requires only a sense that the relationship is based on "good faith" recognition of each other's contributions' (Organ, 1990: 63). Social exchange presupposes trust, reciprocity relations, interdependencies between the parties to it, connection. Fairness in the social exchange with the organization also entails appraisal of how gender relations have been constructed at the symbolic level in the imagination of the male and the female, and at the level of social practice in men/women relationships. It is, therefore, an appraisal of the symbolic order of gender.

Gender citizenship as civic discourse

Gender and citizenship have much more in common than appears at first sight. Both – as Scott (1986) and Saraceno (1989, 1991) suggest – are symbolic constructs that contain ambivalences, tensions and contradictions which express themselves in contradictory practices: the equality at the basis of equal opportunity practices conflicts with the inequality and difference between men and women, but also among men and among women; individualism contrasts with needs for solidarity; the value of independence and autonomy contrasts with needs for nurturing and therefore for dependence and interdependence.

Gender and citizenship are symbolically interwoven with the dichotomy between public and private: a public woman is she who grants public access to the supremely private dimension – sexuality; a public man is he who influences the collectivity, the man of power. The woman symbolizes the private domain, of nurture, of individuality, of difference and of specificity; the man symbolizes the public, the political, the rights and the citizenship that homogenize. Symbolically, therefore, women are non-citizens, second-class citizens, excluded by law, the embodiment of inequality and discrimination; at the same time, however, by practising the dual presence, women in the Western democracies, in the welfare state, are the principal actors in the interdependencies between private and social life (consider redistributive social policies), between institutions and individuals (consider nurturing and solidarity work) and between the suppliers of a service and its users.

The figure emblematic of all these interdependencies is the 'working mother', a term for which there is no corresponding 'working father'. The 'working mother', at the level of rights and of social meanings, is the social representation of the individual who has both social work and public responsibilities and responsibilities for family care. If the 'working mother' tries to shift the work involved in caring for children, the elderly, the family on to the collectivity, or if she questions the social division of labour in her family, then she is 'playing dirty', she is surreptitiously attempting to change the rules that govern the production of common goods. But the ambiguity of the construct 'working mother' goes further: according to whether it is framed by an egalitarian or traditional ideology of gender a different paradox arises. 'Working mothers' take part in organizational cultures in which they find their identity negated in the responsibility of nurture when an egalitarian gender regime cancels its difference, or negated in social responsibility when a traditional ideology of gender assigns the 'working mother' a priority role in the family. When an organizational culture 'thinks' in terms of egalitarian gender citizenship, it assumes that men and women have the same work behaviours. When it 'thinks' in terms of traditional gender citizenship, it presumes that there is a pattern of male working life and a female one, the job remaining equal. Consequently, there are two philosophies and two practices of human resource and career management.

So organizations too produce a culture of citizenship and not only reflect the conception of citizenship institutionalized in society. This, of course, is implicitly to accept the metaphor of organization as a democratic political system, and to acknowledge that every metaphor illuminates certain aspects of organization while leaving others obscure (Morgan, 1986). We should bear in mind, however, that the extension of the conception of citizenship from an exclusively political sphere to one of everyday rights is a historical process which has also affected the economic and productive spheres. Civil society demands democracy and citizenship in other areas apart from politics: the economy, the social, the private, and gender relationships.

I consider citizenship to be principally a practice; that is, a way of life pursued by people – inside and outside organizations – who share a historical context in which they contest the meaning of social or legal norms and struggle to define collective and individual identity. I shall develop this argument by examining how different conceptions of citizenship give rise to diverse organizational cultures, and how these cultures contain a plurality of conceptions of what is 'fair' in the relationships between the sexes.

Western thought has developed two principal conceptions of citizenship (Oldfield, 1990, 1991), and these have given rise to different definitions to the nature of individuals and to the social ties that exist among them *qua* citizens. On the one hand, there is the liberal or liberal-individualist conception of citizenship as status; on the other, the classical or civil-republican conception of citizenship as practice. The difference between the two can be summarized thus:

(a) The constitutive elements of citizenship as status are needs and rights. Individuals are sovereign and morally autonomous beings whose duty is to respect the analogous rights of other citizens, to pay their taxes, and to defend the state when it is threatened. They have no other obligations to society except those freely accepted by contract. Social ties are therefore contractual ties.

(b) Citizenship as practice is based on duties which individuals must fulfil if they are to be granted the status of citizens. Individuals are members of a community, and they are citizens because they not only respect the autonomy of others, but commit themselves to a socially defined practice. The social ties among individuals derive from the fact that they share and establish a life-system.

In the former case, individuals born in democratic countries need do nothing to become citizens because they are so by right, while in the latter case individuals prove themselves to be citizens by what they do. Action sustained by a mental attitude constitutes, in this latter case, citizenship, and it maintains a community whose members assume joint responsibility for its continuity and identity.

Translated into an organizational setting, this analogy prompts a crucial question: are the members of an organization such by virtue of a status created by a contract which sanctions rights and duties, or are they such by virtue of a practice of responsibility towards the community? Depending on the answer to this question, the problem of membership, of its role and of organizational boundaries assumes different connotations. And the individual/organization relationship, too, takes on a different meaning: Oldfield, like Rousseau before him, admits that the practice of citizenship is an unnatural practice, that it is the price to pay for entry into social life.

Citizenship	Gender citizenship
Citizenship as universality and as a legal construct	Gender citizenship as legal ratification
Citizenship as neutrality	Gender citizenship as permanent membership and cultural integration
Citizenship as communality and participation	Gender as the affirmation of specific gender resources
Citizenship as amelioration of class conflict	Gender as tension towards substantial equality
Citizenship as self-sufficiency	Gender as moral obligation to work
Citizenship as hermeneutic endeavour	Gender as civic discourse

Figure 6.1   *Conceptions of citizenship and gender citizenship*

Since citizenship is a complex and ambiguous topic, before examining its general implications I shall first explore a more specific issue: how the ability to construct a social practice of gender citizenship varies according to the way an organizational culture constructs the idea of fairness in gender relationships, and consequently the way in which it reacts to the set of juridical norms that guarantees/imposes equal opportunities and translates them into personnel policies on the one hand, and into culture on the other.

Put otherwise, organizational cultures differentiate themselves according to the concept of gender citizenship that they express and make possible (see the second column of Figure 6.1). For ease of exposition I shall use the six models of citizenship (as universality; as neutrality; as communality; as the amelioration of class conflicts; as self-sufficiency; as a hermeneutic endeavour) set out in Alejandro (1993), since I share his assumption that citizenship is a problem of interpretation and of the discourse-based construction of meanings within a community of practices. The analogies with gender citizenship are my own responsibility.

Gender citizenship as legal ratification

In the conception of citizenship as universality and as a legal construction – as, for example, Dahrendorf (1974) has written – citizenship is viewed primarily as an idea expressed in law. It produces a social order based on ties which are not natural but which are instead created *ad hoc* by the law. It protects citizens against each other and against outsiders. This, therefore, is the liberal notion which conceives first the individual and then the citizen as a right-bearer and which expresses an abstract dimension of equality: citizenship is a generalized right. The citizen has neither gender nor sex!

The abstract universality of rights is a notion of especial significance in both what it says and what it leaves unsaid: the historical-social formation of these rights, their origin in conflicts and struggles between the strong and the weak. Citizens have rights *qua* individuals, that is, as abstract persons; but they conduct their daily lives as members of specific groups and within a social order fragmented by class, race and gender. The discourse of universality and of rights silences the narration of particular identities, of the origins and evolution of equality/inequality. But simultaneously it marks out and guarantees a political arena in which the abstract principle can be challenged.

When we shift this concept to an organizational setting, we have an organizational citizenship based on the legal definition of membership. The labour contract and trade union agreements define a sphere of consensual obligations which turn the organization's members into participants in a system of rules for economic and social exchange.

A definition of organizational citizenship based on the abstract universality of rights creates a discourse space where the logic of the labour law may prevail and trigger social struggles based on the principle of equal wages and equal working conditions. Thus expressed is the idea of social justice as the safeguarding of the contractual positions of the weaker components of the labour force: immigrants, women, young people. What this discourse obscures in organizational life is effective participation and the exercise of rights: those who are disadvantaged in a class system are also largely unable to join a citizenship system and to render citizenship substantial rather than formal.

As regards gender citizenship, the discourse of rights is the discourse that eclipses difference and every difference: citizens have rights *qua* individuals, and the legal definition of the individual transcends every particularity. Women are no longer women; they are individuals, and the relationships between men and women are subject to the same rules of social communality that regulate the relationships between men and men or between women and women. The problem of justice in gender relationships does not arise, since gender plays a secondary role in the constitution of individuality. Women may constitute a disadvantaged social group, but a woman is a bearer of rights on a par with a man. That she is then unable to exercise them is another matter. Thus, women who participate in the organization are individuals with the same rights and duties as their male colleagues, and they will be assessed and rewarded according to their effective performance. They will participate in the social and political life of the organization according to their position in the internal hierarchy of power and prestige. Social differentiation will operate internally to groups, and among women and among men, according to a class structure. The specific action of gender in creating occupational segregation, in the marginalization of discretionary power, in effective political participation, has no place in this discourse which founds citizenship on individuality.

Gender difference is denied or ignored in norms establishing the formal equality of rights, and the ban on discrimination is the symbol of cultural commitment and sensitivity to the problematics of gender. An organizational culture based on this conception of gender difference usually refrains from taking specific measures to promote equality, and it uses the ban on discrimination more as an excuse for failing to act than as a goal to achieve. Non-discrimination is only formal, while invisible barriers, for example, are not a topic of organizational discussion. Occupational segregation is the 'natural' outcome of the unequal social distribution of human capital. Economic theories of human capital, from Mincer (1958) until today, have explained the inequality between men and women in the workplace in terms of unequal investments in education and training. Under this conception of gender citizenship, the organization bears no moral or social responsibility for inequalities.

Gender citizenship as cultural integration

In Rawls's view of citizenship as neutrality, the moral and political diversity of citizens is based on the distinction between the public and private spheres. Citizenship is both permanent membership of a well-ordered society and an effort, in the context of a democratic society, to found justice on a political conception of justice.

In Rawls's model of citizenship, the state is neutral with respect to what constitutes a good civic life. On the other hand, it is the interests of justice which guide the actions of citizens, as well as the separation between their most profound private convictions and the principles of the public search for consensus.

The private is the sphere of the moral personality, of pluralism and of diversity. The public, by contrast, is the sphere of stability, of order, of agreement, and of an 'overlapping consensus' on justice. For Rawls (1971), modern societies are characterized by non-commensurate conceptions of what a good life is. For this reason the state is neutral *vis-à-vis* the definitions that citizens give to it. In the public sphere, citizens are free individuals who have the right not to be identified, or not to identify themselves, with a specific system of ends; in the private sphere, both personal and associative, citizens may possess strong attachments and commitments which they refrain from displaying in public.

The construction of political consensus through the exercise of public neutrality presupposes a social order in which everyone cooperates by accepting this political assumption and by freely choosing to mutilate the public self and to confine the more authentic self to restricted, private or internal, ambits. On the one hand, this entails reasoning in terms of multiple selves, of the end of comprehensive doctrines, of the interweaving of the differences and pluralities of the worlds of sense in which they are simultaneously immersed. On the other hand, this calls to mind the well-known model of the double moral standard whereby, for example, adultery committed by a man or a woman is judged differently. Or, they recall societies of weak democracy where a person's most profound convictions are revealed in private not in public.

By analogy, organizational citizenship as neutrality commits the organization to neutrality *vis-à-vis* the ways in which its members elaborate the contents of a democratic culture and put the principles of a good life into practice. And its members in turn are committed to guaranteeing civil consensus on the idea of justice. The good organizational life should thus be founded on the beliefs of its members, and, as a system of government, the organization should respect these beliefs.

If we look specifically at the citizenship of gender, the above assumption entails that both men and women enjoy permanent membership. However, what is considered 'fair' in gender relationships is elaborated by the local culture and within social relationships among people of different sex. The organization is not affected by the private values of its members. Since public life is based on the effort to reach consensus, and since the power relationships between the genders is a private matter, it is highly likely that consensus will be reached on male values and on the cultural hegemony of male over female. Cultural integration, homosociability, becomes the ticket of entry to civil society and civil organizations.

Gender difference is indeed recognized but minimized in its effects on social relations: male workers and female workers must be considered equal despite the fact that they are different. If there is historical inequality in the initial opportunities available to each sex, this can be corrected by measures designed to achieve egalitarian goals. Emblematic of this conception and of the limits of formal equality is, for example, the prohibition on dismissal for pregnancy. Although originally designed to render women equal with men in the workplace, this provision in fact penalized women because employers were reluctant to hire them in case they became pregnant and incurred costs for the organization.

Like the culture oriented to legal ratification, an organizational culture which embraces this assumption on what is fair in gender relationships denies the consequences of gender difference although it acknowledges such difference. This is the culture of formal equality which considers as equal only those who achieve the same performance or who embrace the same values, and these have been historically inscribed in the body of the male worker. In this culture, the organization's social responsibility is expressed in its respect for formal equality and in its even-handed treatment of workers who achieve commensurate performances. But the organization bears no responsibility for the fact that formal equality may have a backlash effect on those rendered unequal by gender, race or class. Here too, one notes with interest how economic theories on the labour market have sought to explain gender inequalities, and how certain cultural constructs such as gender citizenship are conveyed by similar discourse practices in different disciplines. How, though, does one account for that part of discrimination (by sex or race) which differentials in productivity fail to explain? Becker (1971) introduces the concept of 'taste of discrimination' to define the situation where employers, but also occupational communities, will sustain extra real costs rather than assume the psychological cost of working with people for whom they feel an aversion. This amounts to saying that, performance and behaviour remaining equal, there is a further 'irrational', non-economic-cultural, factor which induces discrimination.

Gender citizenship as a specific resource

The conception of citizenship as communality and participation gives priority to the construction of communal life by means of active political participation. Citizenship is a mode of social being, and the citizen is the product of a process of participation within a community. Walzer's (1983) conception of citizenship, for example, assumes a community of shared values in which citizens share a culture, and are determined to continue to do so in the future, since the community is in itself the most important good to be distributed. The community and the sense of a communal life cement together the traditions, conventions and expectations which underpin the shared experiences and values that almost everybody subscribes to.

What is obscured here is the fact that not everybody attributes the same value to the same traditions, that a universal category like 'people' is composed of a diversity of components which live the same communal experience differently, and that traditions can be questioned and criticized, as well as provoking conflict. The presumption is, therefore, that the community in question is solely a legitimate community, one in which all its members are equally committed to preserving its dominant values.

Organizational citizenship in analogy to a conception of communality and participation is almost synonymous with a conception of organizational culture where the members of an organization are such because they participate in a historical community of meanings shared by the pooling of sensitivities and intuitions.

Gender citizenship within this conception of organizational democracy is recognition of the diversity of human types, but only within the legitimate community. Contribution to the community and participation in the common good is also acknowledged of organizational citizens of female sex, but only within the confines of their traditional social position as the affirmation of the specific resources of the female. Occupational segregation results from different modes of participation in the formation of the organization as a common good by men and women.

In this conception, gender difference no longer arises as the attribution of otherness, difference-from, the biologically determined social destiny of the previous conceptions. Instead, the female body becomes a resource, the means to enter domains barred to the male. Femaleness becomes a resource for the organization, which develops special policies for the management of female human resources.

The definition 'in positive' of femaleness and the assertion, in theory and practice, of its superiority swiftly turned into an urge to dominate which transformed the traditional male/female dichotomy but did not change its philosophy of asymmetric power. This conception has given rise to mostly circumscribed organizational cultures, like the committees for affirmative action in large organizations, or women's organizations within trade unions, or the cultures of specific feminist organizations. Most organizations contain a cultural nucleus, of varying size, which conceives the female as a specific resource and attributes special skills to women *qua* women. The implicit risk here is of a unilateral, as well as normative, definition of femaleness.

Research programmes display the same conception whenever, in different ways and for different purposes, they compare working groups of different sex seeking to quantify the variance engendered by the variable 'sex' and endeavour to define the femaleness that women have and men do not. This formulation, the poverty of its results, and its evident character as a self-fulfilling prophecy, have been widely criticized (see Calás, 1988, as regards management).

Nevertheless, the glamour of female leadership, by way of example, remains intact because it is part of the same discourse strategy which, in the past, femaleness employed to justify discrimination and occupational segregation and, today, employs to obtain a competitive advantage. Organization rhetoric has always exalted the specifically 'female' virtues – in the past to celebrate the secretary, today to extol the woman manager: the contents of gender change, but the trap of gender and of fixed identities for men and women is still firmly in place, and the winner is always the hunter. Paradoxically, the moral responsibility coherent with this conception is the responsibility to exploit – to a greater or lesser extent – this resource.

Gender citizenship as tension towards substantial equality

Marshall (1950) divides citizenship into three successive phases between the eighteenth and twentieth centuries: civil, political and social. Marshall discerns a constant historical improvement in class conflict, because the extension of citizenship rights has weakened the system of privileges even if social inequality has not been eliminated.

Citizenship rights have assaulted the entire structure of social inequalities, and whatever inequality still remains no longer constitutes a class distinction in the sense given to the term in the past. A major factor in the progress of citizenship towards greater economic and social equality has been the expansion of social services backed by more egalitarian legislation.

The welfare state, especially in the eighties, was of crucial symbolic importance because it represented the idea of a more equable system of income distribution and of social reproduction. The task of the social services was to mark out new boundaries between production work and reproduction work, and one of their principal intended effects was the releasing of new productive forces – especially female – for the market.

By analogy, the organization has undergone a similar evolution towards the elimination of the system of class inequalities, although in this case it would be more accurate to say that it was class conflict and workers' struggle which brought an extension of citizenship rights. Organizational citizenship rights, in this sense, signify opposing and assessing the justice of the inequalities system within the workplace, in particular the inequalities of gender in access to the status of organizational citizen. For example, the persistent obligation for women to work what Hochschild (1989) has called 'the second shift' in order to denote the accumulation of family, domestic and nurturing work, impedes women from acquiring full citizenship in organizational life. Since women have a second job outside the workplace, their investments of time and emotional resources are smaller; or, if they wish to maintain these investments at the same level as men, they incur psychological and real costs which men do not. Consequently, those able to exercise citizenship rights, able to discuss them and to enjoy them, are those organizational citizens who are freed from the second shift either by gender privilege or by economic privilege.

Gender difference is formulated in terms of the elimination of inequality: male and female workers are socially and economically unequal; accordingly, they must be made equal. Compensation for inequality is the symbolic action which affirms the value of difference and of the search for equity. The organizational culture which conceives gender citizenship as the elimination of the causes of inequality is that which, in consequence, commits itself to democratic participation in the construction of organizational life. Policies of substantial equality pursue two goals: re-equilibrating women's chances of effective participation, and ensuring just and equable participation for both women and men. As an example, recall the Italian debate on night work for women and whether or not it should be abolished. Simultaneously with the abolition of this protective measure, the demand was advanced for regulation of the practice in the interests of men and women and in order to safeguard workers outside the workplace.

As regards my personal experience in this area, I find that the philosophy of equal opportunities committees in organizations has changed in recent years. From measures aimed exclusively at women, the emphasis has now shifted to ones addressed to all workers in order to redress the balance between working life and family and extra-work life in general.

Gender citizenship as the equal moral obligation to work

Under this conception, the principal component of citizenship is the duty to work, and citizens are defined as self-supporting members of the community. This conception often crops up in debates on poverty, unemployment and so-called 'welfare mothers', that is, women who choose to live on welfare rather than work in low-paid jobs (Mead, 1986).

This debate is being conducted in the United States of America, and therefore in a socio-economic context which differs in many respects from Europe's and from its approach to labour policies, but the basic concept remains the same. The legal character of citizenship is not sufficient: a citizen cannot only be the bearer of rights; s/he must work, for this is the entry ticket to society. Having a job means being empowered to enjoy a series of other rights by virtue of one's status as a worker; an assertion whose validity is proved *a contraris* by the status of unemployed worker. But there is in this conception a worrying ambivalence between 'duty to work' and 'right to work'.

Work, as a means of sustenance, is part of a final vocabulary and assumes the force of a moral obligation, like paying taxes and ensuring that they are paid. The presumption is that work, any work, is gratifying, that full employment is possible, and that to work is to perform a political as well as a normative act. This assertion suppresses or overlooks the fact that non-work is also a political act, but more importantly it induces us to interrogate ourselves about the 'goodness' of work, about the intrinsic equity of its allocation, and about the justice of its social distribution. In the debate between welfare dependency and subsidiarity, the two opposing views are in fact complementary, and they coincide in accepting the justice of an economic structure which produces both work and unemployment.

What is the analogy with organizational citizenship here, if being a worker in an organization means already being self-sufficient? In this case the moral obligation to work is paralleled by the obligation to be committed to the organization. Being an organizational citizen means responding to the organization's appeal to identify with it, to share the organizational culture, to join a collective 'us', to be motivated workers. The commitment thus required is based principally on an emotional and ethical investment, while economic or 'contractual' exchange is secondary. The organization not only pays money in exchange for work, it also disburses more important and intangible things: identity resources, social position, prestige, priority access to welfare benefits, and therefore opportunities to become first-class citizens.

The fairness of the exchange cannot be subjected to open scrutiny and it is therefore regulated in private: it is only in their own hearts that workers judge the goodness of their contracts with the organization and decide how motivated they are willing to be.

Regarding the justice of gender relationships in society and in the organization, much has already been implied: female citizens, precisely because they are women, have less chance of being self-sufficient; they are often self-sufficient not as themselves but because they are tied to a man; and they frequently slide into poverty because they have fewer resources to offer in exchange for citizenship. That one talks of 'welfare mothers' is indicative of the fact that the theoretical model does not take account of the gender structuring of social relationships and therefore of the unequal distribution of chances of being first or second-class citizens. The same

applies to the structuring between male and female workers of participation in the organization.

In this case, gender difference is seen neither as difference nor as
inequality. Indeed, the assumption is that women exploit loopholes in the
system to avoid badly paid and unrewarding work. Doubt is cast on their
loyalty to the organization, the insinuation being that their primary
dedication to their families may induce them to treat work as of secondary
importance, as merely providing a second wage, and that family
responsibilities may subtract effort and time from work. This conception is
akin to that of gender citizenship as cultural integration. Both aspire to
formal equality despite the fact that female participation in the labour
market has not changed patterns of the sexual division of labour in society
or in the household, and women are therefore forced into double job-
holding. The two conceptions differ to the extent that those who look with
suspicion on women's contribution to the organization may nevertheless
turn a blind eye, for it is a private matter and does not concern the
organization, or they may regard it as a factor which reduces competition
between men and women over the distribution of income, restricting
women's aspirations to female work. The organizational culture based on
this conception may be called 'traditionalist' in its view of gender
relationships because it believes that women are predominantly oriented to
the home.

This is a cultural model too well known to require further elaboration.
However, it is worth noting that, while on the one hand a person
acquires citizenship if s/he works, on the other, women may or may not
become citizens via the family. When workers are considered not to be
individual suppliers of labour but as constituting households rationally
deploying their resources and choosing to allocate time between domestic
and extra-domestic work, value-assumptions on the social role of the
division of labour come to light. For example, the New Home Economics (Becker, 1965, 1971; Mincer, 1972; Gronau, 1973) argues that,
since male activities receive greater remuneration in the market, the
maximization of the family's utility will induce the man to invest his time
outside the home, while the woman will seek extra-domestic work only
when the wage on offer is higher than the loss of productivity in
domestic work.

This justifies the lesser value of extra-domestic work by women based on
the rigid sexual division of labour in society, but it does not call into
question the conditions of employment connoted by a rigid temporal
model. In other words, women do not resort to domestic work because
their extra-domestic work has lower value; it is work that has lesser value
because women are in any case committed to domestic work. An
organizational culture that takes the priority commitment of women to
domestic work for granted is an organizational culture which considers
men to be free from such encumbrances and therefore entirely available –
as regards their time, mental energy and priority interest – to the

organization. Paradoxically, this is an organization which systematically under-utilizes female human resources and systematically abuses male ones; although it considers both men and women to have an equal moral obligation to work, it believes that their jobs are not of equal weight in their lives.

Gender citizenship as civic discourse

Alejandro's (1993) critique of citizenship models and his proposed reading of citizenship in hermeneutic terms lays primary emphasis on citizens' interpretation of what constitutes citizenship and how this interpretation is a historical and social construct. The legal model, the productivist and participative models, Marshall's conception of the extension of social rights and Rawls's notion of the exclusion from politics of comprehensive doctrines, all fail to recognize the importance of the interpretation of legal principles and social practices or the diversity of interests in contemporary society.

Alejandro's proposal is to conceive citizenship as a terrain – a hermeneutic horizon or a space of memories and struggles – on which individuals interpret the past, re-examine their traditions, accept or reject social practices. Claiming that citizenship is a social practice is to imply that 'citizenship as a practice has to do with the discourses and symbols that establish the collective identity of a community' (Alejandro, 1993: 37). Citizenship can thus be conceived as a text which opens itself to a plurality of readers, a text which can be used in different settings and for different purposes. As a text, citizenship represents the possibility that its subjects – the citizens – are also the authors of the text; that is they reflect and act upon the meaning of constructing a communal life because they are concrete persons, who belong to specific social groups, who have conflicting political agendas, specific interests, and contrasting systems of meanings for the same concepts. Citizenship within a hermeneutic model 'appears as a social construction; namely, as a dimension of connectedness and distance as well as a metaphor of fluid borders' (Alejandro, 1993: 39).

The analogy with my conception of gender as a discourse practice interpretable in the light of two metaphors of separation and inseparability, and as positionality in the interaction between the symbolic universes of gender, should at this point be evident. Organizational citizenship thus becomes the terrain on which the interpretations and interests of the various members of the organization meet and clash over definition of membership, everyday rights, justice; namely, citizenship.

Gender citizenship is therefore a text which expresses what is deemed 'fair' in the social relationships between the sexes in a certain context and in a certain historical-social setting. In any given organizational culture, gender citizenship constitutes that discourse terrain on which different interpretations confront each other, and where different collective identities struggle to define not only their contents but also the material contexts – circumstances, groups and ideas – that produce them. It follows that every organization produces its text on citizenship in that organization, on the fairness of the relations between men and women, and on how the symbolic universe of male and female is socially constructed. An organization culture is also characterized by its particular narrative structure of gender citizenship and by the voices and silences which confront each other over gender inequalities.

The social processes whereby individuals are differentiated are now slowly changing according to distinctions more complex and subtle than sex. The social construction of gender relationships is a dialectical process which makes it possible to overcome the dichotomy between two and only two genders, or types of individual. The reciprocity of the relationship acquires concrete form through discourse practices which position gender as one of the many principles of differentiation. The ethics of difference thus become a key criterion in assessment of the fairness of gender relationships, and a key instrument in increasing freedom for gender identity. Equal and different, as a basic concept of equality, begins to change its meaning when it abandons the unquestioned foundation of diversity, looks to the dual presence and moves increasingly further into the field of ambiguity, of the fluid boundaries between the genders, of the liminarity condition between one gender and another; that is, as it moves towards an unstable process of difference and in-differentiation. It is the possibility of in-differentiation – contingently inherent to specific social practices – which may give innovative contents to differentiation, map out game-spaces of reciprocal gender positioning, less stereotypical and less tyrannical.

I have not yet encountered an organizational culture truly aware of and committed to a discourse on gender citizenship as a civic duty and as a civil practice. However, I have seen nuclei of awareness emerging, and I have met people ready to assume the risk of uncertain, changing and fluid gender boundaries.

Initiating a discourse on the positioning of gender within organizational ethics entails the organization's commitment to developing discourse practices which are not paternalistic or discriminatory in their effects. Such an undertaking involves the assumption of a moral and political stance in which one accepts or declines to take part in discourse practices which, with their tenets, images or metaphors, are contrary to the beliefs of those who participate in the conversation or to one's own beliefs.

Since I am not a political scientist, I prefaced my remarks on theories of citizenship by pointing out that they would be somewhat superficial and that my interest in the concept of citizenship lay in its potency as a symbol of societal participation. Gender citizenship in organizations is the metaphor that I propose in order to position gender discourse differently in organizations, and which I used in my foregoing discussion to show the various ways to gender an organizational culture:

(a) An organizational culture which claims to be neutral and which denies every relation between organization and the gender of the people who work in it establishes a gender regime based on universality as the negation of gender differences.

(b) An organizational culture which expresses the belief that women are as good as men, and which promises equality of treatment for equality of performance, establishes a gender regime based on cultural integration.

(c) An organizational culture which regards the female to be a specific resource for the organization establishes a gender regime based on the dichotomization and stereotyping of what is specifically female and male.

(d) An organizational culture which declares itself committed to substantial equality is one which implements an equal opportunity policy and recognizes that men and women are not equal but should be made so. The value inspiring this culture is emancipation, although one rarely finds a gender regime systematically predicated on substantial equality.

(e) An organizational culture which expresses a traditional conception of gender roles establishes a gender regime where, despite its commitment to both genders, the work of men is primary and that of women is auxiliary.

(f) A postmodern organizational culture is aware of the gender trap and seeks to establish a gender regime which respects the constant deferral of the meaning of gender and of the practices that sustain it.

The endeavour to give gender citizenship as an interpretative task of civic discourse helps to break the tyranny of gender as a discourse based on dichotomy and hierarchization, and it may become a discourse of liberation from biological destiny for both men and women.

In this sense it moves towards in-differentiation – not to negate it, however, but to incorporate it into a network of manifold differentiation – where gender is only one of the criteria for the formation of identity and difference. In order to link the argument once again to the organization, I shall illustrate how the term 'difference' has changed in very recent times. I shall map three semantic paths and refer to the field of labour law, since this is automatically reflected in managerial philosophies of human resources management.

There is an extremely interesting debate in progress within labour law which, although it takes different forms in different countries, links all the European countries together and has inspired common female labour policies throughout the EC. The principal issue of debate is the passage from neutral law to sexed law, or from the rights of women to rights for women (Andrini, 1991; De Leonardis, 1991). The metaphor of sexed law (Holtmaat, 1989; Pitch, 1991) raises a theoretical challenge to a policy of justice. Admitting a situated and partial subject, with differences recognized as legitimate and safeguarded in their constitutive elements, signifies that differences are no longer differences from the norm (the abstract individual); they are differences among subjects, they are interdependencies (Minow, 1990). The problem for law is the creation of a system of rights which are neutralistic but not neutral, impartial but articulated on differences (De Leonardis, 1991; Forbes, 1991). This debate has touched upon the role of law itself to reveal an alternative use for it, where the law is not solely normative but also serves to motivate behaviour worthy of social recognition and enhances the humanity and dignity of subjects. The acceptance of these norms and of the principles that inspire them has helped, together with the demands of women in the workplace, to alter the cultural meaning of sexual difference.

Admitted that it is possible to talk in general of an organizational culture as a set of meanings shared by a group of individuals in a certain time-span, we can identify a number of stages in the semantic change undergone by the concept of difference since the Second World War. Difference used to be almost exclusively sexual difference, biologically given, from which stemmed a social destiny which differed between the sexes and was naturally unequal. Within certain limits, there was no labour law for women (apart from the tutelage of their reproductive function). Their unequal status was due to childbearing and to the other impediments that their social function raised against their productive function. A first phase of women's struggle pursued the goal of the social valorization of participation by women in the labour market and of their contribution – economic as well – to society's resources through domestic and family work. Stressing that housework was work in every respect, and not just love, highlighted the interdependencies between market and non-market, between direct remuneration, transfer systems and the production of non-market wealth, between production and reproduction. It became no longer natural to be discriminated against, and women demanded equal treatment.

The era of equal rights and egalitarian goals was thus born. Difference had a substantially negative meaning; it was the attribution of otherness. The woman represented diversity and all the social attributes of the diverse: inferiority, inadequacy, the 'second sex'. The equality demanded had the significance of formal equality, because it was supposed to fill a void, to compensate for a loss or a distancing from the norm. It was agreed that all people – male workers and female workers – should be considered equal. The principle of equality was not descriptive of a situation but prescriptive of a desirable state. This ushered in the period of what, with hindsight, has been called 'emancipationism' and which witnessed the mass entry of women into new occupations and the attenuation of occupational segregation.

Equal rights, however, soon revealed the contradictions that arose from the failure to take initial diversities into account: full achievement of workplace parity between the sexes required the affirmation of the specific rights of women and measures which compensated for initial disparities. Thus the subjects who had always been the embodiment of the norm, the paramount object of the law, found themselves discriminated against, found themselves to be the bearers of further differences, expressed anxieties and fears of discrimination.

Alongside formal equality stood substantial equality, and a sharper distinction was drawn between personal differences (of race, sex, religion, political opinion, etc.), which were to be recognized, respected and safeguarded, and inequalities which were to be eliminated or compensated for in order to create equality. Formal or political equality was ensured by 'rights of' (freedom), and diversity, in this sense, was a positive value to be guaranteed. Substantial or social equality was ensured by 'rights to' (work, dignity), and in this case diversity was a negative value to be eliminated. The distinction between difference and inequality marked the transition from the doctrine of equality to the doctrine of difference in the course of the 1970s. The same process of thought that had opposed the definition of difference as otherness first discovered that a definition 'in positive' was necessary, and then absolutized difference into superiority. This was made possible by the discovery of difference as a resource, and of the female body as a specific resource for knowledge and an epistemic relation with the world.

The theoretical path pursued by Luce Irigaray is emblematic of what happened in the many European feminisms, but the repercussions of this debate were less explosive within organizations than at the level of the theoretical and political practice of feminism. Nevertheless, and ironically, in organizational practices the female as a resource encountered a certain managerial ideology which was receptive to it, and which sought to destabilize certain excessively single-dimensional features of masculinity that were impeding the flexibilization of production processes. There thus appeared a rash of management courses which acknowledged and developed nurturing skills and attitudes, and there likewise arose the metaphor of the 'listening organization' (Crozier, 1989), one able to assimilate, to be passive, to receive rather than to dominate. The organizational exploitation of the female resource was only at the beginning, but it was not envisaged as an equal exchange, as a relationship between adults, as a guarantee of citizenship, nor as a predatory act or the replacement of one type of workforce with another that the passage of time and the exigencies of production had made more attractive because its diversities had acquired market value.

With their spread and self-recognition in a condition of postmodernity, all the phenomena varyingly involved in the dialectic between diversity and inequality, between rights to difference and rights to compensation – in short, all the requests for citizenship – demanded a different position and posited the issue not of the subject's autonomy but of the subject's interdependence, in a complex social network, with other subjects.

Today, citizenship is becoming the theme of a new historical cycle – no longer as an institution guaranteeing social integration under the banner of universalism, but as a factor in the development of new solidarities under the banner of respect for differences and substantial equality. The critique of modernity has evidenced how certain features of the segmentation of the social are changing: the social movements that brought collective actors (from the proletariat to feminists) to the fore are in constant decline, and are unable to ensure a stable cultural identity. Certain strong distinctions such as public/private, state/market are blurring into much more indistinct social and economic organizations, like proximity services. Or again, as Eisenstadt argues (1992), there has been a decline in demand for a centre (ideal and symbolic) which seeks to govern functional differentiation, and a burgeoning of autonomous spheres which are ideologically and concretely independent from the centre. According to Eisenstadt, what is changing is the relationship between *volonté generale* and *volonté de tous*, in the sense that there is a tendency for new and different arenas to appear in which the *volonté de tous* can be exercised without the ideological totalitarianism of the *volonté génerale*.

This historical-cultural climate has engendered numerous movements for civil liberties, for the reconstruction of rights, one of which may be the right to sexual difference and to gender citizenship.

Like all differences, gender difference is symbolic terrain for the image-making of an otherness and of a plurality of othernesses which are neither subordinate nor totalizing. A semantic path of postmodern gender difference is an interpretation of difference as liminarity, as irresolvable ambiguity which defers – in time and in interpretation – the meaning of gender as the symbol of difference/*différance* – that is, of becoming. Symbolically standing at the threshold is the image of suspension, of repeatedly traversing the symbolic universes of male and female, of living the dual presence and denying the dichotomous and hierarchical relation between them. What divides and differentiates also unites.

7

Conclusions: The Symbolics of Gender Citizenship

Gender citizenship within organizations is a metaphor, a prospective symbol, which this book has proposed in order to create and develop an account of gender relationships.

Why citizenship? To contrast the metaphor of exclusion with the symbols of law, of civil society and of the civilizing process. Paramount for many years was the gender discourse based on exclusion, on the blindness of gender, on the need to reinscribe gender difference in history and culture. Today the discourse on gender must base itself on an imaginary able to prefigure qualitatively different gender relationships.

Organizations and the organizational communities internal to them are a social laboratory for the everyday negotiation of gender relations. They constitute one of the social arenas in which the dual presence is manifest and has begun to change the boundaries between the symbolic universes of male and female. Women have entered symbolic ambits of maleness (occupations, professionalism, authority) to a much greater extent than men have entered organization settings marked by female-ness, although the feminization of jobs – as the progressive decline in the status associated with the work role – proceeds with the growing impoverishment of the content of work. The other principal arena for the study of the dual presence is the family and the presence of men in the symbolic universe of the female. Unfortunately, this is not my area of study, although the interface between production and reproduction is of growing interest to organization scholars. What is certain is that these two arenas are the principal site for the social construction of gender.

Gender – as a socio-cultural product – is constructed at both the symbolic and the interactional levels. It gives rise to social structures which reflexively institutionalize gender relations. Persons 'do' gender when they celebrate each other's gender identity and repair offences to the symbolic order of gender. As they do so, they defer the meaning of gender as they cope with the ambiguity of the blurred boundaries between universes of meaning.

Organizations do gender too. Gender is an organizing principle and an organizational outcome. Gender charactistics are presupposed, imposed on people and exploited for productive ends, and there are organizational dynamics which create them. However, the belief that there is one sole culture of gender or that there are only male or female organizations is simplistic.

Gender is much more pervasive than binary categorization would have us believe. The culture of gender is a code of differentiation which supplements the other cultural codes: what borders on violence but is still acceptable in the gender relationships of a working-class community may not be accepted in a white-collar community of the same organization. It may not be considered fair by either the men or the women of that community. Or gender cultures may differ even within the same group of men or women. Difference as a social stigma, the labelling of a form of behaviour as 'female' and thereby devaluing it, is a cultural belief that can be expressed just as much by men as by women. For example, the view that women's interests lie primarily outside work may be a conviction which blames their lack of work motivation on gender identity and justifies a discriminatory career policy to the point that behaviour that violates this assumption throws doubt on people's gender identity. But the same principle applies to men who do not subscribe to the ethic of success. Are they true men?

The culture of gender also varies across generations and age cohorts. I gave an example of how a case of potential sexual harassment was interpreted by cultural codes which varied between younger and older women, and simultaneously between occupational communities which had differing organizational relations with the alleged offender and the victim. The culture of gender is the source of further differentiation within organizational cultures, because it already presupposes the differentiation of organizational experiences according to role, job and other occupational characteristics. Gender adds a further dimension to the experience of an organization; an experience which depends less on the sexual identity of the person than on the gender relation that is produced by her and with her. I have shown the variability of gender experiences in diverse organizational cultures by recounting the experiences of women pioneers in male work settings. Theirs is the experience of the outsider, the traveller in a strange land who is socially constructed as guest, holidaymaker, enemy or marginal member in the relation between the host community and her modality of entry to it.

I do not deny the dominance and cultural hegemony which organizations – as components of the patriarchical system – also impose on cultural expressions which seek to withdraw and define themselves in an autonomous and contrary manner. Instead I have sought to articulate the system of differences by drawing on experiences and images, both when the differences were between male and female and when they were internal to the male and the female. I have employed the archetypes of the Greek goddesses to connote the female with such traditional male virtues as independence or rationality, and to illustrate the differences among women in their patterns of organizational behaviour. In conflict, in opposition or in the negotiation of roles, male and female are separate, but there is also a bond of friendship in their coexistence which establishes the relationship and maintains it through conflict.

A limitation of this book – one which I regret – is that it does not give adequate representation to men's gender experiences. I am aware that in discussing cooperation between men and women in the production of gender relations, I have given priority to women's experiences. I too have inherited a tradition which only recently has become aware that half of the history of gender is missing if the social construction of masculinity is not considered. Due to the lack of research and analysis of the direct experience of gender by men, they appear much more undifferentiated than women. I hope that this limitation will be taken as an invitation to join a conversation that has only just begun.

To introduce the argument of gender difference and of the differences between men and women, I used two metaphors which illustrated diametrically opposed modalities of social relationality. On the one hand, the contractual relationship – the sexual contract – framed my analysis of sexuality, the body and eroticism in terms of exchange, of negotiation and of convergent and asymmetrical interests. Woman is the symbol of lasciviousness, of the body as opposed to the mind, of instinct, of the low, of the impure. Organizations erase the sex of people, they deny any involvement with sexuality, they oppose 'work' to 'sensuality'. But while they avow public virtue, they exploit the sexual characteristics of their workforce. They are the places of the systematic abuse, not only sexual, of people; they endorse sublimated (or otherwise) forms of sexual perversion. But are workers solely victims, or are women mainly the victims because they are in turn victims of organizations and of the men who work for them? Organizational life is complex and ambiguous because the dynamics of power and pleasure map out both covert and overt territories. The underground life of occupational communities has a rich vocabulary of allusions. The instruments of work are often rebaptized in accordance with a sexual imaginary. Work situations are often eroticized and eroticizing, and parasexual behaviour in a place consecrated to its opposite may become a form of resistance, of challenge, seeking to appropriate 'private' space and time in the exercise of a 'public' activity. Organizational sexuality is a social practice which lays down explicit and culturally elaborated rules of behaviour with local validity. Behaviour that scandalizes and may constitute sexual harassment in one occupational community may be entirely acceptable a few floors up or down in the same building. It is not necessary to study distant and exotic tribes to describe rites of sexual initiation.

The second metaphor used in this book – Jerosgamos – enables us to think difference as the profound union symbolized by marriage and as the particular – alchemic – union which yields transformation, transcendence, sacredness, fulfilment. The bonds of friendship and solidarity are expressed in recognition of the sacred spark conserved by the archetypes of femaleness and maleness, and in the reciprocal bond between one type of femaleness and the corresponding maleness that it calls forth (and vice versa).

The dynamics of gender, like family dynamics, are an interpretative key that this metaphor makes possible.

The alchemic wedding as a metaphor for transformation prompted examination of gender identity as a process of reciprocal positioning and social construction, not of one but of many and even conflicting identities. It also suggested the use of a well-known symbol of transformation: the journey. I had already alluded to women as travellers encountering an alien culture. I now employed the journey as a symbol of transformation. Travelling is ultimately an inward experience, and outer events provide the occasion to expand one's inner horizons. Travellers are changed by their journeys, but they also bring innovation to the places they visit. A different awareness of the culture of gender will produce different gender relations.

The journey as an interior experience of knowledge and as an expansion of opportunities to communicate induced me to compare it with the process of civilization. Change in gender relations is part of the civilizing process, which is based on the repression of instincts and on the social construction of the emotions. That is, it rests on a paradox: to be able to enjoy greater freedom – in social customs, for example – we accept the greater suppression of our urges. The gender that we 'do' today, this analogy suggests, arises from the education of our sphincters. Gender citizenship should therefore be the logical continuation of the vote for women, as part of the same historical process which has seen women enter civil society and the public domain. If the co-penetration of symbolic universes is part of the same process, we may expect, not the disappearance of the gender distinction but greater richness, articulacy and creativity in the social production of gender relations.

Gender is produced amid ambiguity, amid the pervasiveness of its manifold forms which resist classification, and in its elusive relationship with nature. Gender experiences tell us that reality is not monolithic but multiple and ambiguous. It is in liminarity that the emergence of the determination is grasped.

Both gender and citizenship have been revisited by postmodern thought, for they necessitate and make possible the expression of a plurality of differences, of relations which differentiate. Differentiated universalism is an endeavour which seeks to conjugate the generalization of fundamental values in all the spheres of the social with the specification of those values according to the particular context.

Gender and citizenship express a membership which in complex societies can no longer be merely ascribed, but which must become richer in choice and more productive of social innovation. Both concepts stress that difference is unclassifiable, that it cannot be given labels which force it into dichotomizing categories (man/woman, citizen/outsider). Both express awareness of partnership in life-situations and in the social construction of systems of social meanings and practices which confound distinctions. Both concepts have given life to a social repertoire which is expressed in the image of a plurality of voices, of conversation as a means to construct society, as creativity bred of multiplicity.

Bibliography

Abravanel, H. 1983. 'Mediatory Myths in the Service of Organizational Ideology.' In *Organizational Symbolism*, edited by L.R. Pondy, P.J. Frost, G. Morgan and T. Dandridge. Greenwich, CT: Jai Press.

Acker, J. 1990. 'Hierarchies, Jobs, Bodies: A Theory of Gendered Organizations.' *Gender and Society* 4: 139–158.

Acker, J. 1992. 'Gendering Organizational Theory.' In *Gendering Organizational Analysis*, edited by A. Mills and P. Tancred. London: Sage.

Alcoff, L. 1988. 'Cultural Feminism versus Post-Structuralism: the Identity Crisis in Feminist Theory.' *Signs* 13(3): 405–436.

Alejandro, R. 1993. *Hermeneutics, Citizenship, and the Public Sphere.* New York: State University of New York Press.

Allaire, Y. and M. Firsirotu. 1984. 'Theories of Organizational Culture.' *Organization Studies* 5(3): 193–226.

Alvesson, M. and P.O. Berg. 1992. *Corporate Culture and Organizational Symbolism.* Berlin: de Gruyter.

Alvesson, M. and Y. Billing. 1992. 'Gender and Organization: Toward a Differentiated Understanding.' *Organization Studies* 13 (2): 73–106.

Andrini, S. 1991. 'Differenza e In-differenza.' *Democrazia e Diritto* 5–6: 237–263.

Armon-Jones, C. 1986. 'The Social Functions of Emotions.' In *The Social Construction of Emotions* edited by R. Harré. Oxford: Blackwell.

Averill, J.R. 1980. 'A Constructivist View of Emotion.' In *Theories of Emotion* edited by R. Plutchik and H. Kellerman. New York: Academic Press.

Averill, J.R. 1982. *Anger and Aggression: An Essay on Emotion.* New York: Springer-Verlag.

Balbo, L. 1979. 'La doppia presenza.' *Inchiesta* 32: 3–6.

Barnard, C.J. 1938. *The Function of the Executive.* Cambridge, MA: Harvard University Press.

Bateman, T.S. and D. Organ. 1983. 'Job Satisfaction and the Good Soldier: The Relationship between Affect and Employee "Citizenship".' *Academy of Management Journal* 26: 587–595.

Baudrillard, J. 1981. *For a Critique of the Political Economy of the Sign.* St. Louis: Telos Press.

Becker, G.S. 1965. 'A Theory of the Allocation of Time.' *Economic Journal* September: 725–739.

Becker, G.S. 1971. *The Economics of Discrimination.* Chicago: University of Chicago Press.

Benson, S.P. 1986. *Counter Cultures: Saleswomen, Managers and Customers in American Department Stores, 1890–1940.* Urbana and Chicago: University of Illinois Press.

Berg, P.O. 1985. 'Organizational Change as a Symbolic Transformation Process.' In *Organizational Culture* edited by P. J. Frost, L.F. Moore, M.R. Louis, C.C. Lundberg and J. Martin. London: Sage.

Bergin, J. 1993. 'On Organizational Abuse: Evil is a Robust Organization.' Paper presented at SCOS Conference, Collbato.

Black, M. 1962. *Models and Metaphor.* Ithaca, NY: Cornell University Press.

Bolen, J. 1984. *Goddess in Everywoman.* New York: Harper & Row.

Bolen, J.S. 1989. *Gods in Everyman.* San Francisco: Harper & Row.

Bolognini, B. 1986. 'Il mito come espressione dei valori organizzativi e come fattore strutturale.' in *Le Imprese come Cultura* edited by P. Gagliardi. Milan: Isedi.

Bowles, M. 1993. 'The Gods and Goddess: Personifying Social Life in the Age of Organization.' *Organization Studies* 14(3): 395–418.

Brown, H. 1993. *Women Organizing*. London: Routledge.

Brown, R.H. 1977. *A Poetic for Sociology*. Cambridge: Cambridge University Press.

Brown, R.H. 1989. *Social Sciences as Civic Discourse*. Chicago: University of Chicago Press.

Brunsson, N. 1989. *The Organization of Hypocrisy*. Chichester: Wiley.

Burrell, G. 1984. 'Sex and Organizational Analysis.' *Organization Studies* 5: 97–118.

Burrell, G. and G. Morgan. 1979. *Sociological Paradigms and Organizational Analysis*. Aldershot: Gower.

Burris, B. 1989. 'Technocracy and Gender in the Workplace.' *Social Problems* 2: 165–180.

Burton, C. 1992. 'Merit and Gender: Organizations and the Mobilization of Masculine Bias.' In *Gendering Organizational Analysis* edited by A. Mills and P. Tancred. London: Sage.

Butler, J. 1970. *Gender Trouble: Feminism and the Subversion of Identity*. London: Routledge.

Calás, M. 1988. '"Gendering" Leadership: the Differ(e/a)nce That Matters.' Paper presented at the Academy of Management Meetings, August.

Calás, M. and L. Smircich. 1991. 'Voicing Seduction to Silence Leadership.' *Organization Studies* 4: 567–602.

Calás, M. and L. Smircich. 1992a. 'Re-writing Gender into Organizational Theorizing: Directions from Femminist Perspectives.' In *Rethinking Organiaztion* edited by M. Reed and M. Hughes. London: Sage.

Calás, M. and L. Smircich. 1992b. 'Using the "F" Word: Feminist Theories and the Social Consequences of Organizational Research.' In *Gendering Organizational Analysis*, edited by A. Mills and P. Tancred. London: Sage.

Calás, M. and L. Smircich. 1993. 'Dangerous Liaisons: The "Feminine-in-Management" Meets "Globalization".' *Business Horizons* March–April: 73–83.

Carroll, L. 1980. *Alice's Adventures in Wonderland*. Milan: Rizzoli.

Cassano, F. 1989. *Approssimazioni: Esercizi di Esperienza dell'altro*. Bologna: Il Mulino.

Cassirer, E. 1923. *Philosophie der Symbolischen Formern*. Berlin: Malik.

Castoriadis, C. 1987. *The Imaginary Institution of Society*. Cambridge: Polity Press.

Chetwynd, T. 1982. *A Dictionary of Symbols*. London: Granada.

Chodorow, N. 1978. *The Reproduction of Mothering*. Berkeley: University of California Press.

Cirlot, J. E. 1985. *Dizionario dei Simboli*. Milan: SIAD.

Clegg, S. and D. Dunkerley. 1980. *Organization, Class and Control*. London: Routledge & Kegan Paul.

Cockburn, C. 1983. *Brothers. Male Dominance and Technological Change*. London: Pluto Press.

Cockburn, C. 1985. *Machinery of Dominance: Women, Men and Technical Know-How*. London: Pluto Press.

Cohen, M. and J. March. 1974. *Leadership and Ambiguity*. New York: McGraw-Hill.

Cohen, M., J. March and J. Olsen. 1972. 'A Garbage Can Model of Organizational Choice.' *Administrative Science Quarterly* 17: 1–25.

Collinson, D. 1988. 'Engineering Humour: Masculinity, Joking and Conflict in Shopfloor Relations.' *Organization Studies* 9: 181–199.

Collinson, D. 1992. *Managing the Shopfloor: Subjectivity, Masculinity and Workplace Culture*. Berlin: de Gruyter.

Collinson, D. and M. Collinson. 1989. 'Sexuality in the Workplace: The Domination of Men's Sexuality.' In *The Sexuality of Organization* edited by J. Hearn, D. Sheppard, P. Tancred-Sheriff and G. Burrell. London: Sage.

Cooper, R. and G. Burrell. 1988. 'Modernism, Postmodernism and Organizational Analysis: An Introduction.' *Organization Studies*, 9/1: 91–112.

Crocker, P. 1983. 'An Analysis of University Definitions of Sexual Harassment.' *Signs* 8(4): 696–707.

Crozier, M. 1989. *L'Entreprise a l'écoute*. Paris: InterEditions.

Crozier, M. and E. Friedberg. 1977. *L'Acteur et le Systèm*. Paris: Ed. du Soleil.
Czarniawska-Joerges, B. 1991. 'Culture Is the Medium of Life.' In *Reframing Organizational Culture* edited by P.J. Frost, L.F. Moore, M.R. Louis, C.C. Lundberg, J. Martin. Newbury Park: Sage.
Czarniawska-Joerges, B. 1994. 'Narratives of Individual and Organizational Identities.' In *Communication Yearbook* edited by S.A. Deetz. London: Sage.
Dahrendorf, R. 1974. 'Citizenship and Beyond: The Social Dynamics of an Idea.' *Social Research* 41(4): 673–701.
Davies, B. and R. Harré. 1990. 'Positioning: The Discursive Production of Selves.' *Journal of the Theory of Social Behaviour* 1: 43–63.
De Beauvoir, S. 1949. *Le deuxième sexe*. Paris: Les Editions de Minuit.
Dégot, V. 1985. 'Editorial.' *Dragon* 1: 3–6.
De Lauretis, T. 1984. *Alice Doesn't*. Bloomington: Indiana University Press.
De Leonardis, O. 1991. 'Diritti, differenze e capacità. Sulla giustizia come processo sociale.' *Democrazia e Diritto* 5–6: 197–218.
Deleuze, G. 1969. *Logique du sens*. Paris: Les Editions de Minuit.
Demetrio, D. 1994. 'Diventare adulti nelle organizzazioni.' In *Apprendere nelle Organizzazioni* edited by D. Demetrio, D. Fabbri and S. Gherardi. Rome: Nuova Italia Scientifica.
Denzin, N. 1992. *Symbolic Interactionism and Cultural Studies*. Oxford: Blackwell.
Derrida, J. 1967. *De la Grammatologie*. Paris: Seuil.
Derrida, J. 1971. *L'Écriture et la différance*. Paris: Seuil.
Diamond, I. and N. Hartsock. 1981. 'Beyond Interests in Politics: A Comment on Virginia Sapiro's "When are Interests Interesting? The Problem of Political Representation of Women".' *American Political Sciences Review* 75: 712–721.
DuBois, E.C., G.P. Kelly, E.L. Kennedy, C.W. Korsmeyer, L.S. Robinson (eds). 1987. *Feminist Scholarship: Kindling in the Groves of Academe*. Chicago: University of Chicago Press.
Durkheim, E. 1912. *Les formes élémentaires de la vie religieuse: le système totemique en Australie*. Paris: Alcan.
Ebers, M. 1985. 'Understanding Organizations: The Poetic Mode.' *Journal of Management Studies* 11(2): 51–62.
Eco, U. 1979. *Lector in fabula*. Milan: Bompiani.
Eisenstadt, S. 1992. 'La perdita di carisma dei centri politici.' *Democrazia Diretta* 7(1): 53–60.
Eliade, M. 1952. *Images et symboles. Essais sur le symbolisme magico-religieux*. Paris: Gallimard.
Elias, N. 1978. *The Civilizing Process: the History of Manners*. Oxford: Blackwell.
Elshtain, J. 1982. 'Feminist Discourse and Its Discontents: Language, Power, and Meaning.' *Signs* 7(3): 603–621.
Elshtain, J. 1987. 'Against Androgyny.' in *Feminism and Equality* edited by A. Phillips. New York: New York University Press. pp. 139–159.
Elster, J. (ed.). 1986. *The Multiple Self*. Cambridge: Cambridge University Press.
Empson, W. 1935. *Some Versions of Pastoral*. London: Chatto & Windus.
Fabbri, D. and L. Formenti. 1991. *Carte d'identità*. Milan: Angeli.
Feldman, H.S. and J.G. March. 1981. 'Information in Organizations as Signals and Symbols.' *Administrative Science Quarterly* 26: 171–186.
Ferguson, K. 1984. *The Feminist Case against Bureaucracy*. Philadelphia: Temple University Press.
Ferguson, K. 1991. 'Interpretation and Genealogy in Feminism.' *Signs* 16(2): 322–339.
Fineman, S. (ed.). 1993. *Emotions in Organizations*. London: Sage.
Flax, J. 1987. 'Postmodernism and Gender Relations in Feminist Theory.' *Signs* 12(4): 621–643.
Flax, J. 1992. 'The End of Innocence.' In *Feminists Theorize the Political* edited by J. Butler and J. Scott. London: Routledge.
Forbes, I. 1991. 'Equal Opportunity: Radical, Liberal and Conservative Critiques.' In *Equality, Politics and Gender* edited by E. Meehan and S. Sevenhuijsen. London: Sage.

Foucault, M. 1966. *Le Mot et les choses*. Paris: Gallimard.

Foucault, M. 1984. *L'Usage des plaisirs*. Paris: Gallimard.

Franks, D. and E. McCarty. 1989. *The Sociology of Emotions: Original Essays and Research Papers*. Greenwich, CT: Jai Press.

Frost, P.J., L.F. Moore, M.R. Louis, C.C. Lundberg and J. Martin (eds). 1985. *Organizational Culture*. Beverly Hills: Sage.

Frost, P.J., L.F. Moore, M.R. Louis, C.C. Lundberg and J. Martin (eds). 1991. *Reframing Organizational Culture*. Newbury Park: Sage.

Gabriel, J. 1991. 'Turning Facts into Stories and Stories into Facts: a Hermeneutic Exploration of Organizational Folklore.' *Human Relations* 8: 857–875.

Gagliardi, P. (ed.). 1986a. *Le Imprese come Cultura*. Milan: Isedi.

Gagliardi, P. 1986b. 'The Creation and Change of Organizational Cultures: a Conceptual Framework.' *Organization Studies* 7(2): 117–134.

Gagliardi, P. (ed.). 1990. *Symbols and Artifacts*. Berlin: de Gruyter.

Garson, B. 1975. *All the Livelong Day: The Meaning and Demeaning of Routine Work*. Garden City, NY: Doubleday.

Gergen, K. 1982. *Toward Transformation in Social Knowledge*. New York: Springer-Verlag.

Gergen, K.J. 1991. *The Saturated Self: Dilemmas of Identity in Contemporary Life*. New York: Basic Books.

Gergen, K. and K. Davis (eds). 1985. *The Social Construction of the Person*. New York: Springer-Verlag.

Gherardi, S. 1978. *Il Lavoro Femminile nel Trentino*. Trento: Uomo, Citta, Territorio.

Gherardi, S. 1982. 'Mercato del lavoro femminile: le rilevazioni statistiche in Italia.' *Inchiesta* 56: 57–66.

Gherardi, S. 1985. *Sociologia delle Decisioni organizzative*. Bologna: Il Mulino.

Gherardi, S. 1990. *Le micro Decisioni nelle Organizzazioni*. Bologna: Il Mulino.

Gherardi, S. 1991. 'L'ufficio come luogo di costruzione simbolica del femminile e del maschile.' *Sociologia del Lavoro* 43: 116–136.

Gherardi, S. 1994. 'The Gender We Think, the Gender We Do in Everyday Organizational Life.' *Human Relations* 47(6): 591–609.

Gherardi, S. 1995. 'When Will He Say: "Today the Plates Are Soft?" Management of Ambiguity and Situated Decision-Making.' *Studies in Cultures, Organizations and Societies* 1(1): 25–43.

Gherardi, S. and A. Masiero. 1987. 'The Impact of Organizational Culture in Life-cycle and Decision-making Processes in Newborn Co-operatives.' *Economic and Industrial Democracy* 8(3): 223–248.

Gherardi, S. and A. Masiero. 1988. *Parità e Discriminazione*. Milan: Angeli.

Gherardi, S. and B. Turner. 1988. *Real Men Don't Collect Soft Data*. Trento: Quaderni del Dipartimento di Politica Sociale 13.

Gilligan, C. 1982. *In a Different Voice*. Cambridge, MA: Harvard University Press.

Goffman, E. 1967. *Interaction Ritual*. Garden City, NY: Doubleday.

Goffman, E. 1971. *Relations in Public*. New York: Harper & Row.

Goffman, E. 1976. 'Gender Display.' *Studies in the Anthropology of Visual Communication*. 3: 69–77.

Goffman, E. 1977. 'The Arrangement between the Sexes.' *Theory & Society* 4: 301–331.

Grafton-Small, R. and S. Linstead. 1985. 'The Everyday Professional: Skill in the Symbolic Management of Occupational Kinship.' In *The Symbolics of Skill* edited by A. Strati. Trento: Dipartimento di Politica Sociale.

Graham, J. 1986. 'Organizational Citizenship Informed by Political Theory.' Paper presented at the Academy of Management Meeting, Chicago, August.

Grant, J. and P. Tancred. 1992. 'A Feminist Perspective on State Bureaucracy.' In *Gendering Organizational Analysis* edited by A. Mills and P. Tancred. London: Sage.

Gronau, J. 1973. 'The Intra-Family Allocation of Time: the Value of the Housewife Time.' *American Economic Review* September: 415–434.

Gutek, B.A. 1989. 'Sexuality in the Workplace: Key Issues in Social Research and

Organizational Practice.' In *The Sexuality of Organization* edited by J. Hearn, D. Sheppard, P. Tancred-Sheriff and G. Burrell. London: Sage. pp. 56–70.

Harding, S. 1986a 'The Instability of the Analytical Categories of Feminist Theory.' *Signs* 11(4): 645–665.

Harding, S. 1986b. *The Science Question in Feminism*. Ithaca, NY: Cornell University Press.

Harré, R. 1984. *Personal Being*. Cambridge, MA: Harvard University Press.

Harré, R. (ed.). 1986. *The Social Construction of Emotions*. Oxford: Blackwell.

Harré, R. 1987. 'Enlarging the Paradigm.' *New Ideas in Psychology* 5: 3–12.

Hearn, J. 1985. 'Men's sexuality at Work.' In *The Sexuality of Men* edited by A. Metcalf and H. Humphries. London: Pluto Press.

Hearn, J. 1994. 'The Organization(s) of Violence: Men, Gender Relations, Organizations, and Violence.' *Human Relations* 47(6): 731–754.

Hearn, J. and W. Parkin. 1983. 'Gender and Organizations: A Selective Review and a Critique of a Neglected Area.' *Organization Studies* 4(3): 219–242.

Hearn, J. and W. Parkin. 1987. *'Sex' at 'Work': the Power and Paradox of Organization Sexuality*. New York: St Martin's Press.

Hearn, J., D. Sheppard, P. Tancred-Sheriff and G. Burrell. 1989. *The Sexuality of Organization*. London: Sage.

Heidegger, M. 1969. *Zur Sache des Denkens*. Tübingen: Niemeyer.

Hekman, S. 1990. *Gender and Knowledge – Elements of a Postmodern Feminism*. Cambridge: Polity Press.

Henley, N. and J. Freeman. 1979. 'The Sexual Politics of Interpersonal Behaviour.' In *Women: A Feminist Perspective* edited by J. Freean. Palo Alto, CA: Mayfield.

Heritage, J. 1984. *Garfinkel and Ethnomethodology*. Cambridge: Polity Press.

Hillman, J. 1975. *Revisioning Psychology*. New York: Harper & Row.

Hillman, J. 1979. *The Dream and the Underworld*. New York: Harper & Row.

Hillman, J. 1985. *Archetypal Psychology: a Brief Account*. Dallas: Spring.

Hirsch, P. and J. Andrews. 1983. 'Ambushes, Shootouts, and Golden Parachutes: The Language of Corporate Take-overs.' In *Organizational Symbolism* edited by L.R. Pondy, P.J. Frost, G. Morgan and T. Dandridge. Greenwich, CT: Jai Press. pp. 145–155.

Hochschild, A.R. 1979. 'Emotion Work: Feeling Rules and Social Structure.' *American Journal of Sociology* 85: 551–575.

Hochschild, A.R. 1983. *The Managed Heart: Commercialization of Human Feeling*. Berkeley: University of California Press.

Hochschild, A.R. 1989. *The Second Shift*. London: Viking.

Holtmaat, R. 1989. 'The Power of Legal Concepts: the Development of a Feminist Theory of Law.' *International Journal of the Sociology of Law* 17(2): 18–37.

Irigaray, L. 1974. *Speculum. De l'autre femme*. Paris: Les Editions de Minuit.

Irigaray, L. 1977. *Ce Sexe qui n'en est pas un*. Paris: Les Editions de Minuit.

Jeffcut, P. 1994. 'From Interpretation to Representation in Organizational Analysis: Post-modernism, Ethnography and Organizational Symbolism.' *Organization Studies* 15(2): 241–274.

Johnson-Laird, P. and K. Oatley. 1988. 'Il significato delle emozioni: una teoria cognitiva e una analisi semantica.' In *Psicologia delle Emozioni* edited by V. D'Urso and R. Trentin. Bologna: Il Mulino.

Jones, K. 1990. 'Citizenship in a Woman-Friendly Polity.' *Signs* 15(4): 781–812.

Jung, C. 1963. *Mysterium Coniunctionis*. London: Pantheon Books.

Jung, C. 1966a. *Psychology and Alchemy*. In *Collected Works*. vol. 2. London: Routledge & Kegan Paul.

Jung, C. 1966b. 'Two Essays on Analytical Psychology.' In *Collected Works* Vol. 7. London: Routledge & Kegan Paul.

Kanter, R. M. 1977. *Men and Women of the Corporation*. New York: Basic Books.

Knights, D. and H. Willmott. 1987. 'Organizational Culture as Management Strategy: A Critique and an Illustration.' *International Studies of Management and Organization* 3: 40–63.

Konecki, K. 1990. 'Dependence and Worker Flirting.' In *Organizational Symbolism* edited by B.A. Turner. Berlin: de Gruyter.

Kristeva, J. 1981. 'Women Can Never be Defined.' In *French Feminism* edited by E. Harks. New York: Schocken.

Kvande, E. and B. Rasmussen. 1994. 'Men in Male-Dominated Organizations and Their Encounter with Women Intruders.' *Scandinavian Journal of Management*, 10(2): 163–174.

Lakoff, R. 1975. *Language and Women's Place*. New York: Harper & Row.

Latour, B. 1986. 'The Powers of Association.' In *Power, Action, and Belief. A New Sociology of Knowledge?* edited by J. Law. London: Routledge and Kegan Paul.

Laville, J. 1992. *Les Services de proximité en Europe*. Paris: Syros.

Levine, D.N. 1985. *The Flight from Ambiguity*. Chicago: University of Chicago Press.

Levitt, B. and J.G. March. 1988. 'Organizational Learning.' *Annual Review of Sociology* 14: 319–340.

Linstead, S. 1993. 'From Postmodern Anthropology to Destructurate Ethnography.' *Human Relations* 46(1): 97–120.

Linstead, S. and R. Grafton-Small. 1990. 'Theory as Artefact: Artefact as Theory.' In *Symbols and Artifacts: Views of the Corporate Landscape* edited by P. Gagliardi. Berlin: de Gruyter.

Linstead, S. and R. Grafton-Small. 1992. 'On Reading Organizational Culture.' *Organization Studies*, 13/3: 331-355.

Lorber, J. and S. Farrell. 1991. *The Social Construction of Gender*. London: Sage.

Luciano, A. 1993. *Tornei: Donne e Uomini in Carriera*. Milan: Etas.

Lutz, C. and G. White. 1986. 'The Anthropology of Emotions.' *Annual Review of Anthropology* 15: 405–436.

Macfarlane, R. and J. Laville. 1992. *Developing Community Partnerships in Europe*. London: Directory of Social Change.

McIntosh, P. 1984. *Feeling like a Fraud*. Wellesley: Work in Progress.

MacKinnon, C.A. 1979. *Sexual Harassment of Working Women*. New Haven: Yale University Press.

March, J.C. 1981. 'Footnotes to Organizational Change.' *Administrative Science Quarterly* 26: 563–577.

Marks, E. and I. de Courtivron. (eds). 1980. *New French Feminisms: An Anthology*. Amherst: University of Massachusetts Press.

Marshall, J. 1984. *Women Managers: Travellers in a Male World*. Chichester: Wiley.

Marshall, T. H. 1950. *Citizenship and Social Class*. Cambridge: Cambridge University Press.

Martin, E. 1991. 'The Egg and the Sperm: How Science Has Constructed a Romance Based on Stereotypical Male–Female Roles.' *Signs* 16: 489–497.

Martin, J. 1990. 'Deconstructuring Organizational Taboos: the Suppression of Gender Conflict in Organizations.' *Organization and Science* 4: 339–359.

Martin, J. and P. Frost. 1995. *The Organizational Culture War Games: A Struggle for Intellectual Dominance*. Research Paper n. 1332: Stanford University.

Mead, G.H. 1934. *Mind, Self and Society*. Chicago: University of Chicago Press.

Mead, L. 1986. *Beyond Entitlement: The Social Obligations of Citizenship*. New York: Free Press.

Mennerick, L.A. 1975. 'Organizational Structuring of Sex Roles in a Nonstereotyped Industry.' *Administrative Science Quarterly* 20: 570–586.

Merton, R.K. 1957. 'The Role-set: Problems in Sociological Theory.' *British Journal of Sociology* 2: 105–115.

Mills, A. 1989. 'Gender, Sexuality and Organization Theory.' In *The Sexuality of Organization* edited by J. Hearn, D.L. Sheppard, P. Tancred-Sheriff and G. Burrell. London: Sage.

Mills, A. and S. Murgatroyd. 1991. *Organizational Rules: A Framework for Understanding Organizations*. Milton Keynes: Open University Press.

Mills, A. and P. Tancred. (eds). 1992. *Gendering Organizational Analysis*. London: Sage.

Mincer, J. 1958. 'Investment in Human Capital and Personal Income Distribution.' *Journal of Political Economy* 66: 24–42.

Mincer, J. 1972. 'Labour Force Participation of the Married Woman.' In *Aspects of Labour Economics*. Princeton, NJ: Princeton University Press.

Minow, M. 1990. *Making All the Difference*. Ithaca, NY: Cornell University Press.

Morgan, G. 1986. *Images of Organizations*. Beverly Hills: Sage.

Morin, E. 1974. 'La Complexité.' *Revue Internationale des Sciences Sociales* 4: 44–66.

Mumby, D. and L. Putnam. 1992. 'The Politics of Emotion: A Feminist Reading of a Bounded Rationality.' *Academy of Management Review* 17: 456–486.

Murray, K. 1989. 'The Construction of Identity in the Narratives of Romance and Comedy.' In *Texts of Identity* edited by J. Shotter and K. Gergen. London: Sage.

Nieva, V. and B. Gutek. 1981. *Women and Work: a Psychological Perspective*. New York: Praeger.

Noe, R. 1988. 'Women and Mentoring: A Review and Research Agenda.' *Academy of Management Review* 13: 65–78.

Oldfield, A. 1990. 'Citizenship: An Unnatural Practice?' *Political Quarterly* 2: 123–135.

Oldfield, A. 1991. *Citizenship and Community*. London: Routledge.

Organ, D. 1990. 'The Motivational Basis of Organizational Citizenship Behaviour.' *Research in Organizational Behaviour* 12: 43–72.

Ortony, A. (ed.). 1979. *Metaphor and Thought*. Cambridge: Cambridge University Press.

Ouchi, W. and A. Wilkins. 1985. 'Organizational Culture.' *Annual Review of Sociology* 11: 457–483.

Owen, M. 1983. *Apologies and Remedial Interchanges*. New York: Mouton.

Pateman, C. 1988. *The Sexual Contract*. Cambridge: Polity Press.

Paton, R., R. Duhm, S. Gherardi, J.L. Laville, C. Otero-Hidalgo, R. Spear and A. Westenholz. 1989. *Reluctant Entrepreneurs*. Milton Keynes: Open University Press.

Perrow, C. 1972. *Complex Organizations: A Critical Essay*. Glenview, IL: Scott Foresman.

Perrow, C. 1991. 'A Society of Organizations.' In *Theory & Society* 20/6: 725–762.

Pitch, T. 1991. 'Differenza in comune.' *Diritto e Democrazia* 5–6: 219–235.

Podmore, D. and A. Spender. 1986. 'Gender in the Labour Process – The Case of Women and Men Lawyers.' In *Gender and the Labour Process*. Aldershot: Gower.

Polanyi, M. 1958. *Personal Knowledge: Towards a Post-Critical Philosophy*. London: Routledge & Kegan Paul.

Pondy, L., P.J. Frost, G. Morgan and T. Dandridge. 1983. *Organizational Symbolism*. Greenwich, CT: Jai Press.

Pringle, R. 1989a. 'Bureaucracy, Rationality and Sexuality: the Case of Secretaries.' In *The Sexuality of Organization* edited by J. Hearn, D. Sheppard, P. Tancred-Sheriff and G. Burrell. London: Sage.

Pringle, R. 1989b. *Secretaries Talk*. New York: Verso.

Rafaeli, A. and R. Sutton. 1987. 'Expression of Emotion as Part of the Work Role.' *Academy of Management Review* 1: 23–37.

Rafaeli, A. and R. Sutton. 1989. 'The Expression of Emotion in Organizational Life.' *Research in Organizational Behaviour* 11: 1–42.

Rawls, J. 1971. *A Theory of Justice*. Cambridge, MA: Harvard University Press.

Ray, C.A. 1986. 'Corporate Culture: the Last Frontier of Control?' *Journal of Management Studies* 23(3): 287–296.

Raymond, J. 1981. 'The Illusion of Androgyny.' In *Building Feminist Theory*, edited by C. Bunch et al. New York: Longman. pp. 59–66.

Rich, A. 1984. 'Compulsory Heterosexuality and Lesbian Existence'. In *Desire: The Politics of Sexuality* edited by C. Stansell and S. Thompson. London: Virago.

Rorty, R. 1989. *Contingency, Irony and Solidarity*. Cambridge: Cambridge University Press.

Rothschild, J. 1990. 'Feminist Values and the Democratic Management of Work Organzation.' Paper presented to the XIIth World Congress of Sociology. Madrid, July.

Sampson, E. 1989. 'Foundations for a Textual Analysis of Selfhood.' In *Texts of Identity* edited by J. Shotter and K. Gergen. London: Sage.

Sandelands, L. and G. Buckner. 1989. 'Of Art and Work: Aesthetic Experience and the Psychology of Work Feelings.' *Research in Organizational Behaviour* 11: 105–132.

Sapiro, V. 1981. 'When are Interests Interesting? The Problem of Political Representation of Women.' *American Political Sciences Review* 75: 701–716.

Saraceno, C. 1987. 'Division of Family Labour and Gender Identity.' In *Women and the State* edited by N. Showstack Sassoon. London: Atkinson.

Saraceno, C. 1989. 'La struttura di genere della cittadinanza.' *Democrazia e Diritto* 5: 273–295.

Saraceno, C. 1991. 'Statuto di genere e cittadinanza nelle società di Welfare.' *Problemi del Socialismo* 5: 137–155.

Sarbin, T. 1986. 'Emotion and Action: Roles and Rhetorics.' In *The Social Construction of Emotions* edited by R. Harré. Oxford: Blackwell.

Savage, M. and A. Witz. 1992. *Gender and Bureaucracy*. Oxford: Blackwell.

Schneider, S. and R. Dunbar. 1992. 'A Psychoanalytic Reading of Hostile Take-over Events.' *Academy of Management Review* 17(3): 537–567.

Schutz, A. 1971. *Collected Papers*. The Hague: Nijhoff.

Scott, J. 1986. 'Gender: A Useful Category of Historical Analysis.' *American Historical Review*. 91(5): 1053–1075.

Shotter, J. and K. Gergen. (eds). 1989. *Texts of Identity*. London: Sage.

Sievers, B. 1990. 'Curing the Monster: Some Images of Considerations about the Dragon.' In *Symbols and Artifacts: Views of the Corporate Landscape* edited by P. Gagliardi. Berlin: de Gruyter.

Simmel, G. 1908. *Soziologie*. Leipzig: Duncker and Humblot.

Sims, H. and D. Gioia. (eds). 1986. *The Thinking Organization*. San Francisco: Jossey-Bass.

Singer, J. 1976. *Androgyny: Toward a New Theory of Sexuality*. Garden City, NY: Anchor Press.

Smircich, L. 1983. 'Concepts of Culture and Organizational Analysis.' *Administrative Science Quarterly* 28(3): 339–358.

Smircich, L. and M. Calás. 1987. 'Organizational Culture: A Critical Assessment.' In *Handbook of Organizational Communication* edited by F. Jablin, L. Putnam, K. Roberts and L. Porter. Beverly Hills: Sage.

Smith, D. 1990. *The Conceptual Practice of Power. A Feminist Sociology to Knowledge*. Boston, MA: Northeastern University Press.

Smith, D. 1993. *Text, Facts, and Femininity: Exploring the Relations of Ruling*. New York: Routledge.

Spender, D. 1980. *Man Made Language*. London: Routledge & Kegan Paul.

Spivak, G. 1974. 'Translator's Preface.' to J. Derrida, *Of Grammatology*. Baltimore: Johns Hopkins University Press. pp. ix–xxxvii.

Strati, A. 1986. 'Lavoro e Simbolismo Organizzativo.' *Studi Organizzativi* 2–3: 65–85.

Strati, A. 1992a. 'Organizational Culture.' In *Concise Encyclopedia of Participation and Co-management* edited by G. Szell. Berlin: de Gruyter.

Strati, A. 1992b. 'Aesthetic Understanding of Organizational Life.' *Academy of Management Review* 3: 568–581.

Sutton, R. 1991. 'Maintaining Norms about Expressed Emotions: the Case of Bill Collectors.' *Administrative Science Quarterly* 36: 245–268.

Sutton, R. and A. Rafaeli. 1988. 'Untangling the Relationship between Displayed Emotions and Organizational Sales: the Case of Convenience Stress.' *Academy of Management Journal* 31: 461–487.

Synnot, A. 1987. 'Shame and Glory: a Sociology of Hair.' *British Journal of Sociology* 38: 381–413.

Tancred-Sheriff, P. 1989. 'Gender, Sexuality and the Labour Process.' In *The Sexuality of Organizations* edited by J. Hearn, D. Sheppard, P. Tancred-Sheriff and G. Burrell. London: Sage.

Tannen, D. 1991. *You Just Don't Understand*. New York: Ballantine Books.

Thompson, J.D. 1967. *Organizations in Action*. New York: McGraw-Hill.

Trebilcot, J. 1982. 'Two Forms of Androgynism.' In *'Feminiinity', 'Masculinity' and 'Androgyny': a Modern Philosophical Discussion*, edited by M. Vetterling-Braggin. Totowa: Rowman and Littlefield.

Turner, B.A. 1990a. *Organizational Symbolism*. Berlin: de Gruyter.

Turner, B.A. 1990b. 'The Rise of Organizational Symbolism.' In *The Theory and Philosophy of Organizations* edited by J. Hassard and D. Pym. London: Routledge. pp. 83–96.

Turner, B.A. 1992. 'The Symbolic Understanding of Organizations.' In *Rethinking Organization* edited by M. Reed and M. Hughes. London: Sage.

Turner, V. 1969. *The Ritual Process. Structure and Anti-Structure*. Chicago: Aldine.

Van Maanen, J. and G. Kunda. 1989. 'Real Feelings: Emotional Expression and Organizational Culture.' *Research in Organizational Behaviour* 11: 43–103.

Wajcman, J. 1991. *Feminism Confronts Technology*. University Park: Pennsylvania State University Press.

Walzer, M. 1983. *Spheres of Justice*. New York: Basic Books.

Watzlawick, P., P. Beavin and D. Jackson. 1967. *Pragmatics of Human Communication: a Study of Interactional Patterns, Pathologies and Paradoxes*. New York: Norton.

West, C. and D. Zimmerman. 1987. 'Doing Gender.' *Gender and Society* 1(2): 125–151.

Williams, R. 1981. *Culture*. Glasgow: Collins-Fontana.

Witkin, R. 1974. *The Intelligence of Feeling*. London: Heinemann.

Witkin, R. and P. O. Berg. 1984. 'Organization Symboling: Towards a Theory of Action.' Paper presented at SCOS Conference, Lund, June.

Witz, A. and M. Savage. 1992. 'The Gender of Organization.' In *Gender and Bureaucracy* edited by M. Savage and A. Witz. Oxford: Blackwell.

Woolf, V. 1978. *The Voyage Out*. London: Grafton Books.

Zanuso, L. 1987. 'Gli studi sulla doppia presenza: dal conflitto alla norma.' In *La Ricerca delle Donne. Studi femministi in Italia* edited by M. C. Marcuzzo and A. Rossi Doria. Turin: Rosemberg & Sellier.

Zincone, G. 1984. *Gruppi sociali e Sistemi politici – Il Caso donne*. Milan: Angeli.

Zincone, G. 1992. *Da Sudditi a Cittadini*. Bologna: Il Mulino.

Index